To Daddy for your Birthday
of "1976"
With our love,
Steve, Donna & Jeff

THE COURT-MARTIAL OF
GEORGE ARMSTRONG CUSTER

The
Court-Martial of
George Armstrong
Custer

DOUGLAS C. JONES

CHARLES SCRIBNER'S SONS
New York

Copyright © 1976 Kemm Inc.

Library of Congress Cataloging in Publication Data
Jones, Douglas C
    The court-martial of George Armstrong Custer.
    1. Custer, George Armstrong, 1839–1876–
Fiction. I. Title.
PZ4.J7534Co [PS3560.0478] 813'.5'4 76-12606
ISBN 0-684-14738-6

1 3 5 7 9 11 13 15 17 19 H/C 20 18 16 14 12 10 8 6 4 2
Printed in the United States of America

For

Colonel Benjamin Rush III

soldier and friend—
whose idea this book was

*This is a fantasy which needs no apology,
for who among us has not been intrigued
by the alternatives history never reveals?*

PART ONE

The General

I

The flagstones of the Manhattan Battery are slick and black, varnished by the cold November rain coming across the harbor in swirls and clouds of mist. People hurry toward the ferry slip clutching cloaks and mufflers tight about their necks against the wind blowing in from Staten Island, that low, gray mass to the south. On such a wet, early morning everything is gray: the surface of the water and the lacy foam where the wind ripples; the gulls that sweep down for bits of garbage floating between the Battery and Brooklyn; the buildings of that shore lying blocky and tumbled like dominoes left scattered by some careless child; the East River stretching like a highway to the horizon where the dark turrets of the new bridge—they are calling it the Brooklyn Bridge—rise steeply into the rain like the towers of some medieval castle on a gray Scottish moor; the houses and church spires along Manhattan's south side; the Fulton Fish Market, where even now—at 7 A.M.— Lorenzo Delmonico does the daily shopping for his famous restaurant at 26th Street and Fifth Avenue; all a jumble of brick and unpainted lumber and faded white panels set under a half-daylight sky; the Hudson with tiny sails far out like puffs of sodden cotton; and the Jersey shore beyond, a dismal prospect, low and unmagnificent this far south—not yet the Palisades. The smell is gray, too, like all waterfronts in November in the rain.

Near the ferry slip—a long covered wharf that points toward

Governor's Island—a newsboy hawks his papers, waving one about but protecting the rest under a strip of canvas, the whole perched on an old cement cannon trunnion. It is the *New York Herald*, resting with no great dignity under a dirty tarpaulin, but at least on the foundation where once a proud rifle rested, facing the Narrows and daring anyone with evil intent to enter. Perhaps Mr. James Gordon Bennett, Jr. would approve, for after all he and his father before him have always been noted for their enterprise.

"General Custer trial," the boy shouts, and his business is brisk—which most certainly Mr. Bennett will approve.

The front page of the newspaper, like everything else, is gray. The headlines are only one column wide as they proclaim the great and small events of the day. On this day: "Custer Goes Before a Court-Martial," "Boy General Charged with Neglect," "Long Silence Will Be Broken." Each succeeding statement appears beneath the preceding one, until halfway down the page the type grows smaller, smaller, and yet smaller, until the story itself begins. The trial will be held on Governor's Island, that block of land sitting in New York's harbor only a short distance from the southern tip of Manhattan. Normally there are rowboats and barges between the Battery and the island, but for the crowds expected and the press reporters the Army has hired a steam ferry. From the trolleys that come down Broadway and Hudson Street people hurry toward the slip, and where their paths converge the newsboy stalks them.

One of the men most prominently mentioned in the *Herald* story has come to the Battery on the Broadway trolley, just as he has every day for a month. He is rather tall but he is beginning a paunch which the unbelted Army officer's uniform of the period does little to hide—in fact, accents it. This day he wears a cape, hiding his insignia of rank, major, and his branch of service, Judge Advocate General's Corps. His face is bony, with a long nose remarkable only for the large, fleshy bulb on the end. His mouth is large and sensuous, and over it is a wide but well-clipped moustache. It, like the hair protruding from under his French forage hat, is a mousy brown. His eyes are light blue but on this morning seriously bloodshot—which they always have a tendency to be when he is staying in his native New York City.

The newsboy knows his name and calls it, making other people

turn and watch him. He is Asa B. Gardiner, they whisper, who will
try Custer. He is the trial judge advocate—prosecutor and chief law
officer of the court. Gardiner is not unaware of the stares, nor is
he completely uncomfortable with the attention. He pays the boy
his usual fee, four pennies, which is twice the asking price for the
paper. But he is a lawyer after all and finds legal ways to supplement
his income, unlike many line officers who are hard-pressed to survive
on what they make—if and when the Congress decides to pay them.
Gardiner is past feeling any embarrassment over such small extrav-
agance. He is uncomfortable about what he spent the night before
at Hoffman House, but that was mostly physical.

He knows what the *Herald* will have to say about Custer. He has
been reading it for a long time now, almost three months that he
has been in New York preparing his case. The hero of a thousand
battles, standing like Horatius at the bridge, fending off the vicious
Etruscans—Grant Republicans. There would be the usual spate of
scenes replayed, the past glories of a *Herald* favorite paraded, a
mish-mash of half-truth and absolute guessing. He had never liked
it, and as the trial drew nearer he liked it even less.

The whole unpleasant business had begun when old Billy Dunn,
the Army's Judge Advocate General, had called Gardiner in to
announce that he had been selected to try the case. The most famous
case in the history of the Army, it was bound to become. There
had been some argument—somewhat gentle, of course, for a major
is seldom violent in his arguments with a brigadier general. Then
the magic word had been dropped into the conversation, like a hot
lead shot into a barrel of cold water—Sherman! From that moment,
Gardiner knew it was useless to protest. But he had not stopped
thinking: I'm a city man, a staff officer, a claims lawyer. What am
I doing trying an outdoorsman, a line officer, one of the best
cavalrymen in the Army—a national hero? And after all these
months of work and the damaging depositions stacking higher and
higher, after weeks of knowing more and more surely that there had
to be negligence on that Montana battlefield, after feeling with each
passing day the increased weight of the most brutal witness of all,
those 260 dead and mutilated soldiers along the Little Bighorn—
after all of that, and despite his growing conviction, Gardiner was
still unhappy about having to do it.

For a short time during the war Gardiner had been a cavalry officer himself, serving under Wesley Merritt in Virginia. But when some of his lawyer friends in Washington had discovered that he was wearing a uniform but not doing what he had done in New York before the fighting started—that is, practicing law—they saw to it that the Army took better advantage of his talents. Between 1860 and 1865 there had been a lot of law to practice in the Army. He'd had no intention of liking it, but he did. He came to enjoy the Army's closed society, its strict code of conduct, its camaraderie, and after the shooting stopped he decided to stay, at least for a while. Four years ago he had been promoted to major, a remarkable accomplishment in the peacetime Army for a man only thirty-seven years old, and now he is one of only eight officers in the Judge Advocate General's Corps.

On the ferry to Governor's Island Gardiner braces himself against a rail, and even though he has seen much of it before, he begins to read:

> . . . General Custer has maintained a long silence due to the serious nature of his wounds received on that frightful day. It is expected now at last that the world will know the details of the glorious fight against overwhelming odds. Only that part of the fight made by Reno and the gallant Benteen has been brought to public light in these pages. As to the fate of Custer's battalion, we have been required by sad circumstance to wait this day. But at last it comes, and we rejoice that General Custer, hero of many a fight on the Plains and in Virginia in the recent unpleasantness, is alive to tell his tale. We know not what occurred. That the court will determine. Yet we cannot but feel that General Custer will weather this as he has so often weathered disaster in the past. We see him in our mind's eye now, as he stood at Little Bighorn, pistol in one hand, saber in the other, head high. . . .

Dear God, Gardiner thinks. People who survived that battle have been publishing their stories by the ream, and every one says the officers of the 7th Cavalry did not carry their sabers into the fight. Yet here's one of the world's greatest newspapers still gasping about unsheathed cold steel in the gallant Custer's hand. No, that was

Benteen they call gallant. They call Custer hero. Significantly, they do not call Reno anything. . . .

Across the choppy water he sees Bedloe's Island. Only last week the Congress approved this chunk of rock near New Jersey for the giant statue the French sent. The Statue of Liberty. Gardiner has been to Madison Park and seen the hand holding the torch—it has been on display there for months, the rest of the casting in a waterfront warehouse awaiting a place to be erected. Now it would be Bedloe's, and Gardiner tries to estimate how high above the harbor surface 151 feet would be—I read that somewhere, he thinks. The Statue of Liberty to Enlighten the World. That's the whole name. I read that, too.

His mind leaps to the number 260—260 officers and men and civilians with Custer who didn't come back. There is an unreal quality to it all. The thought of the Yellowstone campaign last year against the Sioux and Northern Cheyenne, the long marches, the choking dust, the blinding heat, the smell of wet horses and leather and gun oil, the sudden boiling fight, the battle cries, the guidons snapping, bursts of rifle fire, the frenzied ponies, the blood, the thirst. Now it was ending, two thousand miles away, in a cold November on a small damp island in New York Harbor. With officers and ladies, polished boots and saber chains, brocade bustles and lace cuffs, and newspaper reporters with their stubby pencils and lined pads. And none of them had the vaguest notion of what a High Plains battlefield looks like, sounds like, smells like. In fact, Gardiner thinks, neither do I.

2

———

The rain in Washington drives down straight and hard. At his window in the War Office, the Commanding General of the Army looks out at the dismal panorama of marble, brick, and red clay. Directly under the window they are paving the alleyway. Flagstones are stacked along either side of the red mire, like the walls of a narrow fort. The reddish puddles in the tiny thoroughfare recall the color of the creek running through the battlefield after Shiloh. Beyond the alley is the long swell of the Mall and then the Washington Monument, cut off squarely at 156 feet, as it has been since the society which was building it by popular subscription fell into serious public controversy in 1854. So now for twenty-three years it has stood, like a noble Egyptian column ravaged by barbarians. Each day William Tecumseh Sherman stares at it. The obelisk without its point—like himself, the general without an army.

At least they've begun to recognize me, Sherman thinks, as he turns away from the window. Operational orders from the Secretary come across my desk. Which is about twice as good as it was a year ago, when they sent me nothing.

But he knows the only real power he has is his personal influence in the Officer Corps. He makes the sour smirk which means either that he is amused or that his stomach is upset. Even in this system dominated by politicians and, worse, political and bureaucratic brass, there are options open to him. He glares at his single window. That damnable window has become to him the symbol of his low station. One window. The Secretary has seven— and two fireplaces.

I wish Sam Grant were here, he thinks, and not in Europe parading his old ass among the silver snuff boxes and crinolines. We should be watching together this thing we've let loose.

His restless mind darts from Grant to President Hayes, who has succeeded Grant in the presidency, but there is nothing about Hayes that particularly interests him. Though without political ambition, Sherman sometimes wonders if perhaps he could have followed Grant into the White House. Although he feels, and rightfully, that official Washington has often mistreated him, he is proud of the fact that he is a popular man. People see him on the streets and nod, even tip their hats and bow. It often confuses him—people are so kind even though they live in a city he loathes. But elsewhere, too, next to Grant he is the most remembered, most respected leader of the Civil War. Hero of Atlanta, the newspapers call him. He cringes each time he thinks of it. He had once said to his aide, Colonel Nelson Wright, "Nellie, I never see my name in print without feeling contaminated."

Nothing was worse than a newspaper and the people who infested it. He had near hanged that *Herald* reporter during the war. . . . What was his damnable name? Knox. Thomas Knox. I hear he has gone off to southern Asia to help build a telegraph line. Or perhaps it was New Guinea. I fervently hope each day to hear that he has been devoured by cannibals.

He had remained in the public eye after the war, commanding the Division of the Missouri—not a unit but a geographic area that included the domains of all the Plains wild tribes. Sioux, Cheyenne, Arapaho, Kiowa, Comanche.

The names make him shudder. Not out of simple dread or revulsion. But, rather, disquiet in the face of strange and somehow dangerous societies dancing and chanting at a murky distance, then suddenly flashing out, screeching, painted like devils—and fighting like devils, too. He had come quickly to realize the plight of the Plains tribes, and like many Army officers serving on the frontier, had come to grant them grudging respect and even admiration. He is uneasy with the feeling and tells himself often that soldiers usually do develop respect for their enemies—he had certainly admired and respected the Rebel armies.

But you do not maintain an army for its sweetness. By God, you are aggressive and, yes, even brutal if that finishes it quickly. The kindest thing anyone can do for an enemy is to finish him off quickly. It's a dirty job. But that's the nature of armies.

Sherman knows that his Army—for although he thinks himself powerless, it is still called Sherman's Army—sees few passive Indians. The Indian Bureau can handle the passive ones. The ones fighting for their old lands—those are the ones the Army sees and comes to admire. After all, fighters will naturally admire fighters. But he has no illusions about the Army job or about the outcome. The nation is growing, exploding in every direction. Nothing can stop that. The idea of Manifest Destiny is not lost on him, nor is it at all dead in 1877. It is a simple, even primitive, society standing against the inexorable advance of a highly technological one.

We need room, he thinks, we need resources. It is sad, but their time is finished now. It is someone else's turn.

But all this is no help to the Army. Sherman, who would talk to anyone about anything, whether he knew anything about the subject or not, has for years been telling everyone how unproductive Indian wars are—and he knows a great deal about wars. You need fifty thousand regulars to patrol a frontier where only fifty young bucks on good ponies and with guns can pop up anywhere and start taking settlers' hair—or threatening to. As for calling state militia to Federal service, that's like deputizing a drunken mob. But everyone screams for the Army. Whites take shots at passing Indians just for the pure hell of it, or perhaps out of stupid fright, and there's a sudden war and the Indian Bureau doesn't have a single company of cavalry. You go into action with everything you can muster, and all you do is chase dust. You can never catch them until they want to be caught.

Sherman grinds his teeth and makes his smirk again, this time because he has a pain. Finally there is a chance, he thinks, after you have sweated, eaten dust and sometimes your own horse, gotten frostbite and been gut-shot riding point, and have never seen anything of the enemy you're supposed to be fighting except his horse shit . . . finally there is a chance. You've picked the terrain and the time, you've got your troops up in solid strength. And the enemy decides to make a stand and fight. A regular cavalry fight. And there they are, not disappearing into the hills but coming right at you. And Custer botches it. Somehow. Like a green, glass-eyed lieutenant who hasn't the dimmest idea of how to use his troops and the ground.

Sherman frowns. I think about every soldier we've sent out there, his pants stuck to his saddle, his eyes glued shut with dust or frost, his fingers raw on the reins while he pushes on ahead to catch something—any damned thing he can shoot at—and I think of the damnable Indian Bureau traders warm in their posts, their fat asses straddling profits they've taken from hornswoggling the Indians. And I think of Custer and the chance we had to close out a large part of this mess once and for all. I can't do anything about the traders, but I'm damned if I will ever allow another soldier to serve under Custer. He doesn't deserve even the wickedest, filthiest, non-English-speakingest recruit that ever enlisted to dodge a sheriff's warrant.

It is exactly 7:30 A.M. and there is a light tap at the door. Sherman makes no answer and the door opens and Colonel Nelson Wright enters with a tray. On it there are two tin cups—Army field mess style—and a pewter coffee pot. Wright says nothing as he places the tray on Sherman's desk, turns, and inspects the fire. He takes the poker and jabs at the flaming logs, producing a shower of sparks, most of which escape into the room. He quickly turns away from the fireplace, knowing that the lack of draft is a sore point with his chief—the Secretary's fireplaces draw excellently.

"The court-martial should be starting now, General," Wright says. Sherman continues to stare into the rain. The aide waits, then speaks again. "Shall I pour a cup, sir?"

"No, Colonel, I can manage," Sherman says. Wright turns without another word and quickly leaves the room.

Wright knows his cues well. Had Sherman called him Nellie, he would have stayed and used the second cup on the tray, sipping as the General mused aloud, which he often did early in the morning. But when Sherman called him by rank, it meant the Chief wanted to be alone.

Sherman lights a cigar, biting off the end and spitting it in the general direction of the brass cuspidor near his desk. He thinks of last year, when the move to court-martial Custer began.

It had been July 6, 1876, two days after the birthday of the Republic, which had been celebrated at the Philadelphia Centennial Exposition. Sherman had been there. Everyone had been there—well, of course, not those gallants along the Yellowstone River trying to herd the Sioux and Cheyenne back onto reservations. But Sheridan and the Secretary, and even Grant for a few days, still President then, his presidential train coming north from Washington with red, white, and blue bunting draped across the engine's cowcatcher and the Marine band on a specially designed flatcar to play at each stop. And the press had been there—damn their eyes—especially that twit from the *New York Herald*, James Gordon Bennett, Jr. He was worse than his father, if that was possible, and still is, sending his reporters nosing into everyone's business.

Sherman grunts at the memory, gulping the bitter coffee and filling the room with blue cigar smoke. What a beastly time that was for news of an Army disaster to arrive.

There had been a rumor out of Salt Lake City. A news story sent by the Associated Press, but it was most likely the wild ramblings of a frontier scout named Muggins Taylor, who had seen nothing except a few dead bodies. Sherman had bided his time because he knew the press always made these things bigger than they were and because frontier scouts were infamous spinners of tall tales. Besides, if anything had in fact happened, an official report would soon reach Sheridan—who was in charge of what went on in the Yellowstone country.

The report arrived in Philadelphia on July 6. It was a "confidential" message to Sheridan from his commander in the field, Brigadier General Alfred Terry. After reading it, Sheridan passed it to Sherman. To the Commanding General it sounded as though Custer had disobeyed orders and gotten his regiment badly mauled—much of it destroyed. The worst rumors were confirmed. Over 250 dead, Custer himself found at the point of death and not expected to live. Terry had sent an earlier message, delayed in transmission, which cast no shadow on Custer's conduct. But the one in Sherman's hand did.

The Commanding General had never wished dead any officer wearing the uniform of the United States Army. Even those he most disliked. When later it turned out that Custer would live, Sherman was happy that an officer of the Army should survive. But he had other reasons to be happy. If Custer died, the Army would have a martyr, beyond reach of mortal hand. Living, perhaps hero worship would not come so easily; but most importantly, living, Sherman *could* get at him.

On that hot day in Philadelphia, Sherman with the confidential message in his hand, nobody knew what would happen. But Sherman acted almost instinctively, without hesitation—as he did committing Schofield's Corps at Atlanta. He made the move that would ensure public controversy and perhaps bring Custer to account, even though he knew it probably would divide the Officer Corps. He gave the story to the press.

Still holding the Terry message, Sherman had turned away from Sheridan, his knuckles white as he crushed the paper in his hand. The Army and all it meant was like a hammer pounding in his chest: officers and men struggling to maintain a fighting force amidst all the political bickering for funds; in-house backbiting between staff and line officers; his own struggle to make operational sense of the scattered, thankless little wars always sprouting on the frontier. And now this Custer pup . . .

Standing nearby in the crowd were a number of messengers and couriers available to the Commanding General. Pointing to one man, he called him over and thrust the paper into his hand.

"Courier, take this message to the Secretary of War at once," Sherman said. "He's staying at the Station Hotel."

The reporter stood there gaping for an instant.

Sherman repeated his order quietly, but forcefully. "Courier, take this message to the Secretary of War at the Station Hotel, damnit."

None of the real messengers would realize what was happening, not having seen the paper in Sherman's hand. Sheridan's back was turned as he talked with another group of officers. Later, it could only be assumed that Sherman had mistaken the reporter for one of his couriers.

When he thinks of it, Sherman snorts and almost chuckles. My

God! To think I would be unable to recognize one of those literary hyenas. I can spot one at the maximum range of the Springfield 45-70 infantry rifle.

Yet it is a secret he has never told. Much as he enjoys talking, arguing, speculating, baiting. He has never spoken to a soul about what he did intentionally that day and let pass as a mistake.

The next day the complete text of the message appeared in the *Philadelphia Inquirer* and in the *New York Herald*. The Secretary got the report, but only after the startled and happy reporter had copied it word for word.

The Terry report appeared in the *Herald* along with details of the bloody fight sent by a Bismarck, Dakota Territory, newspaper editor named Emmit Lounsberry, who had taken the story directly from survivors. He had telegraphed more than six thousand words to James Gordon Bennett, Jr., and the *Herald* had printed every one of them.

Reading the *Herald*—God, how he hated getting details of military operations from the press—Sherman had let the thing take shape in his head. ". . . Lt. Bradley reported that he had found Custer with 190 cavalrymen dead. Imagine the effect! Words cannot describe the feeling of these, his comrades and soldiers. General Terry sought the spot and found it to be true. Of those brave men who followed Custer, all had perished."

The swashbuckler, his luck finally had run out. And those poor soldiers paying the price. Is that the best the Army can offer its troops and the public? Sherman had doubted it then—he doubted it more each passing day that he thought about it. And he thought about it constantly. Custer had been a good cavalry officer, some said, because he got results. And Sherman admitted that. The man was personable, difficult not to like. But his successes too often came by a hair's breadth, a result of brashness. It had always bothered Sherman's sense of military correctness. He, better than any man alive, knew how quickly a battlefield gamble can turn into utter disaster. In any professional one would expect to find that same awareness.

Well, then, what? If the Army must be protected from such disregard for all logical consequences of recklessness, where is the reckoning? Court-martial! The thought had made him physically ill at first. He recalled the trial of Fitz-John Porter. An example made of a good officer. That was hardly the case with Custer. But remembering the Porter court had helped him decide. In any court-martial there are side effects. Most important of these was that the press scooped up all the filth that filtered through and spread it about the countryside among the people like manure. It was repugnant to him. Yet he was well enough aware of how difficult a conviction might be against the Golden Cavalier. The next best thing was to anoint him with the odor of it.

And so his decision had been made. Characteristically, once made, he hove to it with a grim determination unmatched since Pickett's Charge. Cashier if possible—reveal, in any event, the nature of an officer unfit for command. It would make the entire Officer Corps shudder and perhaps create enemies tomorrow among friends of today. But everything had to be considered in light of the Army's good.

Two people would need convincing. Phil Sheridan, who had always liked Custer, but who was also Sherman's subordinate and a good soldier. And the President. Sherman had scribbled a note to Grant in his own hand.

"Dear Sam . . ."

3

His cigar dead and soggy in his mouth, the coffee cold on the desk before him, Sherman looks once again at the note he has just received from Grant. Postmarked London, it is short and uninformative—like one of his field orders, Sherman mutters. Queen Victoria herself has welcomed him to Buckingham Palace and he has reviewed the Coldstream Guards. A job he understands better than the one he had on Pennsylvania Avenue, Sherman thinks.

Sherman drops the one-page letter and rests his hands on the thick folder lying in the center of his desk where Colonel Wright has placed it every morning for the past week. Across the top of the folder, hand-lettered, is the file identification: "LB." And below that, "Orders and press clippings, June 1876 to date. OFFICIAL. For use only by the Commanding General, USA." Inside is the history, insofar as Sherman knows it, of the Custer fight in Montana. Also in the file is Custer's testimony before the Congressional committee on the impeachment proceedings of various members of Grant's cabinet, which took place just prior to the fight. Sherman knows it word for word.

He opens the folder and his mind rushes back to August 1876, the detail sharp in his memory. The response to his note to Grant had been immediate, a White House messenger with word that a meeting was appropriate as soon as Sheridan could be summoned from Chicago.

The General

It had been one of those hot and humid days in Washington, and Grant had scheduled their conference for late in the evening. Sheridan arrived by train in the afternoon. Sherman gave him no hint of what was afoot. But the jaunty Sheridan was sure it had something to do with the report his own headquarters had sent the Commanding General just a week before—that George Custer was responding well to treatment in the Fort Lincoln hospital and that despite previous gloom over his chances, he now appeared certain to live.

There had been a head wound of small consequence, with another much more serious injury to the thigh. It was what had come to be called a Hancock wound, named after that famous Union hero who sustained such a hit to the thigh by a spent ball during the fight at Gettysburg. The ball had broken the femur and had driven foreign matter into a deep wound, and this had festered and caused great pain and long suffering. It was supposed that the ball which struck Custer had hit some sort of weapon first, sending bits of metal and wood into his thigh. Luckily, lockjaw had failed to develop. Yet it was the kind of wound that could cause continuing problems and Sheridan had already approved a year of sick leave. Custer was being attended by the best doctors on the frontier and, of course, by his wife, Elizabeth.

For their meeting place, Grant had chosen a small basement library at the White House. It was a room still clogged with books and small statues, built some years before by a now-forgotten First Lady who wanted a reading room away from the "dust and bustle" of the main floors above.

The President had looked rumpled and out of temper when he first came in, Sherman and Sheridan having been ushered into the room already by a liveried black who, smiling and bowing, had told them that he was a survivor of the Battle of the Crater at Petersburg. Grant's irritation was the result of a meeting he had just had with a political delegation from Colorado, a chore he disliked as much as Sherman would have, but this one was unavoidable. Colorado had just been admitted to the Union as a state.

His spirits rose as he greeted his old friends and comrades-in-arms. He shook their hands warmly, smiling through his graying beard. He looked older than his fifty-five years, his face was lined and his eyes peered red-rimmed from puffy sockets. There were the usual jokes passed between old soldiers—recalling other officers, incidents of the war. Nothing was said to Sheridan about the progress of his campaign against the Sioux and Cheyenne. They all knew it was going very badly.

Mostly it had been banter between the President and Sheridan, Sherman standing back, watching and thinking of what he had to do. No one, least of all Sherman, had any doubts about Little Phil being tough when he had to be. The despoiler of the Shenandoah valley had, after all, initiated the policy on the Plains of attacking villages in winter, when the warriors were packed into tepees, immobile, lying close to fires with no thought of fighting in the cold and snow. Sheridan's policy meant war on non-belligerents—the women and children—but then it had been said how hellish war can be. Besides, Sheridan had explained often that in an Indian village under attack the only non-belligerents are those too young or too old to hold a weapon in their hands.

But tough or not, Sherman was unsure of Sheridan. Everyone knew of Sheridan's fondness for Custer. Barrack walls from Fort Hays to Indian Town Gap—wherever the 7th Cavalry had been— boasted photographs of Custer, Sheridan, Libby, and the Custer wolfhounds gathered in friendly reunion about the steps of some officer's quarters. The problem in the musty little White House library was for the Commanding General to win willing support from his highest-ranking subordinate without too much hide being scraped off either party. It would be better to have Sheridan as a friend than an enemy.

The man from the Crater brought cigars and a bottle of brandy, which he placed on a small table between two easy chairs. Grant and Sheridan seated themselves, and the President was much pleased at the sight of the dark liquor pouring into his stemmed glass. Sherman remained standing in the center of the room, too tightly strung to sit. As the other two sipped their brandy and puffed at cigars, he began.

Everyone now knew, he told them, that the leader of the 7th Cavalry at the Little Bighorn would likely survive his wounds. Already the newspapers were speculating on what he would say when he was well enough to relive those terrible hours in the high

Yellowstone country. No doubt the story would be self-glorifying. Already Elizabeth had been telling the press what a great hero Custer had been, but she always added that only her Autie should tell the tale of that dreadful field.

"I want no brash, headstrong, self-centered egomaniac," Sherman said emphatically, "telling the story of that fight for the press to gobble up like one of those dime novels the news stalls are flooded with." He watched the effect of his words on Sheridan. Typically, Sherman was doing his best to be blunt, no matter what the cost. "I want it told by the Army."

"But, Cump," Sheridan said softly, "only Custer can tell what happened to his troops. None of the others survived to tell it." He realized at once that he had said one of the things Sherman wanted him to say.

"Exactly," Sherman replied, "but we will have him tell it under oath and under conditions chosen by the Army. It will not be told by the *New York Herald*."

Sheridan sipped his brandy, nodding slowly. "A court of inquiry?"

"No," said Sherman harshly. "A court-martial."

Sheridan made no reply, but his face slowly changed color—from red to purple. Sherman was aware of Sheridan's temper. It had been legend among the troops of the Civil War. He could suddenly erupt in an uncontrollable frenzy. Sherman knew that not having been consulted earlier was exactly the kind of thing to set him off. The President, too, knew of Little Phil's maddening flights into mindless rage. He watched closely from deep in his chair, at this point well aware of his role and holding back his comments. Sherman moved in quickly.

"The time has finally come, Philip, to cut off all this public adulation of a man who for years has created constant irritation and dissension in the Officer Corps and the Army as a whole. The controversy he creates! His use of the press! The ambition! My God, the ambition! And he cannot be trusted. Now he wastes men as if they were fishing minnows, and he ruins a well-thought-out campaign. Damnation, Philip, you should know that. It was *your* campaign."

Sheridan, stiff in his chair, bit his cigar. His mouth was grim under his moustache.

"I propose to court-martial him myself," Sherman said. "I will convene the court, make the appointments. I want no doubt as to where the impetus for this is located."

Sherman was finished. He took a cigar from the box on the table and chomped off the end with his front teeth, spitting the nub into a corner. After he had it smoking he stood back and waited for Sheridan to speak.

"I must admit," Sheridan said, "that for some time he has disturbed me with his conduct. During the war it seemed the more responsibility we gave him, the more he tended to exaggerate his successes. He once told me he had captured a Rebel train protected by an entire infantry division with artillery. In fact, the train had had practically no protection at all—one battery, I recall. Yet he did get results for us. Sometimes with brashness, but he got results."

"What kind of man is he who takes part in all these charades and play-acting?" Grant said. "In New York society, the Racquet Court Club people. Wearing costumes and play-acting!"

"None of that is a court-martial offense, Sam," Sheridan said rather testily. "Remember that each of us here has been accused of worse."

It was an awkward thing to have said. Grant had been called a drunk at one point in his career—Sherman crazy. Sheridan was embarrassed that he had said it.

"He did get results," Sheridan insisted.

Sherman's face twisted into the familiar scowl. "What kind of result did he get us at the Little Bighorn, Philip?"

Sheridan's face flushed with anger. "Then do we try every officer who loses a battle?"

"Yes," Sherman instantly shot back. "If it's for the good of the Army we do. I'm concerned with the Army here. Not one officer. Not one battle. The Army. That is my sole concern."

"Who decides which of the unsuccessful officers we will try and which will go free?" Sheridan said, a trace of rancor in his voice.

"*We* damn well decide," Sherman said.

Looking down to allow his temper to cool, Sheridan turned his glass on the small table, leaving wet rings. "We set a terrible precedent," he said softly.

"No, we react to a situation."

"Then we break a long-standing precedent."

"Philip, stop all this concern with precedent," Sherman said. "In battle, no one knows better than you that a commander must react to the situation."

The point was not lost. All three men knew that Sheridan was much more adept at handling tactical situations than was Sherman. It was like a concession requiring a concession in return, and because of that each man also knew that Sherman was, as he had always been, the better of the two strategically.

"Besides," he said, "precedent exists for one reason—to guide those who have no ambition for devising new and better solutions to their problems."

"I hope you had more regard for precedent when you were practicing law."

Sherman laughed, a snort that left his expression mostly unchanged. "I had little ambition in law."

Although Sheridan had thus far refused to commit himself, both men knew he would not fight the Commanding General on whatever charge might be made against Custer. It was up to Grant to decide. If the President was against it, there would be no charge, no trial, no cashiering. But Sherman was sure of his ground with Grant. He only waited now for the President to state what to Sherman was the obvious.

"I think Custer handled the fight in Montana badly—very badly," Grant finally said. "All those dead men—it rests on his head. And it has made all our troop units on the frontier too cautious."

Grant looked for a moment at Sheridan. Across the room Sherman settled into a straight chair and crossed his legs, folded his arms.

"It's bad from another standpoint," Grant continued. "The Congress is stingy with money at best during this depressed economic period. Now, they're squealing about raising troop levels—but that's from fright. As soon as that's past, they'll calm down and look back, and this performance on the Little Bighorn may not help loosen the purse strings. It was a sad performance."

"But, Mr. President, it was only once——"

Grant stopped Sheridan with a lifted hand and a slight shake of his head. "No, it is not just this once," he said. "Custer has long been the center of some kind of controversy. Now take those Congressional hearings just before the Montana column left Fort Lincoln. . . ."

He sipped his brandy and the generals waited. Knowing that the hearings on impeachment of cabinet members were an embarrassing point with the President, neither had dared mention them.

"He came up here to Washington and testified, snorting about wanting to rid the frontier of graft and corruption. Every accusation he made was against one of my people—and my own brother—and these were serious accusations. Yet everything he said was hearsay. I know I got all kinds of criticism for suspending him from command for that, no matter what excuses we made for it. But, damnit, what kind of man will make accusations like that on hearsay evidence? I didn't feel capable of trusting him. Maybe my motives were partly political, but that's what I am, now, a politician. Custer is not. He's a soldier. But he was acting like a scheming politician. You could say he was only disloyal. *Only* disloyal. To his Commander-in-Chief. But there was something worse, much worse, for a man you are getting ready to trust with troops—oh, we'd trusted him before, yes. But a man can change. Look at me. . . ."

He turned toward Sheridan then and smiled sadly, shaking his head.

"You want to stay out of Washington as long as you can, Phil, it's no place for a good soldier. You'll be here one day, but stay out as long as you can."

Sheridan poured the President another drink and Grant took it and sipped it. He winked at Sherman, his smile broader now.

"I will have to admit I've always detested Custer a wee bit. But I think we have good cause to get rid of him. If for nothing else, then for stupidity. That testimony he gave is beyond my comprehension. . . ."

And so it was decided. Once a decision was made, there was no doubting Sheridan—he would support it.

"About politics," Sheridan said. "The Democrats seem interested in Custer for the November presidential conventions."

"God help us and the Republic if he ever moves into this place," Grant said, waving his glass upward toward the main floors of the White House.

"He has a considerable public and press following," Sheridan said.

"In November, according to what the doctors tell us, Philip, he will still be an invalid," Sherman said from across the room. "He could even die. His wounds are debilitating. But just to be on the safe side, I'll speak with my brother over in the Senate. He's a Republican, of course, but a word from him to the Democratic leadership would do no harm. He's a respected man, I think. But most important, I doubt if the Democrats would nominate a man under indictment."

"The court can't possibly be held before the conventions?" Grant asked.

"No." Sherman shook his head. "It will take too much time. Without a previous investigation or court of inquiry, a great deal has to be done. I'll ask Billy Dunn to spare no effort. But I judge we won't get it to trial before next spring—perhaps not even then."

Sheridan frowned, his fiery temper held somewhat uncertainly in check just beneath the surface of all this talk. "I suppose the Army's Judge Advocate General should be able to do a decent job of this kind of thing."

"Dunn is a good lawyer and a smooth old bastard besides." Sherman chuckled. "He'll see our requirements and find us a good trial judge advocate from among his legal folk. He'll push the investigation, too, and we'll spare him no time or expense when his lawyers start digging up evidence."

"Perhaps we need a pre-trial investigation. . . ." Sheridan started.

Sherman cut him off quickly. "I have made all the investigation required for a charge to be made," he said. The sour smile touched his lips. "Although, of course, what the charge will be remains to be seen."

"How will the Secretary of War react to all of this?" Sheridan asked.

"You needn't worry about Taft," Grant replied. "He thinks Cump hung the moon. He knows he can reverse a court-martial finding if it looks good for him politically. But right now I think he sees Little Bighorn as something to stay completely out of, with half the press and probably the people, too, screaming for Custer's scalp, the other half calling him hero."

Sherman explained how he expected to convene the court himself and to have Terry make the charges. With the proper explanation, he was sure Terry would go along. This left Sheridan out of the official proceedings against his former favorite.

"Do we have him arrested and confined?" Sheridan asked. "I think regulations require it."

"Regulations do require it," Sherman said. "But regulations, like precedents, are guides only, made to be circumvented. It's one of the privileges we have at this level, Philip. We want no excuse for his wailing admirers. We will treat him more than fairly."

Sheridan shook his head. "I wish you had a better idea of what you expect Terry to charge him with."

"Tomorrow I expect to meet with Billy Dunn and we'll have something for Terry within the week. As Judge Advocate General of the Army, Dunn will assist Terry in drawing up charges. Then Dunn will visit Custer. I expect Terry will inform Custer of the charges against him, but I want Dunn out there, too, so he can warn Custer to keep his mouth shut about what happened to his battalion. Anything he might say could be prejudicial to this case. I want Dunn to caution Libby about the same thing—not that it'll do much good."

"Why would she listen to the man coming to tell her husband he's to be tried?" Sheridan asked.

"Oh, Billy will go as a friend to the family. I'll be the son-of-a-bitch in the picture."

"Cump, you've thought this all out," Grant said. "But how are you going to charge him if you don't know what happened to his battalion?"

"We won't try him for anything that happened after he split the regiment, we'll charge him with what he did before he split the command. We've got witnesses to that, and we know the results. It's all we need."

Sheridan thought a long time, scratching his moustache and frowning, lips pursed. Grant and Sherman remained silent, letting the junior member ponder it all.

"Where do we try this, at my headquarters?" Sheridan asked.

"New York," Sherman said, and Grant for the first time showed surprise.

"Why New York?" he asked.

"It's the center of things, Sam. Easy to get to. Plenty of accommodations. It's close to many of the officers we'll appoint to the court. And it's removed from the scene. Chicago—and certainly Terry's headquarters in St. Paul—that's too close to the action, too close to the people involved."

"Hell, I can't see why Chicago doesn't fit into all of that, too," Sheridan protested. "What's your real reason for wanting New York, Cump?"

"I want Schofield for the president of the court, and he's at West Point. I want it all easy for him, he's a temperamental man."

"Schofield's good," Grant said.

Sherman made his sour grimace. "But there's a better reason," he said. "New York is where the big newspapers and magazines are."

"But I thought you said you didn't want the press telling it. . . ."

"I want the Army telling this story on its own terms, on its own ground. But I want every word printed for people to see and read."

Grant nodded, his cigar jutting from his beard. Sheridan stared a long moment at Sherman.

"And I'm willing to wager that his being loose in New York— among all his high-powered friends, and perhaps a few enemies— will work more to our advantage than to his," Sherman said.

"Cump, I had never really appreciated the depth of your dedication, once you get something treed."

"The treeing has been too long coming, Philip."

"Speaking of the press, who tells them about all of this, with Custer keeping still?" Sheridan asked.

"My aide does a tolerable job of such things. We will announce the charge and give them the court-martial order naming the members. Here in Washington. We will also explain why they should not be hounding Custer for information. His health—and, of course, the prejudice."

"I would prefer not being shown as any part of this," Sheridan said.

"No, it will be shown as my decision," Sherman said.

Grant rose, his eyelids heavy. They said their goodbyes in the library, but as they walked to the west entrance, up a flight of narrow stars and down a darkened hall, Grant touched Sherman's sleeve and the two men paused at the entranceway as Sheridan went on and entered the waiting carriage.

"Cump, I won't be here to back you when the trial takes place," the President said. "I don't know where I'll be."

Sherman stood patiently, looking down at the smaller man. From the Potomac a cool breeze had started up, driving some of the day's humidity away.

"We've always thought alike," Grant said. "It's the same on this Custer business. You've got to keep at it, you've got to do it, Cump. No matter who is elected next fall."

Sherman nodded. He knew Grant still had something to say so he waited.

"You think we should . . . don't you think it best to place him in arrest in quarters?"

"No, Mr. President, we don't want to arouse sympathy in the press. He'll have enough of that at best."

"I suppose so. Well, it's your battle, so fight it." His hand remained on Sherman's arm. "He won't fly the coop?"

"Where would he go? The Army is his home."

Grant nodded slowly. "Yes. That's the worst part of all this. He loves the Army as much as we do, in his strange way. But now the Army can no longer afford him."

"Sam, the presidency has turned you into a philosopher." Sherman chuckled softly. He squeezed Grant's hand. "Good night, Mr. President."

4

Fussy Billy Dunn had finished his work, and Sherman was satisfied with it. Elizabeth Custer had not remained silent—nobody really expected her to. But at least in those months before the trial she had given no hint of what happened to her Autie and his battalion that day on the Greasy Grass—the Indian term everyone now knew meant the Little Bighorn River valley. It had become fashionable for newspapers to use the Indian names for places. A great many people thought Custer had not told his wife about the battle, although that would have been highly unusual. The entire Army and at least half of the country's total population knew he generally told her everything.

The furor in the press over the Montana battle mounted in pitch and tone with each passing week. Concern seemed less with the story Custer would eventually tell and more with who was to blame for the disaster at the Little Bighorn. One view held Terry the culprit, and he was attacked with spirit and imagination. Another group assailed Custer with equal vigor—and in both instances enthusiasm was generally matched only by ignorance. But not always. As Sherman had foreseen, the Army did become involved—had to become involved—in the messy public controversy. Officers were interviewed or wrote their own accounts and opinions, and

Sherman and his aides watched closely. Somehow, miraculously, Custer kept himself aloof. Sherman began to wonder if perhaps there had been some elemental change in the dashing cavalier.

The best among Dunn's judge advocate officers, Major Asa B. Gardiner, had been selected to try the case. Gardiner had been brought into the presence of the Commanding General, and Sherman had heartily approved him. They had chatted for a while, Sherman careful to avoid mentioning the case for fear someone might whisper about command influence. The investigation had begun within a week of the conference in the White House basement. It had gone slowly. Many of the officers and men involved were still engaged in an active Indian campaign. Others were scattered with the occupation Army in southern states—at least until Hayes was inaugurated, when the occupying forces of the Union were withdrawn from the vanquished territory.

Major Gardiner had moved back temporarily to New York, where he built his case with material sent by two assistants assigned him by the Commanding General; the orders actually came from the Secretary, which proved what Sherman and Grant had supposed, that Sherman would be allowed free hand—for the time being at least. Gardiner had found a small flat just off West Street on 33rd, overlooking the Hudson and a short walk from the River Railroad Depot. He spent most of his time studying testimony, penciling in positions on maps and charts, and gazing out at the Jersey shore across the river. As the case began to take form, he went to Governor's Island from time to time, taking the River Railroad cars to Chambers Street, then a trolley to the Battery. At night he traveled much the same route, sometimes to the Mott Street area and a place called Madam Song's, best described as a domino parlor and pleasure palace. Or he might go across town and enjoy an evening near Fifth Avenue and 26th Street—at Delmonico's—or at the Fifth Avenue Hotel or Ned Stokes's Hoffman House. The theaters, too, were nearby, as was the Racquet Court Club.

Both Gardiner's assistants were young officers in whom he had great confidence. Lieutenant George Beakin, an Adjutant General's Corps officer who had graduated from West Point in 1873, was operating out of Chicago, obtaining briefs of testimony from the officers and men in the field. Before the trial Gardiner went to

Chicago twice, and he and Beakin traveled on to Bismarck and Fort Lincoln. From there they took a steamer into the Yellowstone country and, finally, with a company of cavalry as escort, visited the battlefield. A third time, in July 1877, they accompanied the reconstituted Company I, 7th Cavalry—the original company had been destroyed in the fight—back to the scene. The cavalry's job on that trip was to reclaim the bodies of officers for reburial in the East.

Everyone on the expedition had been appalled to find that the field was covered with bleaching bones, scattered in great profusion about the hill above the river. The soldiers had been ill-equipped the year before for grave-digging, and the holes had been too shallow. Many of the bodies had been clawed out of the ground by animals; others had likely been washed to the surface by spring rains.

Gardiner's second assistant, Lieutenant Charles Sommers, Cavalry, West Point class of 1875, had been stationed in Washington City, collecting and studying reports and records. He had also been Gardiner's liaison with General Dunn.

A week before the trial was scheduled to convene, Gardiner arranged for quarters on Governor's Island for his assistants. Both officers were married, but neither could afford to bring his wife to New York. In those final days before the trial there had been little time for anything but work. Frequently one or the other or both officers stayed the night in Gardiner's flat, sleeping on a floor pallet amongst the scattered papers of the prosecution's case.

Beakin was a tall, slender man who at times seemed to be all knuckles. His freckled face was clean-shaven, his hair a flaxen blond and straight. He seldom smiled, but when he did he showed large white teeth behind thin lips, and his pale blue eyes twinkled. Sommers complemented him well, being shorter, somewhat rotund for so young a man, raven-haired with a thick moustache. His face was oval in shape, olive in complexion, his mouth was full-lipped and small, his eyes a sparkling black, with black lashes and brows, almost like the ones painted on the china faces of the expensive dolls at Mr. R. H. Macy's new store on 14th Street. Beakin moved only when required, but Sommers was constantly darting about on errands real or imagined. As a team they functioned well for Gardiner's purposes, and he was grateful for them.

It was Sommers's task to set up the courtroom on Governor's Island. Major General Winfield Scott Hancock presided over the island—indeed, over all the East Coast, militarily—and he cooperated with a wholeheartedness Sommers could hardly understand. Gardiner explained it one evening as the three of them prepared a large map of the battlefield to be used in the course of the trial.

In 1867 Custer and the 7th Cavalry had been a part of a campaign in Kansas to pacify or to intimidate a few unruly Indians. Hancock had been in command, at that time being stationed on the frontier. Unfortunately, due to a few decisions most kindly described as the result of inexperience, the march across Kansas did not pacify—it started a war with the Cheyenne. Custer was dispatched with his regiment to run down marauders. After weeks of chasing dust devils and catching nothing, Custer reached western Kansas, horses and men exhausted. He left the command there and with a special escort rode back to Fort Riley to visit his wife. Hancock court-martialed him.

"What happened?" Sommers asked.

"Convicted and sentenced to a year without pay. But Sheridan needed Custer for a winter campaign in the Indian Territory and talked him right back into the saddle."

"I understand all that," Sommers said. "The battle of the Washita. . . . But surely Hancock got what he wanted with the trial. Is he still so bitter against Custer?"

"It might have been all right, but while Custer was suspended from command he wrote a number of articles critical of the court and of Hancock. They were published widely. Hancock took most unkindly to that."

"I should have known that," Sommers said, running a hand over his dark hair. "But I don't suppose we could use it anyway."

Gardiner smiled and shook his head.

"Let me see," Sommers mused aloud. "When that happened I would have been—let's see—a twelve-year-old urchin in dear old Savannah."

"Get your dear old butt off the edge of the map," Beakin interrupted.

Sommers laughed. "Well, for whatever reason, General Hancock is doing flip-flops to help me get that courtroom set up. It's going to be the grandest of courtrooms anywhere before we're finished."

At that moment the interior of the old mess building where the court would be held was being whitewashed. Later the court facilities would take form quickly under Lieutenant Sommers's direction. The building had not been used for a number of years. It sat on the west end of Governor's Island, a single-story, long stone structure with an anteroom at one end, an empty kitchen at the other, and in between a dining hall that took up most of the floor space in the building. There were high windows on either side of the long room—which would be the courtroom—and as one entered it from the anteroom through a large double door, the windows on the left opened onto the Narrows and Staten Island, those on the right onto lower Manhattan and the mouth of the Hudson River.

The anteroom became an entry hall with chairs and coat racks, one end partitioned off to form a provost guard room where soldiers assigned to the court could rest when they were not on duty and where the court provost—a kind of master-at-arms—could make his headquarters. At the other end of the building, the kitchen would be used as court chambers, where members of the court could ponder their decisions and refresh themselves at the sink still set into the rear wall. A long conference table was placed there, with enough chairs to accommodate the court. A number of legal reference books were placed there as well, among them, the *Manual for Courts-Martial* and Colonel Steven V. Benet's *Military Law and Courts-Martial*. Strips of paper and pencils were provided for voting.

Two doors led from this room into the dining room or courtroom. On the west wall of the courtroom, between these doors, was suspended a United States flag. On the other side of each door was a floor stand for colors. In the stand to the left was a second, smaller national flag and on the right were the colors of a major general, solid red with two large white stars. Directly in front of these flags was the bench—a long table—with chairs aligned along the side next to the wall, facing the long end of the room.

Facing the bench on the left was a single chair standing on a platform about six inches above the floor. The witness stand. It was slightly in advance of the bench and canted at a forty-five-degree angle to it. At the other end of the bench, abutting it at a ninety-degree angle, was a small table with a chair. This was for the court reporter.

There was a large empty space directly in front of the bench—Sommers called it the bull ring—then the tables of the prosecution and defense, each facing parallel to the bench and aligned with each other perpendicular to the side walls. There were chairs around these tables facing the bench. Looking toward the bench, the table to the left was for the trial judge advocate, the one to the right for the defendant and his attorneys.

Behind the tables another space, and then two banks of chairs, aisles along either wall and down the center of the room. Directly behind the trial judge advocate's table were five of the total of nine rows of chairs roped off and marked "press."

Potbellied stoves were placed down the center aisle of the courtroom, in the anteroom, and in the court conference room.

Once the court was convened, armed provost guards would be stationed throughout the court. One would be at each door behind the bench, leading into the conference room; one on either side of the large door between the courtroom and the anteroom; one just inside the entrance to the anteroom from the gravel walk outside; and finally one outside the main entrance—his duty being primarily to direct ladies and gentlemen to appropriate rest facilities in adjacent buildings. The provost guards were soldiers of the 17th Infantry stationed at West Point, selected for their bright and pressed appearance.

On the day when it was all completed, Sommers stood in the bull ring, smiling, well pleased with his work. His eyes swept over the room, then up toward the ceiling. He suddenly stopped smiling. There were no lights. The sixteen soldiers Hancock had assigned Sommers were sent hustling and soon stepladders and brass lamps appeared. Until the trial was finished, Governor's Island troops would have to eat breakfast and dinner in their mess hall under the greasy, yellow glow of coal oil lanterns. By the end of the day—Monday, November 5, 1877—all was ready.

PART TWO

The Charges

5

Newspaper reporters stand on the gravel walk before the main
entrance to the court building, huddled under umbrellas and waiting impatiently for the doors to open. Most are young, in their
thirties, but there are a few older men trying to maintain some
dignity in the press and push of all the others. They stand tightly
packed as cattle in the cold mist and rain, not because there is
inadequate space to spread out, but because of a strong herd instinct
in such weather.

At the front of the mob, holding himself rigid against the contact of the others, is Solomon Buckley, distinguished correspondent
of the *New York Herald*. He is about fifty years old, a tall be-
whiskered man of sharp eye and feature, with a sour disposition
and little inclination toward making friends. He has had a brilliant
career with the Bennett newspaper, starting during the Civil War.
He had been captured by Rebel forces at one time and held in
Castle Thunder Prison in Richmond for almost a year before being
released in an exchange of prisoners. He was on the frontier with an
Indian Peace Commission in 1867 and was known and despised by
William Tecumseh Sherman. He has little reason to suppose the
Commanding General's feeling toward him has mellowed and it
bothers him not at all.

A rope has been strung across the hand railings on either side of the four wide steps leading from the gravel walk to the double doors of the court anteroom. On the top step stands a soldier at parade rest, nervously eyeing the crowd a few feet below him. He carries a bayoneted rifle and he is dressed for rough weather with forage cap and rain cape. From time to time the court provost sergeant appears at the door behind him and glances around the area near the court building.

Along the walk leading to the court building is a long warehouse with a wide veranda. In this shelter stand a number of officers and their ladies. Soon after each barge arrives from Manhattan the group is joined by newcomers, and greetings are exchanged in a flurry of loud conversation that lasts only a few moments, then subsides into a murmur as the crowd waits for the court to open. There are a number of civilian men and their wives. They are well dressed and obviously well bred—or at least have been able to buy the appearance of breeding. Of working-class people there are none, for this is a working day in New York. On a Tuesday, during the great depression of '77, one either labors or searches for the privilege of doing so.

In the heavy air the scent of frying bacon comes across from a troop mess. Some of the officers waiting had hoped to enjoy coffee in the officers' club, but the number of officers on the island in connection with the trial has caused all such facilities to be placed off limits to visitors.

With the harbor gulls squawking as they wheel above in the gray mist, the soldiers of Governor's Island start another day. The new relief of guard forms ranks before the flagpole and is counted off and posted by the officer of the day. A flag detail runs up the colors as the guard comes to present arms. A bugle in front of the commanding officer's headquarters blows assembly, and all the troops on duty come grumbling to the edge of the parade ground where first sergeants check off the roll and announce the orders of the day. Then the men return to the buildings where they will work in the offices of General Hancock's Atlantic Division until the bugler plays "Beans" at 11:30. It is an administrative post, with only a few line troops assigned for guard duty.

All of this can be dimly perceived by those waiting for the trial to begin. The press representatives and the other civilians crane their necks to see what is happening, but to the officers and the Army wives it is a routine long remembered, and each sound brings memories of past stations and posts. The ordinary movement of uniformed soldiers gives them a feeling of well-being. The muted notes of the bugle come at intervals they anticipate, with calls they understand.

The warehouse, the court building, and the other structures on the west end of the island are actually outside the walls of Fort Columbus. The fort was completed on Governor's Island in 1833, its purpose to protect the entrance to the East River and the rest of New York Harbor. The guns are still in place, but there is no coast artillery garrison on the island to man them—only a housekeeping crew of ordnance troops. The people who have come for the trial leave the ferry slip and walk past the main gate sally port to this western, exposed area of the island. Their view of what takes place inside the walls of the main compound is almost completely obstructed, but the sounds come to them, and above the forty-foot-high walls, with the deep embrasures for the guns, they can see the top of the flagstaff and the storm bunting that has just been raised there.

A mess attendant appears from the west sally port—the one nearest the court building—and hurries along bareheaded in the mist, carrying a large tray with a coffee pot and a number of cups. His feet make a moist crunching in the gravel as he walks toward the rear of the court building. He kicks on the door there and a provost guard lets him inside. At the sally port a group of officers appears, walking briskly also, talking loudly, smoking. Most are gray-whiskered and somewhat rotund. They pass along the walk as the mess attendant has done and disappear into the back of the building. With members of the court now on hand, the reporters know the trial will soon begin and they press against the rope.

Inside, Gardiner has greeted the nine officers assigned as judges to the court. It has been a frosty meeting—it is not supposed to be friendly. The purpose of the meeting is to allow the trial judge advocate to check roll, to determine how many officers appointed to the court-martial by the convening authority are actually on hand. As soon as Gardiner has taken roll, they disappear again into the conference room.

As the crowd begins to move into the courtroom, the provost sergeant standing at the door says over and over again, "Please do not push or run, please do not push or run, please . . ." Gardiner is back in the bull ring, watching, standing at his table. Lieutenants Beakin and Sommers are at their chairs, talking softly. Neither turns to watch as the press scrambles into the seats directly to the rear of them.

Behind the defense table someone has marked off a number of chairs with a length of white engineer tape. Gardiner knows this is for the Custer party. His eyes move over the people as they come in, and now and then he nods to some officer he knows. The press quickly overflows its area and fills most of the left aisle. Gardiner inclines his head to Solomon Buckley, but the *Herald* man makes no acknowledgment. Women's bright dresses make splashes of color in the right aisle. As planned, when the seats are filled, only a few standees are admitted. The provost sergeant and two of his guards close the doors to the courtroom. In the anteroom extra chairs have been provided. With the double transom open over the doors, spectators can at least hear much of what goes on inside the courtroom.

Although Custer will be represented by a civilian lawyer, the Army has appointed a Judge Advocate General's Corps officer for the defense as well. He is Major William Winthrop, a stocky man with a deep scar across his left cheek and steel gray eyes set wide over a flat nose and lips that seem perpetually pursed. He has been a major since the war and has never worked with Gardiner—whom he resents. Gardiner is aware of this and is disturbed by it.

When Winthrop comes into the courtroom the two ignore one another. Winthrop does so intentionally, but Gardiner is concerned with watching—sizing up—the large man walking down the aisle behind the Army officer. He is a man in his late fifties, graying and balding, with a closely clipped moustache and sideburns. He walks with a shuffle, and Gardiner sees that his right foot is turned in, a deformity he has had since birth. His eyes have a yellow cast as he glances quickly about the room, seeming to take it all in and storing each detail of what he sees for future reference. He sees Gardiner standing at the front of the room and smiles, showing large yellow teeth, and Gardiner realizes the lump under his left ear is a cud of chewing tobacco held tightly in his cheek. He shuffles up to the trial judge advocate and extends his hand.

"Jacobson. Allan Jacobson, of Bacon, Harms, and Benfield in Monroe, Michigan," he says. He is slightly shorter than Gardiner and as he leans forward he gives the impression of gazing intently up Gardiner's nose.

"Gardiner. Major Asa Gardiner." Jacobson's fingers are soft but his grip is firm. They shake hands for a long moment.

"I look forward to this, young man," Jacobson says. "They tell me you're one of the Army's brightest lawyers."

Gardiner glances over at Winthrop and thinks, I'll wager *he* didn't say that.

"With your help, sir, I hope to keep the proceedings in order."

Jacobson laughs. "Of course. All we ask is a fair hearing."

"That is one of my particular duties here," Gardiner says.

Still smiling, Jacobson wheels and clumps across the room, looking back toward the spectators and making his little bow.

Gardiner turns to his table and opens a folder, glancing through the handwritten material that Beakin has collected since it was announced some months ago that Jacobson would defend Custer. Although he has read it before, Gardiner scans it again, now that he has seen the man. Jacobson has a reputation as a trial lawyer in Michigan. He is headstrong and sometimes obstinate, and these characteristics have apparently kept him from partnership in the firm of Bacon, Harms, and Benfield. He does not seem to care particularly, for he could long since have left them and formed his own firm. He comes from a well-to-do Detroit family, has been married twenty-eight years, has seven grandchildren. During the war he was a special counsel for the United States Navy. A Democrat, he nonetheless supported Hayes in '76. He is fond of rye whiskey, oysters, and mutton stew. His education includes the University of Michigan and Harvard Law School. The senior partner in the firm of which he is a part is Elizabeth Custer's father.

The mutter of conversation among the spectators stops as the doors behind the bench open and the nine members of the court come into the room. They continue to chat casually; some still hold coffee cups in their hands and a few are smoking cigars.

"You forgot the cuspidors," Gardiner whispers, leaning toward his assistants. Sommers swears under his breath and jumps up, bolting down the aisle toward the rear of the courtroom.

The members of the court begin to arrange themselves as everyone watches. They appear to be in no hurry. The senior member—who will act as president of the court—moves to the center of the bench, each subordinate rank descending alternately to his right and left. A few of them take their seats and look at the crowd, elbows on the table before them.

Sommers has provided a high-backed armchair for the president, and behind it now is Major General John McAllister Schofield, Superintendent of West Point, a graduate in 1853. He is known throughout the Army as an intellectual, having at one time been professor of physics at Washington University in St. Louis. His Civil War record as a combat leader is solid. He served in Sherman's Army in the West until after Atlanta, then with an independent command was victor over John Bell Hood at the Battle of Franklin. He served for a short while as Secretary of War under Andrew Johnson. He had, from time to time, rather colorful ideas —such as the acquisition of a naval base in the Pacific at a place called Pearl Harbor.

A stout man, Schofield fills his uniform. As is his custom, he has his coat open except for the bottom two buttons, and a red flannel shirt is visible. He has close-set brown eyes under bristling brows. He is bald on top, with gray hair above the ears running down into magnificent muttonchop whiskers. A drooping moustache does not hide sensuous, cupid-bow lips.

He is a brilliant billiards player and he holds a cream-colored cue ball which he will use as gavel. Well liked—although generally from a distance—and trusted by most of the Officer Corps, he has taken no part in the Custer controversy and it is not expected that either defense or prosecution will try to have him challenged from the court.

Gardiner pulls a large watch from his pocket and snaps it open. Almost eight o'clock. He glances toward Schofield and the other officers who seem in no hurry to begin. There is a stir in the rear of the room and all turn to see an entourage of a dozen people coming in as the provost sergeant and another soldier hold the doors. Leading the group is a strikingly attractive woman, her head up, a slight smile on her broad lips. She wears a green taffeta princess gown, trimmed in antique white lace, and it rustles softly as she walks—seems to glide—toward the front of the room. The same color scheme is carried out in the small hat she wears, and all of it complements her deep chestnut hair. The other members of her party follow her closely, as though they are afraid to be left behind. As she glances to either side, Gardiner sees she has gray, clear eyes. Her lashes and brows are finely etched against almost alabaster skin. In her ears she wears two large pearls. Gardiner thinks the neck arching up from the lace of her collar is the most attractive neck he has ever seen.

She moves confidently into the chair behind the defense table. Both Jacobson and Winthrop are standing, waiting for her. She smiles for them and they bow as she arranges her skirt and sits down, the dress billowing out, making it difficult for members of her party to take their places on either side.

The princess skirt was not made for sitting and is infamous for hiking up in front on such occasions, but she is mindful of this and holds her hands over her knees. Even so, the hem of the dress rises enough to expose a lacy battery of petticoats and a dainty pair of green high-button shoes. The members of the court watch closely, but despite the fervent wish of some—the older ones particularly— her petticoats do not lift high enough for them to see her shoe tops and stockings.

Turning her head slightly to the left, her eyes touch Gardiner's. He sees a hard, metallic glint, although she still smiles. He has a sudden desire to move toward her, then she looks away. Well, Elizabeth Custer, we meet finally, he thinks. Little wonder that Custer has been infatuated since his boyhood. What is in the man that can hold so steadfast such a woman? Gardiner pulls his gaze away from her.

The buzz of conversation in the room has hardly begun after Elizabeth Custer's entrance when the doors are opened again. Stalking into the room is George Armstrong Custer. His face is wasted from a long convalescence, but he has been sunning himself and his cheeks are ruddy. His nose is peeling. His hair hangs in long, oiled ringlets to his shoulders, which show the stars of a major general. Gardiner grinds his teeth. During the war Custer had indeed been a major general, and many—including the newspapers—still refer to him as such. But he is actually a lieutenant colonel. Without looking toward the bench, Gardiner knows that these stars will rankle Schofield.

Custer's hair is brushed back behind his ears and one almost expects to see earrings there, shiny and golden like the buttons down his front. His moustache is oiled as well, thrusting out defiantly. His eyes, although red-rimmed, are their usual cold blue. He strides confidently, but with a slight limp, a full-dress, fur-lined cape swinging out behind. Under one arm is a wide-brimmed hat with a plume. He wears light blue trousers with a black stripe, and over his black shoes are gray felt spats. On his left little finger glistens a large diamond ring, the gold burnished, as is the gold of his cufflinks and of a monstrous watch chain that dangles across his belly.

As Custer comes to the defense table he turns and bows slightly toward Gardiner, a sardonic smile showing under his moustache. Then he faces the court, bows once more, and when he speaks his voice is low but audible in the silent room. "General Schofield, sir. Gentlemen."

He seats himself casually, crosses his legs, and tosses his hat onto the center of the defense counsel's table, obscuring most of Jacobson's documents. Gardiner can hardly suppress a chuckle as Jacobson's face contorts for an instant. The defense counsel hurries around his table and beckons the provost sergeant down the aisle, and the sergeant takes Custer's hat back to the anteroom. All of this Custer ignores as his eyes sweep back and forth over the members of the court.

Schofield and the others have taken their places and Schofield is grim-faced. No one on the court has acknowledged Custer's greeting except the second ranking member, Major General Irvin McDowell. When Custer spoke McDowell had smiled and nodded, his fat face crinkled like old tissue paper a long time in the sun and rain. His chins overflow his collar and his chest is concave, allowing a number of bright yellow breakfast cake crumbs to settle there, showing plainly among the brass buttons. They will remain there all day.

Schofield is ready to rap the billiard ball onto the table when Sommers and a soldier hurry into the room and down the aisle, each carrying a spittoon under each arm. As these are deposited behind the bench and before the tables of both prosecution and defense, Schofield watches, the billiard ball held above the table. As Sommers scurries back to his seat, Schofield glares a moment at Gardiner.

The billiard ball taps lightly on the bench. "Because there are a great many ladies present, I would appreciate your cooperation, gentlemen. Let there be no smoking in the courtroom."

Someone in the press gallery stage-whispers, "He doesn't smoke."

Schofield glances in that direction and holds up the billiard ball, turning it slowly in his hand as he speaks.

"I will say this as well. The proceedings here will be closely controlled. There will be no emotional outbursts. Nor will there be any comment or attempt to interfere from spectators, be they officers, civilians, or newspaper people. I will not hesitate to have anyone causing such a distraction ousted from this courtroom and from Governor's Island by the provost guard."

He pauses, looking from the press section across the room to the area most densely colored with blue Army uniforms. He smiles slightly and adds, "And I am sure we have all observed that the provost guard is armed with bayonets."

There is a chuckle from the officers among the spectators and scowls from the press. Solomon Buckley, of the *Herald*, lifts his eyes toward the ceiling and sighs loudly.

Schofield turns to Gardiner. "Major, are you ready?"

"I am, General."

"Is the defense ready?" Turning toward Jacobson.

"We are, Mr. President."

Back to Gardiner. "Proceed to convene the court, sir."

6

The ritual for getting a court-martial underway is somewhat stilted and uninteresting, but each phase has its meaning, each statement its purpose. Of all those in the room, Jacobson appreciated this most acutely, and he watches and listens intently as the court rises and Gardiner positions himself directly before Schofield. As each officer's name is called for the record—by order of rank—that officer seats himself. Thus, out of respect for rank, the senior man on the court is seated first, the junior last.

Looking at each man as he calls the name, Gardiner says, "Major General John M. Schofield, Superintendent of West Point; Major General Irvin McDowell, Commanding General, Division of the Pacific; Brigadier General John Pope, Commanding General, Department of the Missouri; Brigadier General Oliver O. Howard, Commanding General, Department of the Columbia; Brigadier General Edward O. Ord, Commanding General, Department of Texas; Brigadier General Christopher C. Augur, Commanding General, Department of New Mexico; Colonel Thomas L. Crittenden, Commanding Officer, 16th Infantry; Colonel Ranald MacKenzie, Commanding Officer, 4th Cavalry; Colonel George Sykes, Commanding Officer, 20th Infantry."

There is a murmur of appreciation throughout the courtroom at this galaxy of rank as the members of the court settle into their chairs. Gardiner, returning to his table and finding the appropriate paper, waits for Schofield.

"The court is now opened," the president says.

Some of the reporters lean forward or squirm or lick their lips in anticipation of the coming action, but there remains a great deal of official procedure. Gardiner begins to read.

" 'Headquarters, the Adjutant General's Office, Washington, 17 October 1876. Special Orders Number 217. By direction of the President, a court-martial is hereby appointed to assemble in the city of New York at such time as the convening authority may direct, for the purpose of trying certain charges made against Lieutenant Colonel George A. Custer for conduct on and in the vicinity of the Little Bighorn River, Montana Territory, on 23, 24, and 25 June 1876, while in command of the 7th United States Cavalry.'

"The detail for the court has been indicated. In addition, Lieutenant Benjamin Jones II, Assistant Adjutant General, Headquarters, Division of the Atlantic, is appointed court reporter." Gardiner nods toward the young officer at the end of the bench taking everything in shorthand. "And myself, Major Asa B. Gardiner, TJA."

"May I request something?" Jacobson says from his chair. "These numbers and letters . . . could I be told what they mean? It all sounds like hens' cackling to me."

Schofield looks from the defense counsel to Gardiner.

"TJA means trial judge advocate," Gardiner explains. "The number, sir, is a sequence number of special orders issued from the adjutant general's office during a year."

"Calendar or fiscal?" Jacobson asks.

Schofield intervenes testily. "Mr. Jacobson, there are certain administrative procedures which must be accomplished and they do not require long wrangles. Surely your service to the Navy prepared you for this kind of thing. We have enough of substance to occupy us."

Gardiner resumes his reading, ending with " '. . . by order of General Sherman and signed Brigadier General E. D. Townsend, Adjutant General of the Army.' "

Gardiner turns toward the defense. "Are there any objections or challenges to members of this court as seated in the appointing order?"

"Yes, we would like to object to everyone who is not a cavalry officer," Jacobson says, rising and smiling at the court.

"You may challenge for cause, Mr. Jacobson, and branch of service is not a cause," Schofield says.

"Yes, I expected as much," Jacobson continues in good nature. "Then we should like to challenge . . . uh . . . General Ord."

The short, fiery Ord sits with brows bristling over deepset eyes. Knowing what is expected, he rises and moves to the witness stand. Before he sits down he faces Gardiner and raises his hand.

Gardiner begins. "Do you swear the information you are about to provide in matters of this challenge will be the truth, the whole truth, and nothing but the truth, so help you God?"

"I do."

"Please be seated, sir, state your name, grade, and present duty station."

"Edward Ord, Brigadier General, Commander of the Department of Texas."

Gardiner moves back and Jacobson shuffles to the witness stand, smiling at General Ord as he does.

"General, do you know a man named Nelson Miles? A colonel, I believe."

"Yes, I know him."

"Isn't it true, General, that you and Nelson Miles have engaged in a disagreement—a public disagreement—on the conduct of the battle under question in this court?"

"We did." Ord appears surprised that such information would be available to the defense counsel. "I don't know how public it was."

"Did Nelson Miles defend the actions of General Custer in that battle?"

"He did."

"And did you disagree?"

"I did." Ord's face is beginning to grow red.

"Isn't it true, General, that in the company of a number of officers and their wives, you said General Custer was headstrong and incompetent?"

Ord stares at him for a long time before answering. "Something to that effect."

Jacobson turns abruptly and walks to his seat, hands outstretched.

"Thank you, General Ord. Mr. President, I submit such a statement constitutes prejudgment."

Schofield glances up and down the bench. "There being no objection from any member of the court, General Ord is excused."

Ord leaves the stand and disappears into the conference room. Unknown to any of them, his arguments with Nelson Miles are not finished, and eventually he will be forced into retirement in order to make a place on the promotion list for Miles.

The court rearranges itself so that once more order of rank is observed right to left alternately from the center, and someone in the press gallery snickers. Sommers hears a whisper about musical chairs and he cannot suppress a grin himself.

In the short pause Gardiner looks at Jacobson and wonders when he spits. The bulge of the cud is still obvious in his cheek.

"Are there further challenges?" Gardiner says.

"If the court please." Colonel Crittenden rises. "I wish to challenge myself."

As he takes the stand and is sworn, there is a murmur among the spectators and Beakin whispers to Sommers, "I told you he would do it."

From the center of the bull ring, Gardiner explains to the court that on such challenges, questions will be directed by the TJA.

"Sir, explain the nature of your challenge."

"I was appointed to this court over my own objections," Crittenden says. "My oldest son, John, was detailed to the 7th Cavalry for duty last spring from his normal station with the 20th Infantry. He was with Custer at the Little Bighorn."

There is a long silence in the room and Gardiner, realizing the colonel will go no further, does so himself.

"Your son was assigned to Company L, was he not?"

Crittenden, red-eyed now, nods. Gardiner turns to the court.

"Company L was one of those which the accused personally commanded. There were no survivors—except one." He looks back at Custer and Jacobson is immediately on his feet.

"We are supposed to be testing challenges here, not making statements relative to the so-called case against my client."

"Well taken, Mr. Jacobson," Schofield says. "Major?"

"I beg the court's pardon, but I had supposed I was making a simple statement of fact," says Gardiner. "Perhaps I can rephrase. Colonel Crittenden's son was killed while serving directly under the command of the accused."

Having gotten in the barb again, Gardiner wheels to the witness stand and continues—although Jacobson has his mouth open to protest.

"Do you feel you can fairly judge the accused in this case?"

"No." Crittenden chokes but quickly controls himself.

"Colonel Crittenden, do you have any notion why, under these circumstances, you were appointed to this court?" Schofield asks.

"The order was apparently signed before the mistake was discovered," Crittenden says. "When I asked to be taken off the panel, General Sherman's aide—a Colonel Wright, I believe—wrote and told me I should serve, but if at the time the court was convened I felt it impossible to do so, then I should take the action I now take."

Crittenden is excused and once more the court reseats. This time there are chuckles from the press gallery, which cease when Schofield glares in that direction.

"There being no further challenges, read the charges, Major Gardiner."

Lifting a sheath of papers, Gardiner glances toward Custer. The cavalryman seems unconcerned with anything happening in the courtroom.

"These charges were brought by Brigadier General Alfred Terry, Commanding General, Department of Dakota, and were served on accused by Brigadier General William Dunn at Fort Lincoln, Dakota Territory, one year and ten days ago, 28 October 1876. A copy has been provided the defense. Does defense waive reading of the charges?"

"Defense does not," Jacobson says.

Gardiner reads from the charge sheet: " 'Violation of the 21st Article of War, Disobedience of orders. Specification number one. In that Lieutenant Colonel George Armstrong Custer, 7th United States Cavalry, receiving from General William T. Sherman an order not to permit newspaper reporters with his column in campaign against the Sioux in 1876, did willfully disobey same.

" 'Specification number two. In that aforesaid officer did, having received a lawful order from his superior, Brigadier General Alfred Terry, to march up Rosebud River beyond a point where an Indian trail crossed from Rosebud to Little Bighorn and to proceed as far as the headwaters of the Tongue, thus placing himself south of any hostiles in the Little Bighorn valley, did willfully disobey by following said trail directly, thus precipitating battle before other friendly forces were up, resulting in unwarranted loss of animals and men.' "

Sommers has made available on each table and bench pitchers of water and glasses. Gardiner pauses now for a drink. Over the rim of his glass he watches Custer violently flicking at imaginary dust spots on his trousers.

" 'Charge Two, Violation of the 42nd Article of War, Creating a hazard to his command through negligence. Specification number one. In that aforenamed officer did, at the Little Bighorn on or about 25 June 1876, endanger the safety of his command by failure to make an appropriate reconnaissance for information concerning the terrain and the enemy prior to commitment of his command, thus resulting in unwarranted loss of animals and men.

" 'Specification number two. In that aforenamed officer did, at the Little Bighorn, fail to provide adequate security for his command, resulting in surprise and unwarranted loss of animals and men.

" 'Specification number three. In that aforenamed officer did, at the same place, fail to provide orders to subordinates of even the most rudimentary fashion and did himself fail to act as he had indicated he would act in the course of battle, hence resulting in confusion, uncertainty, and the unwarranted loss of animals and men.

" 'Charge Three, Violation of the 92nd Article of War, Conduct prejudicial to good order and discipline. Specification number one. In that aforenamed officer did, due to overriding ambition noteworthy throughout a long period, precipitate a headlong engagement with a vastly superior enemy in order to defeat said enemy before other friendly forces could arrive to assist him, thus insuring virtual destruction of his regiment.' "

Gardiner tosses the papers onto his table and faces the court. "Mr. President, the charges and specifications have now been read in the presence of the accused and in open court."

"Let the record so indicate," Schofield says. He sees Jacobson on his feet. "Does defense counsel have something?"

"Mr. President, defense moves all charges be dismissed."

"On what grounds?"

"On the grounds that each attacks the prerogative required of any commander in the field and in the face of an enemy. Only the judgment of the commander on the scene, carrying the responsibility, is valid."

"Mr. Jacobson, your motion will be noted in the record and due regard given on appeal, but you must understand that the very basis of your request is what this court was constituted to determine. Motion denied. Major Gardiner, swear the court."

The officers of the court and the reporter rise and lift their hands. McDowell coughs, clears his throat. Standing in the center of the bull ring, Gardiner lifts his right hand also and administers the oath. As the others take their seats once more, Schofield remains standing and swears the TJA.

"Do you, Major Asa B. Gardiner, swear that you will well and truly perform the duties of trial judge advocate in the case now in hearing according to law or the rules of land warfare in like cases . . ."

As the oaths drone on, some of the spectators become restless, shifting their feet, settling more securely into their seats, coughing. The provost sergeant moves down the aisle, closing dampers on all the stoves. With the room filled, the morning chill has quickly been absorbed.

". . . so help you God?"

"I do," Gardiner says. "I will now introduce legal counsel. Myself, as named in the appointing order, a member of the bar in New York, Maryland, and the Federal system, a member of the Army Judge Advocate General's Corps. For the defense, Major William Winthrop, a member of the bar in Pennsylvania, Maryland, Virginia, and the Federal system, and a member of the Army Judge Advocate General's Corps. The Honorable Mr. Allan Jacobson, member of the bar in Michigan, Illinois, Indiana, and the Federal system. Are these qualifications correct, gentlemen? Very well. The court will accept the plea."

Throughout most of his opening presentation Gardiner has

MAJ. GEN. JOHN M. SCHOFIELD

spoken without notes and Jacobson is obviously impressed with the TJA's preparation. Now he remains seated, rubbing his chin, as Winthrop and Custer rise.

"How do you plead?" Schofield asks.

Before Winthrop can reply, Custer answers. "Not guilty." As he always does when he is excited or angry, he speaks with a decided stammer.

"Be seated, please. Major Gardiner, proceed with your opening argument."

"Mr. President, I will present no opening argument as such. With your indulgence I should like to outline the general situation of the campaign under consideration here in order to give focus for members of the court and also to provide a complete official record in the minutes of this trial of last summer-a-year-ago's campaigning in Montana."

"I am sure the newspapers," Jacobson says, only half rising and waving a hand toward the press gallery, "have given us all a perfectly satisfactory general view of what took place there. I see no need for this summary."

Schofield cuts him off sharply. "This court will decide what is and is not needed, Mr. Jacobson. Surely you do not expect a court of law to rely on newspaper reports, particularly when you consider that the only newspaper reporter at the scene of the events in question is now dead. It was a battle the Army fought and one which the Army will document. Major Gardiner, please."

Gardiner knew Sherman would not have given Schofield any specific instructions about how to run his court. Yet the president's words were almost identical to ones Gardiner had heard the Commanding General speak in Washington over a year before. Do they begin to think alike at star rank? He doubted it. But it was strange.

As he speaks Gardiner strides back and forth slowly before the bench, gesturing with his hands. As he holds his arms out, many in the room are taken by the eloquence his hands impart. Elizabeth Custer finds herself watching them intently, but then she quickly turns her eyes away. Now and again Gardiner pauses directly before the president of the court and seems to be speaking only to him. Everyone is intent on his presentation—except McDowell, who within a few moments struggles to stay awake in the warm room.

"In 1875 the United States government entered into negotiations with the Sioux Indians at a place called Red Cloud Agency, Nebraska, for the purpose of acquiring the Black Hills in Dakota Territory, a place earlier ceded to the Indians. Precious metals had been found there and white prospectors could not be kept out of the area, although the Army had tried to do so for some time. However the government could not obtain an agreement for the property and the meetings ended in failure.

"The Sioux, feeling that regardless of any agreement white gold-seekers would come into their lands, and perhaps in protest and frustration, left the reservations in great numbers—along with their friends the Cheyenne. When the Secretary of the Interior—who is charged with Indian affairs—was unable to return these Indians to their reservations, he labeled them hostile. Indeed, a number of whites had been killed, but most of these were trespassers in the Black Hills. The President of the United States ordered the Army to return the Sioux and the Cheyenne to their reserves.

"Lieutenant General Philip Sheridan, Commander of the Division of the Missouri, was charged with the task. He planned three columns to converge on the place it was suspected the Indians would be, hoping to surround them and bring them in. One column was to move north from Wyoming—commanded by General Crook, Major General George Crook. Another was to move from Fort Ellis in Montana Territory toward the east—commanded by Colonel John Gibbon. Yet a third was to move from Fort Lincoln, Dakota Territory, marching westward up the Yellowstone River. Thus they hoped to converge in the Powder River country or along the Bighorn, where they expected the Indians would be after wintering there. The expeditions, after some delay, were begun in the spring of 1876.

"The area in question, gentlemen, is a high plain drained by the tributaries of the Yellowstone and is one of the few remaining grasslands where buffalo graze in quantity. The Yellowstone, flowing generally west to east, is fed by a number of streams coming into it from the south. If you could imagine the four fingers of your hand hanging down . . ." Gardiner holds up a hand and allows his four fingers to hang below. "They might represent the streams in that system. From east to west they would be the Powder, the Tongue, the Rosebud, and the Bighorn—with its tributary, the Little Bighorn.

"The eastern column had as its principal mounted unit the 7th Cavalry, commanded by Lieutenant Colonel Custer. The column was commanded by Brigadier General Alfred Terry."

"Don't you mean, Mr. Gardiner, that General Terry had been placed in command after the President of the United States had removed General Custer from that position because of General Custer's politics?" Jacobson cuts in loudly.

"Mr. Jacobson, you will have a turn at defense opening," Schofield says. "And in the course of these proceedings, even though others may not do so, parties to the trial should use present ranks—not the temporary ones of the Civil War." His eyes shift to Custer's shoulder boards. Custer is contemplating the large flag on the wall behind the bench. "And the accused in this case is a lieutenant colonel."

Jacobson immediately smiles and makes his now familiar bow.

"I do apologize, Mr. President," he says. "I am so unaccustomed to the . . . uh . . . ritual of military court-martial. I hope my own ignorance will not reflect adversely on my client."

"Of course not, of course not. . . ." Schofield seems about to say more but changes his mind. He motions Gardiner to proceed.

"As General Terry's column moved up the Yellowstone, General Crook meanwhile began his advance into the area I have indicated. On the upper Rosebud, on 17 June, he was fallen upon by a large body of hostiles and a day-long engagement resulted in no decision. General Crook retired to Wyoming where he waited for reinforcements.

"General Terry, with the 7th Cavalry under his immediate command and unaware of what was happening to General Crook, proceeded and was soon in courier contact with Colonel Gibbon advancing downstream. A scout in force was sent out by Terry under command of Major Marcus Reno, executive officer of the 7th Cavalry. In the valley of the Rosebud—north of where the fight between the Sioux and General Crook was in fact at that moment being fought—the scout discovered a fresh Indian trail going upstream. Reno returned and made his report of this discovery on 21 June.

"These are the facts of the campaign revealed by official records. At this point the government will proceed with its case, for it is here that the questions to be resolved come into play."

"Call your first witness, Major," Schofield says.

For the first time, Gardiner notices that Jacobson spits into the cuspidor placed before the defense table.

PART THREE

The Prosecution

7

"James Brisban, Major, 2nd Cavalry." As he sits slumped over in the witness chair, he appears slender, even gangling. Years of severe rheumatism have given him perpetually sloped shoulders and a humped back. His face, with small beard and moustache, is a well-controlled mask against the constant pain. His skin, exposed to years of wind and sun, is leathery and deeply creased.

"Do you know the accused in this case?" begins Gardiner.

Brisban, knowing the protocol of courts-martial, points toward Custer and says, "Yes. George Custer."

"Recalling the date of 21 June 1876, did you have occasion to see him then, and if so, what were the circumstances?"

As he speaks, Brisban holds his head back, his eyes closed most of the time, brow furrowed as though thinking intently. "Yes, I did. It was the evening of June 21 when General Terry issued his orders. I was attached to John Gibbon's command and we had been coming down the Yellowstone. Our troops were at the mouth of the Rosebud, most of them anyway, when one of Terry's patrols came back with word of an Indian trail up river. We had figured the Sioux were off to the south and west and it seemed like it was certain with that report."

Brisban coughs, pulling a large bandana handkerchief from his inside coat pocket. He chokes for a moment before resuming.

"Terry decided he wanted to get in on 'em. He'd come up river in his supply boat, the *Far West*, a paddle wheeler. She was out of Bismarck and a good boat. Captain Grant Marsh was——"

"Sir, could you tell us about the evening meeting?" Gardiner breaks in.

Brisban blinks at him, then nods. "Sure . . . sure. Terry . . ." Brisban is as carefree about rank as his nickname—Grasshopper— might imply. He usually ignores it, even with general officers. "Terry. He called Gibbon and me into his cabin on the steamer. Custer was there, and his AAG, Cooke, and so was E. W. Smith. Terry's AAG."

"Just a moment," Gardiner says, holding up his hand. He turns toward the defense counsel. "That means assistant adjutant general. An AAG is the principal staff officer to a commander and carries out most of the administration of the command."

"Thank you, thank you," Jacobson says. "I didn't know that."

"Now, Major Brisban, please . . ."

"Sure, well, we were all on board the *Far West* and Terry gave us his plan. He told us . . . he said he wanted to get these Sioux corralled before they could slip off and get away. He wanted to get one outfit north of them and another south, and he told us the main thing was not to let 'em get away from us."

"Did you hear him say to Custer specifically what the 7th Cavalry was to do?"

"Oh sure, he said to John Gibbon he wanted him to bottle up the north end of the Little Bighorn valley—Terry had already decided the Sioux were someplace on the Little Bighorn—he told John Gibbon he wanted him to bottle that up, and he asked how long it would take to get to the mouth of the Little Bighorn. Gibbon thought a while and they looked at some maps, and he allowed it would take him until June 26 before he could get there. His command was mostly infantry and slower afoot than Custer's cavalry would be. Then Terry told Custer to go up the Rosebud to that Indian trail, then on past it so he would be sure of coming into the Little Bighorn valley south of them."

"You heard him tell Custer to go beyond the Indian trail—to go on south of it—before he crossed over into the valley of the Little Bighorn?"

"I did. He told Custer two or three times not to let the Sioux slide around his flank. Maybe get clear of us and off to the Bighorn Mountains. Terry kept saying that to all of us. He wanted to corral them and he said maybe that way the Sioux would see the good sense in coming back to the reservations."

"How did everyone react to this plan?"

"John Gibbon said it looked fine to him and he'd start right off. Custer said it looked fine to him, too, and he'd start the 7th in the morning. Everybody said it looked just fine. There was the usual talk amongst us, and I think it was then that Terry offered Custer part of my command and some Gatling guns he had with his outfit. Custer said he'd rather just do it with the 7th because he felt like control would be easier, and he said the Gatling guns would just slow him up. We all talked a while. It looked fine to us all."

"Your witness, Mr. Jacobson."

Brisban eyes Jacobson suspiciously as the defense counsel shuffles across the bull ring toward the witness stand.

"Now, Major . . . did you hear General Terry say that General Custer was to do this thing without any chance of change—under no circumstance of the field was General Custer to deviate from the plan? Did General Terry say that?"

"I don't think I ever heard an officer say that, except once at a little place in Virginia during the war when——"

"Major Brisban," Jacobson cuts in sharply. "Did General Terry tell General Custer he was not to deviate in any way from the plan of corralling the Indians?"

"No, he didn't say anything like that."

"Thank you." Jacobson shuffles back to his seat.

Gardiner indicates he does not wish to redirect and Schofield excuses the witness. Brisban salutes the court and, as he turns to walk out, winks at Custer, who smiles slightly.

Gardiner calls Captain E. W. Smith, Terry's AAG on the Montana campaign. Smith confirms the testimony of Brisban that Terry's general plan was to place strong forces north and south of the Indian camp. Gardiner introduces a document which the court designates prosecution exhibit A for identification, and he shows it to the witness.

"Do you recognize this document?"

"Yes. It is the written order given General Custer the morning after the meeting on the *Far West*. I wrote it for General Terry."

"Would you read the salutation?"

As Smith reads, Beakin moves along the bench, giving each member of the court a copy. He also passes one to Jacobson, who nods as he glances over the single sheet and tosses it on his table.

" 'Camp at Mouth of the Rosebud River, Montana Territory, June 22, 1876. Lieutenant Colonel Custer, 7th Cavalry. Colonel:——' "

"And now, Captain Smith, the second and third sentences."

Smith counts down the page and then reads. " 'It is, of course, impossible to give you any definite instructions in regard to this movement and even were it not impossible, the department commander places too much confidence in your zeal, energy, and ability to wish to impose upon you precise orders which might hamper your action when nearly in contact with the enemy. He will, however, indicate to you his own views of what your action should be and he desires that you should conform to them unless you should see sufficient reasons for departing from them.' "

"And what were those views which the department commander—General Terry—indicated to Custer?"

"On the evening before and on the morning Custer marched out, General Terry said he wanted the 7th to come up south of the Indian camp and cooperate with Colonel Gibbon to fence in the hostiles."

"Why did Terry bother to have you prepare this written order? Was that usual?"

Smith looks toward Custer, who ignores his glance.

"It is not usual. General Terry told me to give General Custer an indication that he—General Terry—still had great confidence in General Custer's ability. But he also said he wanted no question about how the 7th was supposed to proceed. Based on those instructions, I wrote this order and gave it to General Custer the morning of June 22."

"Please read the rest of the order."

Smith reads it and the instructions are those outlined by Brisban, including instructions to explore thoroughly a small tributary of the Rosebud and to send a courier to Gibbon's column when contact with the enemy was imminent.

"What would you say is the primary concern expressed in this document?" Gardiner asks when Smith is finished reading.

"To surround the Indians by coordinated action."

"And how would you describe this order in regard to its acceptance by those having heard it?"

"They all understood it, at least according to what they said. They all said it was good."

"Was there anything, then, that required coordination in the context of this order?"

"Yes, sir. That there be a convergence of forces on the Sioux on June 26."

Gardiner introduces a second document, the report Terry sent Sheridan marked "confidential" and which Sherman allowed to slip into press hands.

"Prosecution exhibit B for identification," Schofield says, and the reporter marks it. Once more Beakin distributes copies to the court and the defense counsel.

"Do you recognize this, Captain Smith?"

"Yes, this is the report General Terry and I prepared on board the *Far West* after the battle."

"Please read it, sir."

The document is a long one, and as Smith reads there is considerable restlessness in the room, feet-scuffing, coughing, shifting of rears on hard wooden seats.

When Smith is finished, Gardiner says, "Please read the signature on this document."

" 'Alfred H. Terry, Brigadier General.' "

"Thank you, Captain Smith. Cross-examination?"

Jacobson shuffles over, one hand in his pants pocket, his cheek stuffed with a fresh cud. He stands for a long while in front of Captain Smith before beginning

"You know, Captain Smith, I have been reading that order you wrote for General Terry on June 22. Now it occurs to me that that order is very ambiguous. Wouldn't you say it was very ambiguous, Captain?"

"No, sir, when you consider it in the light of oral instructions."

"In your experience, Captain, which carries more weight, historically, I mean, oral or written information?"

"It depends——"

"No, no, no, Captain, please answer my question. Which carries more weight—the spoken word which is gone"—he snaps his fingers—"like that? Or the written word like this"—and he waves his copy of the order. "A document which can be passed down—for *generations*."

"I suppose the written word is more permanent, but——"

"Captain, let us go on here. You said General Terry wanted to let General Custer know that he still had confidence. Why?"

"General Custer had been relieved of command of the entire column from Fort Lincoln. He was finally allowed to go with the expedition but only as commander of his own regiment."

"Why was he relieved and by whom?"

Captain Smith glances around the room nervously. As his eyes touch Gardiner's, the trial counsel nods slightly.

"President Grant—then-President Grant relieved him because General Custer was supposed to stay in Washington to testify in some of the impeachment proceedings against Secretary of War Belknap."

"Oh, yes, that was the announced reason. But what was the real reason, Captain?"

"Objection," Gardiner says, on his feet. "No relevance."

"Overruled," Schofield says. "We'll hear this."

"Captain?" Jacobson smiles, leaning forward.

"I don't know."

"Wasn't it common knowledge that it was because General Custer had said embarrassing things about the Grant administration and was being punished by the President?"

"I have heard——"

"I object," Gardiner cuts into his witness's answer. "If the defense wants these words in General Grant's mouth, let him call General Grant."

"Who, of course, is in Europe," Jacobson mutters.

"Very well, gentlemen," Schofield warns. "I will sustain that objection, Mr. Jacobson."

Jacobson shrugs and smiles at Smith as though it is a pity their conversation has been cut short.

Gardiner rises.

"Captain Smith, in the written order. What do you take the phrase to mean, 'when nearly in contact with the enemy'?"

"I take it now as I took it then—and as General Terry did also according to his explanation to me—that in contact or nearly in contact with an enemy, naturally a commander must have freedom of judgment. But it did not mean he had freedom of judgment on movement to contact—before there was, indeed, any contact with the enemy. On the approach to contact, General Terry's orders had to be carried out, else the entire plan was in jeopardy. A courier had to be sent to Gibbon, otherwise the whole expedition might come to naught—as indeed it did."

"Thank you, Captain."

Schofield looks at his watch. "Gentlemen, it is getting toward noon," he says. "I would like to recess for the day. Mr. Jacobson, Army regulations require a court to recess by 3:30 P.M. In this case I propose to meet at eight each morning, take no lunch break, and recess for the day at about 2 P.M. Since you didn't know that until now, I might be placing unnecessary inconvenience on you if we ran to two today. Therefore, if there is no objection"—he glances along the bench and toward Gardiner, who shakes his head —"I will excuse this witness and recess the court until tomorrow morning at 8 A.M. There being no objection."

8

The Hoffman House on Fifth Avenue is one of the favorite watering holes of New York this November 1877, especially for the socially elite young gentlemen of leisure who seem so much more in evidence during depressions than at any other time. A number of beggars keep returning to the sidewalks outside the main entrance and are run off time and again by the doorman, the police, or even Mr. Ned Stokes himself, the proprietor.

Inside at the Gentlemen's Bar, Gardiner and his two assistants are ending a long afternoon of sipping. They stand with one foot on the brass railing that runs the entire length of the seventy-foot bar. It is of carved mahogany. As Sommers leans against it, his dark eyes glassy, he gazes at the painting over the back bar. It is Bouguereau's *Nymphs and Satyr,* a classic example of the current French crop of voluptuous nudes gamboling in pastoral settings, pursued by creatures half man, half goat, and obviously nimble enough to catch any of the overblown women on the canvas.

"Acres and acres," Sommers mutters. "Acres and acres of undressed womanhood."

"It created a sensation last year when it was brought over from France," Gardiner says. "It cost over ten thousand dollars. Since then offers of over three times that have been made for it."

Sommers is speechless, slightly drunk. The room is becoming

crowded in the early evening, and there is the gruff buzz of male conversation. The lamps hanging from their golden brackets along the walls cast a yellow glow over the derbies and top hats. Polished button shoes and some boots scuff the thick Persian rug of pale cerulean blue, tan, and umber design. At one end of the bar is a sumptuous free lunch that includes shrimp and the best liver pâté available. At the other is a display case of Hoffman House cigars, the boxes with full-color reproductions of *Nymphs and Satyr* on the lids.

Beakin, too, leans on the bar, his blond head lowered over a copy of the *New York Evening Post.* With one finger he traces each line. In his other hand he holds a stein of Bavarian beer. Mr. William Cullen Bryant's newspaper fascinates him, as it does many others, and he reads the editorial prose of the dying editor—he will be dead within the year—as though it were the blank verse of "Thanatopsis."

"Listen to this," he says. " 'Today, in the very beginning of the farce on Governor's Island, the ugly truth began to be shown as Mr. Jacobson boldly spoke against former President Grant's dictatorial punishment of a loyal officer once his trusted subordinate. A brave and true officer was being severed from his rightful place at the head of a major expedition only because of his political leanings. General Custer was criminal because he was opposed to the putrid administration of Grant! And it goes on still, the horrid vendetta. More will be heard, however, thanks to the mighty man of Michigan, Allan Jacobson.' "

Beakin groans.

They have been snacking on Virginia ham and pumpernickel with a sharp mustard prepared only at the Hoffman House, but they plan to dine at Delmonico's. As they finish their beer and prepare to leave, a short dark man comes up and puts a hand on Gardiner's shoulder. His teeth shine under his ebony moustache. His face is a contrast of darkness and light.

"My friend, my friend, welcome, welcome, how long have you been here?"

"Only most of the day." Gardiner laughs.

"Why didn't you come back to my private bar, Asa, you and your friends?"

"We've been admiring the ladies."

The short man glances at the painting and laughs. "Of course, of course, my darlings and the goat."

Gardiner introduces the two officers to Ned Stokes.

"You can help me, gentlemen, you can help me," Stokes says. He beckons a bartender. "Gordon, make one of those new drinks for these gentlemen."

He turns back to Gardiner. "Well, well, my friend, you're becoming very famous in this town. The Custer case is filling the papers."

"Yes, and we've hardly begun."

"You may as well have finished for all they're writing about it. Well, come now, what about it? Is he guilty or innocent?"

"Guilty as hell," Sommers says.

"He did certain things, Ned," Gardiner says. "I think we can prove he did. Whether or not these things were criminal will have to be decided by the court."

"Well, then thank God we aren't on the court, what? The newspapers are about equally divided. Well, here are the drinks."

The bartender places four stemmed glasses on the bar. Each is brimful of a dark red liquid and in each is a cherry.

"Try this," Stokes says. "Icy cold. Be careful, lad, don't spill it on your fingers. Terribly sticky."

Gardiner smacks his lips. It has a strange new bite and warms deep into his body as he drinks. He nods.

"You approve, good, good. I just made it up today."

"What is it?" says Sommers, who obviously doesn't like it.

"The best Kentucky bourbon, about four parts, to one part Italian vermouth, a dash of bitters, cherry," Stokes says, placing his own drink half finished on the bar. "I call it the Manhattan cocktail."

"And you just thought it up today?" Gardiner says.

"That's right, that's right. What's your verdict, sir?"

"You have an amazing life, sitting here all day gazing at your naked women and concocting refreshments."

They all laugh and Stokes shakes hands all around and moves off to "check to be sure all my chefs are not drunk."

"A fine-looking gentleman," Beakin says. "I've never been part of a new cocktail before."

"Fine gentleman," Sommers mutters.

"Yes, but don't abuse him," says Gardiner, taking a purse from his pocket and snapping it open. "He's just out of Sing Sing Prison for killing Jim Fisk with a pistol."

The others stare for a moment.

"My God, I remember reading about that in the newspapers, but I never connected it," Beakin says.

"My wife will never believe it. . . ." Sommers says.

When Gardiner tries to pay, the bartender waves him away.

"Mr. Stokes's treat, sir, Mr. Stokes's treat."

On the street, fastening their capes about their necks, they pause and let the fresh air brace them. Gardiner lights a cigar before they start walking down the avenue.

"I don't trust that Jacobson," Sommers says suddenly. "He smiles too much."

"And all that bowing, too," Beakin says.

There is a cold wind blowing up Manhattan from the harbor but the weather has moderated since morning and it is clear, showing a sickle moon and stars. Still they are inclined to hurry, bent against the wind.

"I don't like the way he cross-examined those two this morning," Gardiner says. "He didn't stick with it long enough. He should have come down hard on that order of Smith's. God, I wish Smith had never written it."

"But it's all in the sense of the thing . . ." Sommers starts and can't find any way to end it.

"I suspect he's holding back the big guns for Terry. There isn't much doubt but that Terry will come, and Jacobson knows it. I wish we could have started with Terry. If only Washington hadn't been so anxious to get the court-martial started. We would have been able to postpone it until Terry could get here."

They all knew that Washington meant Sherman.

"Why did you have Smith read that part about General Terry having confidence in Custer, sir?" Beakin asks.

"Because it made a better impression on the court for us to bring attention to it than if Jacobson had."

Gaslights keep this part of the city well illuminated. In other, darker streets where immigrants crowd together, they would be wary of the young toughs roaming in gangs. As they move along, horse-drawn trolleys clank up and down the avenue, some with dogs trotting along behind, sniffing at the droppings. A policeman with his domed helmet is at the corner of Fifth Avenue and 23rd Street and when he sees their uniforms touches two fingers to his visor. Nearing Delmonico's they see the street crowded with carriages and people moving into the four-story brownstone. Its design is very much like the private mansions along Fifth and Park avenues. Now the press of business from the south of Manhattan is pushing the houses of the rich as far north as 45th Street.

They turn in past the doorman to the heat of a large foyer. They shed their capes and check them with a young woman dressed as a high-fashion housemaid, with black, tight-necked dress and white lacy apron. Sommers stamps his feet although there is no trace of mud on them. This part of Fifth Avenue has been paved with cobblestone for several years.

They pass quickly through a large carpeted waiting room and then through the oyster bar, highly mirrored and lighted with hanging crystal chandeliers. The room smells of the seashore and horseradish. At the entrance to the main dining room, the maître d'hôtel checks his listings and finds Gardiner's reservation. He leads them to a table along one wall where the draperies are as thick as the rugs and wine-red. The walls are covered in red velvet alternating with cherry panels. Busboys are dressed in red sailor suits. Waiters are in formal black and white, but with red cummerbunds. There are candles on each table but they are superfluous in the large room lighted by hanging gas jets that hiss now and then above the subdued music of the string trio in the alcove at the far end of the room. Each jet is enclosed in a crystal globe. The room is filled with well-dressed people, many going to Booth's or perhaps to the Academy of Music afterward. Some of the gowns are daring, cut low across the breast. At throats and on fingers, watch chains, and cuff links there is the frequent glint of diamond or ruby. The two younger officers are fascinated with this, the most elegant dining room in America.

When the waiter brings the menu it is twenty-eight pages long, not counting the wine list. The lieutenants fumble through it, frowning at the French.

"Gentlemen, allow me," Gardiner says. "What shall it be? The Salmon à la Victoria? With Filet of Beef à la Lucullus? With Artichokes Lyonnaise and Peaches Parisienne?"

They stare at him dumbly.

"I'm not sure I would enjoy any of that," Sommers says, and Gardiner laughs.

Eventually they have a four-course dinner of consommé, capons with truffles, chestnut puree, pudding of pears, and a vanilla bread. Gardiner also orders a light white wine which neither of the others drinks.

"Well, then, is it acceptable?" Gardiner asks.

It is and they say so. There is some confusion about which of the many silver spoons and forks to use on which dish, but Gardiner quickly shows by example. The young officers soon realize that a Delmonico meal is a thing to be taken slowly, not attacked like enemy breastworks. Sommers has trouble keeping his napkin tucked into his vest, but other than that they proceed through the meal without incident and with very little talk.

The dinner finished, Gardiner orders Irish coffee for the three of them. The conversation is casual, the younger officers having become more accustomed to the lavish surroundings and grown more at ease. As a waiter passes with a flaming hors d'oeuvre, they glance at it for only a moment.

"Do you know," Sommers muses, "there are twenty-five different veal dishes on the menu here? I counted them."

"Yes, it's an elegant trough," Gardiner says.

Sommers suddenly reaches over and grabs Gardiner's arm. Gardiner nods slightly, his coffee cup to his lips.

"Yes, I see them."

Into the room from the Fifth Avenue entrance comes a party of about ten people. Leading them is Elizabeth Custer and just behind her is George in a major general's uniform complete with gold piping on the seam of his cape and a double row of buttons down his flat front. Beside Custer is a large, robust man with ruddy face and blond bushy sideburns. He is dressed in a highly fashionable gray suit.

"Whitelaw Reid," Gardiner says. "He publishes the *Tribune*." What a strange irony, he thinks. Reid is one of the worst reconstructionists in the newspaper business, still waving a blood shirt over the South and advocating complete Republican rule there, regardless of the vote. Yet here he is, strolling at the side of a man so much a Democrat he almost destroyed himself to fight a Republican administration.

The party moves confidently to a table waiting for them. They attract the attention of everyone in the room and both Custer and his wife smile and nod to a number of people.

Elizabeth's dress is pink with cobalt blue trim. The slight bustle is ribboned and ruffled in blue and her hat is a tiny speck of color with streamers of blue ribbons down her back. Her bodice, tailored tightly to her body, reveals the flesh beneath, although her blouse comes up close around her neck, where she wears a cameo.

"Oh God, what a shame, what a shame," Sommers whispers. "Look at that woman. What a shame."

Gardiner is not sure, but as he quickly finishes his coffee he thinks Elizabeth Custer recognizes him across the room. Her eyes pause for only an instant then quickly move away and she is smiling once more. But there had been a moment when her expression seemed to change.

Custer stands aside and allows someone else to seat his wife, but the Golden Cavalier quickly moves over to hold the chair for another of the ladies in his party.

Gardiner sets his cup in the saucer as though he is afraid he might break it. "Let's get out of here," he says softly.

The younger officers are not finished with the town this early, so Gardiner leaves them on Fifth Avenue and 26th Street, taking a cross-town trolley to Tenth Avenue. He walks toward the river, letting the cold air clear the cigar smoke from his head. He walks uptown for a couple of blocks, trying to jog the heavy clot of food in his stomach into a more comfortable position for sleeping. On 28th Street he buys hothouse violets from an old lady huddled in a doorway. He pauses and watches the reflection of the moon on the Hudson. His mind churns back and forth, rearranging the order of his witnesses. The case has him trapped, and he feels involved in something that will never let him go. To have been selected by the Commanding General of the Army—or at least to be serving only by his specific approval—is a heavy responsibility. He knows what is expected of a trial judge advocate under the Articles of War, but what in addition is expected by Sherman? To make it all worse, the charges are not going to be all that easy to prove. Gardiner is well aware that a man's career could hang in the balance, but that is only a passing thought to him. He cannot feel that Sherman will be vindictive—so long as the trial proceeds honorably and everything legally possible is done to convict. But there are those stories of Sherman's wrath, a disquieting thought that he cannot completely put down. He thinks of Custer . . . of Jacobson's club foot. And of Elizabeth, with that long alabaster neck, an ivory cameo at the throat almost where the little blue vein comes up.

9

'It was before dawn on June 22 and there was a heavy mist along
the Yellowstone when they played 'Boots and Saddles' and I rousted
out me men and we et hardtack and bacon and had the last good
coffee made with clear sweet water we'd be havin' for a dear spell."
The witness speaks with a thick Irish brogue.

"But it was near noon before we were lined out for the start.
We issued a pound and a half of grain to each trooper for his
horse, a wee bite, and I checked me men for ammunition—one
hundred rounds each for the Springfields and twenty-four for the
Colts. I figured the only reason the dear regiment was taking away
from the rest of Gen'l Terry's command was to get into it heavy
with the Sioux. I told my lads to check canteens and saddle gear
careful, fer stragglin' to take a fresh hitch in the cinch might cause
a body to lose some hair, and I told 'em as soon as we get shed of
the Yellowstone, to keep an eye peeled on the ridges and their
carbines handy.

"Gen'l Custer had the band out playin' the 'Garry Owen' as we
formed up. Gen'l Terry was sittin' his horse not far from the river
bank, his staff all around his dear self, and we could see the people
lined along the rails of the boat watchin' the dear old 7th makin'
off towards the fierce Indian country. We passed in review before
himself, Gen'l Terry, just like on parade at Fort Lincoln. He give

each company a salute and a wave of his hat, he did. It was all a grand sight in the clear sunlight day."

"What were your orders, Sergeant?"

"Keep closed up, keep a quiet march, and keep your eyes open, sir. Them was me onlyest orders."

He is First Sergeant William Boyle, Company A, 7th Cavalry, and he has served with Custer since before the regiment was formed.

"Yes, sir, I knew Gen'l Custer in Virginia. I was private in the 1st Michigan Cavalry. He was a fine, brave officer and as good a rider as ever I did see a-horse."

"Sergeant Boyle, were you in the victory parade in Washington City immediately following the war?"

"Yes, sir, I most surely was."

"If the accused was such a fine horseman, how do you account for the fact that his horse ran away during that parade—right past the reviewing stand where the President and General Grant were sitting?"

"Oh, beggin' your dear pardon, sir, that horse niver run away. No horse ever tread earth could run away with Gen'l Custer."

"How do you explain that episode then?"

"Well, sir, all the boys by then already knew, Gen'l Custer, he was a man liked to show off a wee mite now and again."

There is a snicker in the courtroom. Custer nods slightly and glances back at Elizabeth. She smiles at him.

"I object," Jacobson says softly from his chair. "What has all this to do with the case?"

"Sustained," says Schofield. "Get along with your case, Major."

"Sergeant Boyle, troops always have nicknames for officers, do they not?"

Boyle looks nervously toward the line of colonels and generals at the bench and laughs.

"Yes, sir, they generally do."

"What was one such nickname for Colonel Custer—in regard to horses?"

"Some called him Horse Killer."

"I object——"

Gardiner wheels on the court and says vehemently, "It is most assuredly relevant, Mr. President. We are vitally concerned here

73

with the condition of the command when it was committed and with the accused's attitude toward treatment of men and animals on campaign."

"Overruled," Schofield says, without referring to the other members of the court.

"Sergeant Boyle, why did the men call Colonel Custer Horse Killer?"

"He always pushed hard on the march, sir. And he always went back to the quartermaster for remounts more often than any other cavalry commander—that was during the war."

"Now tell us what happened after the parade on the banks of the Yellowstone."

"We had one of the worst marches I can remember," Boyle says. "It was dry, the grain wasn't plentiful enough for the horses, the dust was enough to choke the lads no sooner than we started. After the first day the pace was hard, terrible hard. We went thirty-five to forty miles a day.

SGT. WILLIAM BOYLE

You can't march the horses that hard for long in heat and dust and with little water."

"Were conditions bad enough to make men think of deserting?"

Jacobson's head jerks up and Gardiner knows the defense counsel is suspicious of what is about to be asked.

"Yes, sir, sure and it was but there was no desertin' because there was no time."

"What do you mean, no time?"

"We marched four days and then we was a-fightin', sir. It wasn't like Kansas in '67 when we marched and marched and had no fightin', atall atall."

"There were desertions then?"

"I object," Jacobson says, on his feet, and Gardiner is surprised the defense has let it go this far.

"I'll take this, Mr. Jacobson, subject to objections from other members of the court," Schofield says.

"There were desertions from the regiment in Kansas in 1867, Sergeant? Please explain that."

"We were part of Gen'l Hancock's campaign against the Cheyenne in Kansas and the 7th was sent to scramble the hostiles. But we found none to scramble and we marched for weeks. Some of the lads took to their horses at night."

"You just let them go?"

"No, Gen'l Custer sent us after them every one."

"With what instructions?"

For the first time Sergeant Boyle appears ill at ease. He squirms on the stand and clears his throat.

"Beggin' your pardon, sir," he says softly. "Gen'l Custer told us to catch 'em—or shoot 'em."

There is a stir in the courtroom and some of the newspaper reporters glance at one another.

"Did you ever shoot one?"

"No, sir, I had no stomach fer it, but I know those who did. . . ."

"Mr. President!" Jacobson shouts, red-faced now.

"Yes, Major Gardiner, I think that's enough in this direction. Let's get back to Montana and leave Kansas out of it."

"Very well, Mr. President. Now, Sergeant. Marching up the Rosebud, what about graze along the way for the horses?"

"Army horses don't do well on graze, sir. They was bred on grain and grain is what they mostly need. One or two days might be all right on range grazin', but as we got up the valley of the Rosebud, where the Indian trail started, where we could see the pony and travois tracks in a trail almost half a mile wide, all the grass had been et by the Indian ponies."

"What about water on the march?"

"Sometimes we were too far from the river to get at it when we was halted. From the Indian sign we'd seen, we wasn't too anxious to go sportin' off away from the column. Then sometimes when we could get at it, the water wasn't any good."

"From the standpoint of the horses alone, would you say the 7th was ready for a serious fight after four days of that kind of marching?"

"I allow the dear 7th can fight any time, sir. But it was a bunch of horses in as bad a shape as any I ever seen just before a fight."

"Mr. Jacobson, your witness."

It does not surprise Gardiner that Jacobson declines cross-examination. He's waiting for the big fish, Gardiner thinks. If he goes after only a few of my witnesses, when he does the impact will be greater.

Gardiner calls Captain Thomas B. French, who takes the oath, identifies himself, and indicates that he served as commander of Company M at the Little Bighorn. He testifies that the dust on the march was exceedingly bad and that before the end of the third day horses and men were exhausted from the suffocating cloud and the lack of good water and sleep.

"You've served in the cavalry for many years, Captain French. Would you estimate for us the lengths of those marches?"

French takes a small pad from his inside breast pocket and gazes at it intently. He is a small man with a receding hairline that accents the bushiness of his beard. As he refers to his notes he frowns, finally takes a small pair of steel-rimmed glasses from a breast pocket, and places them on his nose.

"Yes, sir, the first day, that was June 22, we marched about fifteen miles. Then the next day it was near forty. Again on the 24th we marched about thirty and a night march added ten more. On the day of the fight, before we were engaged, most units marched at least twenty-five miles."

"Then what would your estimate be of—let's see—the distance from the mouth of the Rosebud to the point of first contact in the fight?"

"I would say, by the route we marched, about a hundred miles."

"Yes, in four days! On inadequate water, rest, and grain."

"This sounds like a summation," Jacobson says from his chair.

"Is that an objection, Mr. Jacobson?" Schofield asks.

"Never mind, Mr. President, I will go on to another subject," Gardiner says, and he smiles at defense counsel, who bows from his seat and smiles back. He is whittling another chew from a large black plug.

"Captain, we've heard here of a large Indian trail. Can you give us any information about that?"

"It was mid-afternoon of the second day, June 23, when we struck it. A great many unshod ponies and travois had come into the Rosebud valley from the east and started upstream."

"The same direction you were following?"

"Yes, sir. We were following the trail in the true sense of the word. I would judge it was about a week old when we first saw it. We began to see old camp sites, very large. By the end of the fourth day the trail was extremely large. Other bands had joined along the way. It was very fresh as well. I would say a day old."

"Captain French, could you judge how large a body of Indians you were following?"

"General Custer—I heard General Custer say there were likely about fifteen hundred warriors ahead of us. I would have guessed many more."

"Did that number concern you?"

French slides his spectacles back into his pocket and gazes up at the ceiling for a moment. He nods. "Yes, some concern. I knew we had marched with over 580 men and 30 officers and a number of Indians and civilians—scouts and interpreters and whatnot. I had the feeling the regiment could handle almost anything we ran into —but the number of Indians ahead did concern me somewhat."

"All right, Captain, did this trail continue up the Rosebud?"

"No, sir. On June 24, the fourth day, it took a sharp western turn across the divide between the Rosebud and the Bighorn—well, it was the Little Bighorn at that point."

"Of course. The main stream of the Bighorn is farther west, and the Little Bighorn flows between the Rosebud and that main stream until it empties into the Bighorn a few miles south of the Yellowstone."

"Yes, that's correct."

"So the trail turned west toward the Little Bighorn? What reaction was there to that?"

"We were halted for the night and the men were doing what they could for the horses. Some tried to sleep, but there was little time. We weren't making fires, of course. Some effort was made to get grain up from the pack trains, but very little of it was brought up in time. General Custer called his officers together. He told us the trail led west into the Little Bighorn valley and he wanted to move during the night to close the distance on the hostiles. He said we would lay up and rest on the 25th, then attack with Gibbon on the 26th."

"I want to make sure of this point. When the Indian trail turned west Colonel Custer ordered the regiment to follow in that same direction, is that right?"

"Yes, sir, that is correct."

"Are you sure the regiment did not march south of the point where the Indian trail turned west?"

"Absolutely. We followed where it turned."

"Did any unit of the regiment explore any of the Rosebud tributaries south of where the trail turned west?"

"Not to my knowledge."

"Did anyone—Colonel Custer or some member of his staff—did anyone ever say anything to you about going south of where the Indian trail turned west before following it?"

"No, sir. There seemed to be no hesitation about it. We were following it wherever it went."

"Were you aware of Colonel Custer's orders?"

"Not at the time."

"All right, at the time you turned west—immediately on the Indian trail—had Colonel Custer at that time given any indication that the command had been discovered by the Indians and that a quick attack was necessary?"

"No, sir, he made no such indication, not at that time."

"And so the regiment took up a night march to bring it closer, you say. . . ."

"That's correct, sir. For about twelve miles. Then we halted again in the dark. It had been a bad time. Night marches with cavalry are difficult. There was much noise and stumbling and falling about. The terrain was unfamiliar—rough and rocky. We tried to keep closed up tight to avoid straggling. The non-commissioned officers did a magnificent job, else we would have had serious straggling. Finally, though, we halted again. The men fed their mounts what few kernels of grain they had left, then wrapped bridle reins around their arms and went to sleep on the ground under their horses' heads."

"How long did the regiment remain there?"

"Until after dawn—about seven-thirty or eight, I would say. General Custer had gone forward to an observation post with Lieutenant Varnum and his Indian scouts. Varnum was commanding the scouts. We got orders from a courier to move forward, but we had gone only a short ways when General Custer rejoined the regiment and we halted and he called the officers together once more. He said the Crow scouts had said there was a big village in the valley ahead, but he said he hadn't seen it with his glasses."

"Exactly what did he say about the Crows?"

"He said he didn't think they knew what they were talking about and that they were afraid and could not be trusted. Then he said a number of things had happened to make him believe the column had been discovered by the Sioux and therefore we must attack the Indians wherever they were before they could slip away."

"But he did not say how many Indians there might be?"

"He said probably about fifteen hundred. He wasn't concerned with how many. That's the impression I had."

"Were there indications there might be more than fifteen hundred?"

"From the trail I would have estimated more. The Crow and Ree scouts with us were very unhappy about the prospect of getting involved in a fight with the number *they* thought was ahead of us."

"Now, on this second officers' call, your orders were no longer to rest on the 25th and attack with Gibbon on the 26th?"

"No, sir. General Custer said we had been discovered and we must pitch into them before they got away."

"I think that will be all, Captain French, thank you. Cross-examination."

Jacobson shuffles across the bull ring in his usual pose, hands thrust into his pockets, head down, his cheek bulging under the right ear. He smiles at the witness.

"You used the word *exhausted*, Captain, in referring to the command on the third day of the march, isn't that true?"

"Yes, sir, it is."

"What does that word mean to you, Captain? *Exhausted?*"

"It means very tired. In need of rest."

"But doesn't exhausted mean much more—doesn't it mean you cannot continue? That you *must* have rest and food and whatnot?"

"It is near to that, I suppose."

"Near to that, Captain? Now let us be a little more precise here. For the night and the following day after you say the command was *exhausted*, they made a night march and a long day's march and fought a good fight against odds, did they not?"

French hesitates a moment. "Yes, sir."

"Then I would hardly say they were exhausted on the third day, would you, Captain?"

"Well, they were very tired."

"Ah, good, good, very tired. In all this wide experience of yours to which trial judge advocate has alluded, have you ever been involved in a battle where troops were a little *tired* before they were committed?"

"Yes, sir," French says stiffly.

"So there is really nothing unusual in war for troops to be a little *tired* before the battle, is there?"

French hesitates again and Jacobson smiles and turns toward the center of the bull ring. He waves one hand.

"Very well, Captain, I think we see what you really meant now. If this company of yours was tired enough—if you felt as its commander that it was tired enough to be a serious thing, did you report it to your commander?"

Jacobson now turns in the center of the room and stares back at French.

"No, I did not report it, he could see——"

"Isn't it the responsibility of a commander to report anything to his superiors which he feels may impair his combat effectiveness?"

"Yes, I suppose, but——"

"*But at the time, you didn't think it was worth reporting, did you?*" Jacobson shouts. He goes on, happily aware that he has startled everyone in the courtroom and especially the witness. "It was only afterwards, when the whole thing failed and you were looking for someone to blame. Then you suddenly discovered, Captain, that your troops were too tired to fight."

"I object, Mr. President," Gardiner says loudly, too loudly, and it upsets him that he has allowed his anger to control his voice.

"I withdraw that last," Jacobson says, but not smiling now. He stands for a while in the center of the bull ring, head down. Then from beneath his brows he stares at French. "Now then, Captain French, isn't it true that you were itching to get into a fight your-self?"

"I don't know what you mean."

"It didn't matter how large that Indian camp was, did it? You wanted to get in there and tangle with it, didn't you?"

"That's what I was there for," French says with some heat.

Jacobson whirls and his teeth show once more as he looks toward Gardiner. He stamps across to his table, pauses a moment, and looks at the bench.

"Of course, Captain French, and that's what General Custer was there for as well."

French sits red-faced and Gardiner quickly indicates he has no redirect. Schofield excuses the embarrassed cavalry officer, and as he leaves Custer chuckles audibly.

Gardiner's next witness is a show for the court and the press. He had explained to Beakin, whose job it had been to get the witness to New York, that little could be expected from his testimony. But he might make a lasting impression on the court and the newspaper reporters. He is Goes Ahead, one of the Crow scouts with Custer at the Little Bighorn who survived.

As he walks down the aisle alongside his interpreter, the crowd gapes, gasps, and a few even point. He is impassive as he takes the stand, but a flicker of recognition crosses his face as he sees Custer. He wears a white man's coat with the sleeves cut off, a heavy leather belt from which hangs a wolf's hide, cloth trade leggings with beadwork, and fawn moccasins. His shirt is a patch-work of felt and cured doeskin. From his neck hangs a hair-bone breast plate that has begun to yellow with age. His hair is pom-padoured in front, in the manner of the Crows, with two braids down either side of his face. A larger plait hangs down his back. His ears protrude and they are pierced from lobe to crown and set with small mussel shells. His face is flat, leathery, and handsome, a deeper brown than his hands. On his right cheek is a single white spot of paint. Into the room he brings also the pungent odor of grease and wood smoke.

The interpreter, who takes his place beside the witness stand, is obviously a half-breed. He wears white men's clothes, but around his neck is a bear claw necklace and his hair falls loosely to his shoulders.

"Gentlemen," Gardiner says, moving before the bench. "This man was one of Colonel Custer's scouts on the march up the Rosebud. We have with him a man I will swear and who will interpret. He has served many times for the Army on the northern Plains."

"There being no objection to that procedure," Schofield says, glancing at his fellow officers. He looks at Jacobson. "Does defense have any objection?"

Jacobson is grinning as he mouths a new cud. He shakes his head. "No, General, I suspect I'll want to do the same kind of thing with one of my own Indians later on."

The spectators laugh. Gardiner swears the interpreter, Frank Gautier.

"Gentlemen, in way of establishing Mr. Gautier's credentials," Gardiner says to the court, "his father was a French trader along the upper Missouri years before the Civil War. His mother was a Crow Indian."

Gardiner turns to the interpreter, who stands next to the witness chair, where Goes Ahead sits impassively. "Sir, have you ever acted as interpreter for the United States?"

"Yes, sir, many times. I was with General Harney years ago."

"Were you involved in the campaign of 1876 against the Sioux?"

"I was not. That summer I was in the Tetons with some Shoshoni, hunting elk."

"Mr. Gautier, would you ask the witness to tell us who he is, and of what tribe, and if he was with the 7th Cavalry on the Montana campaign."

Gautier and the Indian mutter a few moments. Goes Ahead grunts and a smile touches his thin mouth for an instant. He points toward Custer.

"Yellow Hair," he says, and the spectators giggle and strain forward. Goes Ahead has a deep voice and he speaks softly.

"He says he is Goes Ahead," Gautier explains, "and he is a Crow. He scouted for General Custer on the Montana expedition against his old enemies, the Sioux. He says he knows General Custer well."

"Mr. Gautier, ask Goes Ahead to describe what happened when

the 7th Cavalry came on the Indian trail along the Rosebud on 22 June 1876."

Once more interpreter and Crow confer, their hawking voices barely audible in the quiet room. As Goes Ahead begins to speak, he raises his voice and gestures with his hands. The fingers are long, the skin wrinkled, and the hands expressive as he moves them about before his face, often repeating what he is saying with the same word or phrase in sign language. He continues to stare at Custer as he talks, a dead glint in his eyes.

"He says many ponies were ahead. Many Sioux and Cut Fingers."

"What are Cut Fingers?"

"That's what most of 'em calls Cheyenne."

"Why do they do that?"

"Cheyenne warriors like to take the finger. This one." He points to his left index finger. "They like to take it off any enemy they kill, dry it out good, and make a pendant for a necklace out of it."

There is a faint gasp from the spectators and glancing back, Gardiner sees Elizabeth Custer sitting transfixed by the Crow, staring at him with pale cheeks.

"Ask him if he wanted to fight these old enemies."

After a guttural exchange Gautier says, "He says the Crows and their friends the Rees were afraid. He says there were too many Sioux and Cut Fingers. He says the second day they were following it the trail got so large it made them all afraid, and when it turned west toward the Little Bighorn it was the biggest trail any of them had ever seen."

"Did he tell Custer this?"

Goes Ahead listens as Gautier asks the question in Crow. He is staring directly at Custer and the cavalryman stares back unsmiling.

"He says yes. Him and the other Crows told Custer more than once that he had better be careful because there were too many Sioux and Cut Fingers out there for the regiment. But he says Custer just laughed and called them old women. He says some of the Crows Custer called old women died fighting that day against their old enemies, the Sioux and Cut Fingers."

Gardiner is phrasing the next question in his mind when Goes

GOES AHEAD

Ahead speaks out harshly in English, moving one hand before his face like a fan. "Many ponies. Many travois. Crows say to Yellow Hair"—and he points emphatically at Custer—"too many Sioux and Cut Finger. No fight now. Wait. Fight later. Too many."

The room is absolutely silent. Gardiner stands a moment, undecided. He had expected to take the witness further, yet this is a dramatic pitch he had not counted on. Suddenly he turns and nods at Jacobson.

"Your witness."

Jacobson sits a long time, his lips pursed, his jaw muscles gently working. Then he rises and from his place says, "I do not feel that I can really elicit any information of value from this gentleman, who appears to consider himself an expert on the commitment of United States troops. Thank you anyway, Mr. Gardiner."

There is some confusion as Gautier tries to get Goes Ahead off the stand. The Crow had obviously come to say a great deal more. Finally, with the interpreter pushing gently from behind, the Indian starts up the aisle. Then he pauses and looks at Custer and laughs, a short hard burst of laughter. He waves a finger toward the cavalryman as though scolding a small child.

"Too *many*, Yellow Hair, too *many*."

Everyone in the courtroom stares breathlessly—except for Gardiner and his two assistants. They can hardly avoid looking elated as Custer sits clenching his teeth, obviously furious. God, I wish it was over right now, Gardiner thinks, right this minute.

But of course, it is not. It is hardly beginning.

The man taking the oath is tall, with a weathered face, eyes perpetually squinted against the High Plains sun and wind. He is dressed in a tweed suit, but obviously uncomfortable in it. His hands hang six inches out of his sleeves, wrists brown and bony. On his feet are winter-style Sioux moccasins, highly decorated and beaded, extending halfway up his shin. As he takes the stand the fringes splay out around his feet.

"Fred F. Girard, interpreter and scout with the expedition into Montana in the spring of 1876, sir, and detailed to General Custer when he went up the Rosebud."

"Mr. Girard, what is the Crow's Nest?" Gardiner asks.

"It's a high knoll about halfway between the Rosebud and the Little Bighorn where the 7th Cavalry followed the Indian trail on June 25 of last year."

"Is it a lookout point?"

"Yes, sir. The Crows used it for years, long before the Sioux ever came into that country, I reckon. Anyway, it's about the highest point around. From there you can see a far piece, but it's sometimes deceptive."

"What do you mean, deceptive?"

"That country, it's fair-to-middlin' rough terrain, but as she rolls away from the eye she gets to lookin' flat. In just a little ways —a few hundred yards—a gully or draw can hide a great deal from your view."

Gardiner leans back easily against his table, arms folded across his chest. "Does that mean something could be close to you and you would never notice it—say, like a band of hostiles?"

"Oh, you bet they could, sir."

"So you need to be careful about looking a-round when you know there are hostiles in the area."

"I object, he's leading the witness," Jacobson says from his chair.

"Sustained."

Gardiner nods. "Very well, Mr. Girard, did you have occasion to be at the Crow's Nest on 25 June 1876?"

MAJ. ASA B. GARDINER

"Yes, sir, I'd stayed with the command after the night march on the 24th and was sleeping when General Custer woke me right after dawn and said two of Lieutenant Varnum's Crow scouts had come in from an observation post and they were going to guide him back there. He wanted me to come along, so the four of us—the General and the two Crows and me—rode up to this high ground they called the Crow's Nest. We dismounted just short of it and walked up.

"There was Lieutenant Varnum, and Lieutenant Hare a short ways off—he was commandin' a bunch of Indian scouts too—and there was a whole pack of Crows and Rees. The Rees were back off the hill a ways because this was the Crows' country. The Crows was pretty excited. They claimed they could see a big pony herd and smoke from a big village in the valley, near fifteen miles off. I looked, and General Custer looked, and Lieutenant Varnum looked. There was a haze over the valley—an early mornin' haze—and it was hard to tell if there was really any smoke that far away.

"One of the Crows said there were bluffs down along the Little

Bighorn and the village was hidden by them. But he said you could bet it was there, and a mighty big one, too. He and them other Crows showed they wasn't at all anxious to tie into it. I looked a long time at that valley. There was like a darker patch on the floor of the valley on the far side of the river. It was hard to tell if it moved at all, but now and again it seemed like a big nest of worms, just a-wigglin' a bit."

"How did Colonel Custer react to all of this?" Gardiner asks.

"He said he couldn't see anything. He said he didn't think the scouts saw anything either. He asked me and I told him I wasn't sure but I thought maybe I could make out a herd. He said it was likely just brush blowin' in the wind. But I was pretty sure it wasn't no brush that I'd seen. It was more than that."

"Did Colonel Custer continue to say he saw nothing?"

"Yes, sir, he did. But the way he acted a little later, I think he really did see that herd."

"Why do you say that, Mr. Girard?"

"Like I mentioned, Lieutenant Hare was off a little ways but as the general and me was riding back to the regiment, he come up hard, and he said Mitch Bouyer——"

"Who is Mitch Bouyer?" Gardiner cuts in.

"He was a breed scout with the regiment."

"Where is he now, Mr. Girard?"

"Dead. On Custer's Hill."

"Very well, continue. Lieutenant Hare rode up with a message from Mitch Bouyer."

"Yes, sir, Mitch said he'd seen a couple Sioux and they had seen him. When he got to the regiment General Custer called his officers together and said we'd been discovered and we were going to move right on to the Little Bighorn and attack the Indians wherever they were. So he must have figured they were down there somewhere."

"Did he say anything to his officers about what had happened at the Crow's Nest?"

"Oh, yes, sir, I forgot that. He told them what the scouts said they saw, and he told them he didn't believe them."

"He said they would go into the valley and attack the Sioux wherever they were to be found, even though he said he did not believe his scouts when they said the Sioux were there?"

"Yes, sir, even though he said that."

"Your witness, Mr. Jacobson."

Jacobson is across the bull ring quickly, his deformed foot hardly scuffing the floor at all. He leans close to Girard's face. "It is a pleasure, Mr. Girard," he says, "to have this opportunity to interrogate a civilian. Thus far, all we've had are soldiers." He glances back at Gardiner. "Or an occasional Indian chief."

Custer leads the laughter in the court, and Schofield taps for order, a faint smile on his own lips.

"Now, sir, you say General Custer disbelieved his scouts."

"Yes, sir, that's what he told me and then he told all the officers."

"Good. Now please recall. What was it exactly General Custer did not believe?"

Girard stares at Jacobson a moment, confused. He frowns and scratches his cheek. "He said . . . he said he didn't believe they saw anything."

FRED F. GIRARD

"Yes, General Custer did not believe his scouts *saw* anything. Did General Custer ever say he did not believe there were hostile Indians somewhere along the Little Bighorn?"

"Well . . . no, I can't recall he ever said that."

"So there is no contradiction, is there, Mr. Girard?"

"Sir?" Girard says, more confused than ever.

"That will be all, sir, thank you."

The witness is excused and Gardiner calls Lieutenant Luther R.

Hare. He is a slightly built officer, but with a heavy chest. His eyes are dark and move constantly as he sits on the witness stand. He is the first witness thus far who looks boldly at Custer, and when Elizabeth raises her eyes to his he nods and smiles.

After the preliminaries are concluded, he crosses his legs and seems relaxed as Gardiner moves over to stand near him.

"I was a member of Company K, but during this campaign I was detailed as commander of a detachment of Ree Indian scouts."

"Does the term *Crow's Nest* mean anything to you?"

"Yes, it was the high ground where Varnum and I had our Indians at dawn on June 25, 1876. It was where our Indians claimed they saw a large pony herd and village in the Little Bighorn plain."

"You call it a plain. I have heard it referred to as a valley."

"Yes, sir, it was the drainage basin of the Little Bighorn, but it was so wide and the elevation of so much of it uniform, I think of it as a plain."

"What did you do when the Indians told you what they saw?"

"Varnum and I sent for General Custer. He came up, said he could see nothing, then rode back to the regiment. He took me with him, and I remained with him from then—early morning—until he sent Reno on the attack across the river at about 2 P.M. I was sent with Reno."

"Then you were with Colonel Custer throughout most of the morning of June 25?"

"Yes, very near him most of that time. I had supposed he wanted to have my scouts available for reconnaissance."

"Did he use your scouts in this way?"

"No, sir, they were what I would term on local security station. Just a few yards from the rest of the command."

"Were you present at the officers' call that morning after Colonel Custer rejoined the regiment?" Gardiner asks.

"Yes, sir."

"Then you heard him say the command had been discovered?"

"Yes, sir. He told the officers that. He said we would follow the Indian trail on toward the Little Bighorn."

"Did you hear him say he had not seen any Indian village and that he did not believe his scouts had?"

"Yes, sir. He said that as well."

"But he committed the regiment to the valley. Lieutenant Hare, did he make any effort to determine what *was* in the valley?"

"No, sir, not that I could see. As I have mentioned, our own Indians were just a few hundred yards from the command at most, riding ridges immediately along the line of march."

"Did he dispatch any sort of reconnaissance toward the Little Bighorn ahead of the regiment?"

"No, sir. He did not."

"Did he make any effort to determine the size of the enemy to his front—its strength?"

"No, sir. He did not."

"How many more times is he going to be required to answer that question, Major Gardiner?" Schofield says. There is a raw edge to his voice.

Gardiner, who has been pacing during Hare's testimony, pauses now before his table, glances at a small note pad, tosses it back onto the table, and looks back toward his witness. "As a subordinate of Colonel Custer's on this occasion—when you commanded a portion of his *scouts*—did you see anything unusual in his behavior."

"Objection. He's calling for an opinion." Jacobson remains seated, his chin in his palm, his elbow resting on the table.

"Mr. President, this is a man who served in a special and close relationship with the accused, and I submit that his opinion in the matter, as I have requested it, is nothing more than a part of his duty as a subordinate in the regiment. One must assess the mood of one's commander," Gardiner says.

Schofield frowns and his fingers move restlessly on the billiard ball. He shakes his head with a short jerk. "I'm going to take this, Mr. Jacobson. It seems on shaky ground, yet Major Gardiner's argument is well taken."

As has been the case each time Schofield makes a decision, the third ranking member of the court, Brigadier General John Pope, nods. Schofield ignores him. In fact he leaves the impression with spectators that he has little regard for Pope or McDowell. The impression is exact. Schofield has no tolerance for what he considers ineptitude, and McDowell he believes a pompous ignoramus, Pope an intellectual gelding.

"You may answer, Lieutenant," Gardiner is saying.

"Yes, sir, there were some odd things. Of course I thought it strange that no scouts were sent forward—Indian or white—to see what we were getting into . . . but . . . there were other things. General Custer was always what I would call a close-mouthed commander about his plans. Yet he was vocal in all other ways. He was always talking with his officers, teasing and joking—he teased his brother Tom about women——" Hare stops and flushes, glancing toward the Custers. Elizabeth Custer is staring at him, no expression on her face. Custer is looking at the toe of his boot. "General Custer enjoyed teasing officers he liked when we were on campaign. Usually. But in Montana just the reverse was true. He told us more about what he was doing, and why, than usual, but he was no longer carefree—boastful, perhaps, and confident. He was silent most of the time, frowning. Speaking to no one. He seemed preoccupied. Morose."

"You say he told you more than usual about his plans."

"Yes, sir. Of course that still was very little. But generally, about all we ever knew was that somewhere along the line the bugler would most certainly blow the charge."

There is laughter from the officers in the room and from Custer as well.

"Lieutenant Hare, you said Colonel Custer had said the command had been discovered. In your military judgment——"

"Objection." Jacobson more insistent now. "Opinion."

Schofield shakes his head. "I think the court is capable of understanding a military man's judgment on a detail or two, Mr. Jacobson, in regard to tactics. If that is your area, Major Gardiner, you may proceed."

"In your judgment, Lieutenant Hare, if indeed the regiment had been discovered, what was the major contributing factor to that discovery?"

"That the regiment had followed the Indian trail out of the Rosebud valley too quickly, and——"

"*I object!*" Jacobson shouts, on his feet, waving a finger at the court.

Schofield shakes his head again. "I must agree, Major Gardiner."

"Mr. President——" Gardiner starts but Schofield cuts him short.

"This deals with an element of proof directly concerning one of the charges, and I don't think this court can take an opinion on it from someone involved. The objection is sustained."

Gardiner walks to his table, jaw muscles tightening. Jacobson sits back down and empties his mouth into the cuspidor, wipes his lips with a monogrammed linen handkerchief, and watches the trial judge advocate with eyebrows raised.

"Very well, Lieutenant Hare, that will be all."

"Cross?" says Schofield.

Jacobson does not move, but continues to lean back in his chair, hands laced across his stomach. His eyes shift from Gardiner to the witness and he blinks a few times. As he begins, Hare must look directly across Custer's nose in order to see his examiner.

"At the Crow's Nest did you see the village?"

"No, the Crows said there were bluffs intervening."

"Lieutenant, just answer the question, please, do not give us a tactical analysis. Did you see the village?"

"No, sir."

"Did you know that a certain Mitch Bouyer saw Indians watching the regiment?"

"Yes, he told me that two Sioux had seen him."

"As commander of scouts did you suggest to your leader that your men might follow these two hostiles to determine where they went after they saw Mitch Bouyer and the regiment?"

"Well, I don't think he said they saw the regiment——"

"*Please*, Lieutenant."

"No, I did not."

"Did you suggest, in your capacity as chief of scouts, that your men go ahead to see what was in the valley ahead?"

"No, I did not." The "sir" is obviously missing from Hare's responses by now and his face is growing red. "Only a few officers could suggest to——"

"That will be all, Lieutenant Hare." Jacobson has not left his seat throughout the exchange.

Gardiner is on his feet before Schofield calls for redirect. "Lieutenant Hare, did you have any reason to disbelieve the Crows when they said they saw a pony herd in the valley?"

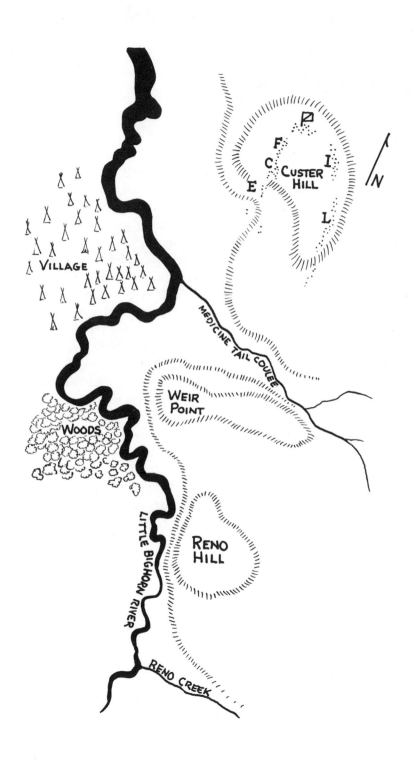

"No, sir, it was too far away to see clearly. They knew the country."

"What did you *believe?*"

"That there was a great village in the valley."

"Thank you. Mr. President, with no further questions to this witness, I request he be excused."

Gardiner now asks permission to set up a map of the Little Bighorn battle area. It is a large affair, and two soldiers as well as Beakin and Sommers get it into place just behind and to the right of the witness stand. The court and all parties to the trial can see it except the witness, who will have to turn slightly to his right. Jacobson objects to it, claiming it is not to scale.

"No, it is not, and for our purposes here it does not matter," Gardiner says. "Its purpose is simply to orient the members of the court on various parts of the battlefield. It is a schematic chart rather than a map, showing the four major geographic landmarks of the battle area. The Little Bighorn River running from bottom to top, then on the right of that the three areas of high ground, from the bottom, Reno Hill, Weir Point, and finally Custer Hill."

Jacobson subsides as Schofield accepts it and asks the reporter to mark it prosecution exhibit C for identification.

Schofield says, "Major Gardiner, I know your people have gone to some lengths here in getting the map—chart—erected. But I feel most parties to the trial are rather tired. Would you object to a recess now until tomorrow morning?"

On recess spectators hurry for the ferry slip and members of the court move out casually, inviting one another for a drink at the officers' bar. Gardiner sits for a long time at his table, slowly gathering his scattered papers. The two younger officers sense his mood and leave him.

10

In his flat Gardiner is sprawled, limp, on a couch he has pulled before the window so that he can gaze out at the sun setting over the Jersey shore of the Hudson. He has on red flannel underwear and black woolen socks. He sips from a bucket of cool beer that he has had sent up from the saloon immediately below on 33rd Street. The thick, oily smoke from one of Ned Stokes's *Nymphs and Satyr* cigars diffuses the sun's late rays.

The brassy November glare turns the entire room bright orange, and Gardiner sits in the cool light, trying to shuck off the tensions of the day on Governor's Island. With each thought he can see Pope's fuzzy head bobbing up and down, or Schofield's finely tapered fingers wrapped lovingly around his cue ball. McDowell catching a few winks.

Strange, he thinks, but I've had little time even to consider the other members. Two days gone and I'm looking at only three of them. Have to do much better than that. Tomorrow, look at each one at least twice during the day.

She is not at all a beautiful woman. But something there always makes a man look a second time. She is striking. With high cheekbones and chestnut hair. Or is it auburn? The movement of her small hand today when Hare looked at her—just the fingers closing ever so slightly. The nails so well manicured they seem not manicured at all. How she lifts the fingertips to her cheek, touching gently! That flashing look when Schofield looks at her.

The charges are all so fragile. If we could only convict him of murdering someone. Or stealing something. If we could only prove he made deals with post traders . . . but that's all absurd. We can't, and he isn't even charged with that sort of thing. He is charged with making a wrong decision—a number of wrong decisions when you get right down to it. And who is expected to dredge up all the bad and throw it into the faces of the court? A man so often and so long a hero now because I say so is a threat to the Army?

Of course he is. But how am I supposed to prove it in a court of law? And in Washington, Sherman is watching. To bring these charges he must want Custer's hide very badly.

His mind darts back and forth and he can see the faces of the people in court and of the members. Then the defense table, Jacobson chewing his cud like a glass-eyed cow.

Her skin is translucent—like very old and fragile Italian marble. And how can anyone sit with such a straight back?

Gardiner sips his beer, the sun in his eyes. Oh damn, why did fussy Billy Dunn and the old man ever decide I was the one for this job?

II

<hr>

Marcus A. Reno is a short, well-built man with dark hair and eyes—the hair parted on the left above a rather high and protruding forehead. He is dressed in blues, a double row of brass buttons set down the front of his tunic and the wide piping of commissioned rank along his trouser seams. The golden insignia of his shoulder boards mark him major of cavalry. He carries neither hat nor saber, having deposited these in the anteroom.

When he is sworn, he settles into the witness chair. His eyes move restlessly about the room. He looks at Custer for only a short moment. Satisfied that he has seen everything that interests him, he turns his attention to the trial judge advocate.

Gardiner, after administering the oath, returns to his table for some papers, and with these held behind him he stands before Reno leaning forward slightly. Quickly he finishes the preliminaries —name, rank, organization, the fact that Reno knows the defendant and served as his second in command at the Little Bighorn.

"Major Reno, tell us what happened on the morning of June 25, 1876."

Reno clears his throat and begins. "At about eight o'clock the regiment began to move. We had been halted since 2 A.M. that morning following a night march. I had no idea what was happening but I moved with the column, doing what I imagined the second in command is supposed to do."

"You had no orders from Colonel Custer at this time, even though you were second in command?"

"None whatever. The night before General Custer had told us we would follow the trail a while, then rest on the 25th. But now we were moving again. Later I was told by one of the company officers that General Custer had gone forward to scout the Little Bighorn from high ground. Soon thereafter instructions came back from General Custer to halt the regiment once more."

"He used mounted couriers, I assume, to send those instructions?"

"Yes, sir."

"To whom did these messengers report, if not to you?"

"To the commander of the leading company in the column. That was Tom Custer on the 25th."

"Why was Custer's brother leading the column?"

"It was purely chance. Normally positions in a line of march are rotated so each company will at one time or another be leading."

"Very well, Major Reno, now, what happened when this halt was called?"

"Custer rode down from where he had been observing and said the Indian scouts claimed to have seen a very large hostile village in the valley. Custer said he did not believe it. He had looked with his glasses. He said we would move the regiment into the valley of the Little Bighorn because he was afraid the Indians would escape."

"But I thought he said he didn't think they were there."

"I don't know if he meant he didn't think they were there or that he didn't think there was a village there as large as his scouts told him there was. He didn't explain."

"All right, as the regiment started its movement this time, did he instruct you at all?"

"No, sir. I was with the other officers when he returned from his scout. But other than the general terms of his announcement at that time, he said nothing to me."

Gardiner asks him to continue and Reno crosses his legs and licks his lips. As he testifies he does not look toward Custer, who watches him with a smile. Now and then Reno's eyes glance toward the ceiling or the windows.

"In a short time, once we were under way, while I was moving back and forth along the column, keeping the men closed up and so on, I saw that Captain Benteen was moving off to the south—to our left—with a number of units. I rode over and asked him what was happening and he said Custer had told him to move off to the left and 'tie into anything' he might find. That was all he said. He had Companies D, H, and K with him."

"Custer sent no information to you indicating why he was dispatching Benteen to the left?"

"He did not, no, sir. We continued the march until about ten o'clock. We had come to a small stream and we were following it. It ran toward the west—toward the Little Bighorn. I assumed it emptied into the stream and it turned out that it did. Lieutenant Cooke, Custer's adjutant, came over and said the General wanted me to take command of Companies A, G, and M."

"Did you know then what he wanted you to do with this battalion, or did you know what he planned for the rest of the regiment?"

"No, Cooke gave me no further instructions at that time. I took command of my companies and moved them along the west bank of the stream, generally opposite and parallel to the rest of the regiment on the far side—I assumed it was still directly under Custer's command."

"You were on Custer's left?"

"That is correct, to the south of him, on his left, and we were marching west. We continued a short time and then Custer waved his hat to me. I had fallen slightly behind and rode along my column bringing it up. As I moved abreast of Custer, but still on the opposite side of the creek, I saw that they had discovered an abandoned Indian tepee. Custer's Indian scouts were highly excited. They were stripping off their clothing and daubing paint on their faces and bodies."

"Which meant what to you?"

"Custer had the Crow scouts—I'm not familiar with them. But from what I have learned of Plains Indians, this meant they were preparing for a fight. They were using quantities of black paint, and black is very nearly the universal color for war and death among Plains Indians."

Reno coughs, covering his mouth with a clenched fist. His hands appear entirely too large for the rest of him.

"Then Lieutenant Cooke rode over to me and said that I should move forward as rapidly as I thought prudent and charge the village and that I would be supported by the whole outfit."

"This order was from Custer?"

"Yes, with the exception of his telling me to take command of the three companies, it was the only instruction I had from him all day."

"Now try to recall, Major Reno, once again—didn't you think it strange that Custer had said before that he did not believe his scouts about the village and that now he was asking you to charge it?"

Jacobson is out of his chair. "I object, it's leading and calls for an opinion."

"Can trial judge advocate justify?" Schofield asks.

"Mr. President, I am asking an opinion which, held at the time of an action, might well have influenced some response on witness's part."

Schofield glances left and right at the other members of the court. "I can understand that, but you do seem to be leading him."

"Allow me to rephrase the question."

"Please do. Won't you have a seat, Mr. Jacobson?" The defense counsel sits down.

"When you received this order—to move ahead and charge the village—what were your thoughts in respect to the morning's events until that time?"

"I thought I had no idea what the commanding officer wanted me to do until that moment, and then I had no idea against what he was sending me. I mean, I didn't know what he thought was in the valley."

"Under such circumstances, doesn't one inquire?"

"Not with General Custer. You do what he says."

"Major Reno, are you afraid of Custer?"

For the first time since he took the stand, Reno looks squarely at Custer for an extended moment. He shakes his head. "I am not personally afraid of him—or of any man, sir. But as my commanding officer I was. Anyone who has ever served under him is frightened of what he may do. He is a cruel and unjust——"

"*I object!*" screams Jacobson.

"Sustained."

"Even his own brother, who served under him? Was he frightened of Custer, too?"

"Mr. President, I *object*," Jacobson fairly screams.

Reno shouts, "Yes, he was afraid!"

The billiard ball is slamming into the bench and Schofield is furious. "Major Gardiner, I will not condone such conduct in the court. That objection is sustained, it is sustained."

Gardiner stands wide-eyed. He turns and looks at Jacobson. "I am sorry, I heard no objection," he says. He smiles broadly.

"The court will disregard that last question and the answer given by the witness."

Gardiner turns again to the court. "Would the court please clarify? Which questions are to be ignored?"

Schofield glares at Gardiner. "I will not repeat the questions because you and I and everyone in this room know exactly what questions I refer to when I say they will be disregarded."

"I am confused, Mr. President."

"You are in serious trouble, Major, if you don't continue the questioning of this witness, confused or not."

Gardiner returns to Reno, who has been visibly shaken by the exchange.

"In his order, did Custer specifically say he would support you, Major Reno?"

"Yes, with the whole outfit."

Reno testifies that his command moved quickly toward the Little Bighorn. As he approached the river he saw more and more Indian signs, the dust along many of the trails deep from being churned by the hooves of many ponies.

"I sent two messages back to General Custer to tell him that I had seen a great deal of Indian country and that I was sure we were close to an overwhelming number of hostiles. He made no reply and soon he struck off to the right and I was committed to the river, straight ahead. Lieutenant Ben Hodgson had joined me as my acting adjutant. He was not on company duty that day and could have remained with the trains, but he didn't want to be left out of a fight. When Custer made no response to my messages, Hodgson laughed and said it didn't matter because, as the General had often said, the 7th Cavalry could whip the whole Sioux nation.

"The banks were steep at the river, but not high, and there was no difficulty in fording. We had to swim only a few feet. On the far side I formed two companies in line, one in rear of them for a reserve, and we swung out into the valley and turned to our right—or toward the north.

"There were trees along the river directly to our front. As we moved beyond these and could see up the valley, we were astonished to catch sight for the first time of the village—it was bigger than any Indian village I had ever imagined. It seemed to stretch for miles out into the valley and out of sight to the north——"

"Major Reno, please clear up one point before proceeding. Why couldn't this village have been seen before you crossed?"

"Just to the north of where we crossed, high bluffs rise all along the east bank of the Little Bighorn. Some perhaps eighty feet high. That country is relatively flat and any such elevation can conceal a great deal of terrain lying in its lee."

"In other words, to anyone approaching from the east, most of the Little Bighorn valley at one point was masked by bluffs?"

"Yes, sir. It was in that particular area where the Indians had erected their village."

"Could Custer have seen it?"

"Not from the point where we separated. At some distance to the north he could have—I would say perhaps three miles north of where our columns diverged he could have seen it. Of course he could have seen it much sooner had he marched close to the edge of the bluffs and looked down."

"Please continue."

"Well, we were riding directly toward the village and as soon as we came into sight a swarm of warriors started riding out to meet us. They kicked up a considerable dust cloud, but even so as we advanced we could still see the village from time to time."

"How far were you from the village when you first saw that you were heading directly toward it?"

"I would say three miles. We continued to close that distance at a trot and the enemy in front were increasing rapidly. They were enveloping my left flank as well in considerable numbers. They made no attempt to close with us but there was firing. I would say at this time there were about four hundred warriors. I saw we needed more power to the front and I drew the reserve company up into line. We had just increased the pace of advance when from out of a ravine immediately to our front a new swarm of enemy—a very large group—broke out and raced toward us firing and screaming."

"Major Reno, from what you could see, did it appear a trap had been laid for you? Did it appear that you had been expected?"

"Oh, no, it seemed our sudden appearance had created great excitement and consternation in the Indian camp. They seemed to be running about rather wildly in the village, as one would expect they might when unexpected danger threatened. But of course the warriors were riding directly out against us on ponies tethered near their tepees."

"At this point, after the group had appeared from the ravine, how many warriors would you say were in your immediate area?"

"I would estimate about nine hundred."

There is a gasp from the spectators.

"What was your troop strength, Major?"

"About 114—not counting a few scouts."

There is an even louder murmur from the room and Schofield gently raps his ivory ball.

"All the Ree scouts except three had disappeared. But I needed no scouting to tell me that offensive action against such a body of mounted men was impossible, and God only knew how many more were behind them in the village, still catching up ponies. I was thrown onto the defensive. We were about a mile, perhaps three-quarters of a mile, from the village when I ordered the troops to their right into the trees along the river."

"You moved into the trees to stand defensively? To what purpose, Major?"

"To save my battalion. And to wait for Custer. In the trees, dismounted, I would at least have something left when he arrived."

"You expected him to come to your support then?"

"It was the last thing he had said to me—through Cooke, of course."

"Did he come?"

Reno stares for a moment at Gardiner as though he is insane, then for the first time what appears to be a wry smile crosses his lips.

"No, he did not come."

"And in the trees, then . . ."

"Dismounted, our fire was effective, and many Indians were dismounting too, crawling close to us. We were taking fire from three sides. It was an intensive fire. I saw a number of warriors with repeating rifles. Then Captain Myles Moylan sent word that the enemy was enveloping our right flank, coming between the battalion and the river. I knew if we waited there any longer we would wait forever. My ammunition was getting low. I had no idea where Benteen was, or the pack trains. Nothing had been communicated to me. I ordered a retreat.

"The battalion moved back from the trees in a column of fours at a gallop. The warriors were soon all about and among us."

"Among you?"

"Yes, they rode into the column, using clubs and hatchets. Others rode parallel to both our flanks, firing into our column. I could see that we would never reach the ford where we had crossed. I led the battalion directly toward the river, although I could see the bluffs were high and sharp at that point.

"Many never reached the crossing. After we left the trees I never saw Lieutenant Don McIntosh again. He was killed trying to reach the river. And at the river it was worse. The Sioux were coming right into the water with us. I saw Lieutenant Hodgson, dismounted and waist-deep in water, facing the Indians and firing his pistol when he was hit. His chest was shattered, and three of them rode over him and he sank beneath the surface."

Reno has been rushing on and now he stops, breathless. A bead of sweat runs down his pale forehead.

"I apologize. Benny Hodgson was the darling of the regiment and my own favorite officer as well. I should have sent him back to the trains where he belonged."

"No apology is necessary, Major Reno," Gardiner says. He pauses a moment but Schofield is becoming impatient and he nods to Reno that he should continue.

Reno testifies that he brought what was left of the battalion up to high ground, the horses struggling and straining on the slope. Almost at once the pressure decreased and then suddenly was gone completely, the Indians having ridden off to some other area. At this point Benteen and his unbloodied battalion rode up and Reno welcomed them with joy and relief.

"Was there still no sign of Custer?"

"No sign at all. Benteen had no notion where he might be, because of course he—Benteen—had been off to the south all morning."

"What were your casualties in killed, Major Reno?"

"In the valley, twenty-seven killed. Half that many wounded."

"Could you still see the village from your defensive position?"

"Actually better than we could see it from the valley. It was huge. It stretched out for miles along the valley. We could tell little about what was happening because of distance, heat waves, and dust. But I heard many troopers remarking on what a great Indian camp we had tied into."

Reno licks his lips and looks toward a pitcher of water on Gardiner's table. The trial judge advocate gets a glass and pours it full for him. Reno empties the glass as everyone watches.

"Thank you, sir," Reno says.

"Major Reno, basing your estimate on what you saw in the valley, what you saw from the defensive position on the bluffs, and what you could see of the village—plus of course your wide experience on the Plains—how many warriors would you say were in the valley of the Little Bighorn that day?"

"I'd say six to eight thousand."

"Jesus," someone in the courtroom whispers. Schofield makes no move to gavel silence but stares at the witness.

Reno sits pressed back into the witness chair. Everyone can see he wishes it were over, but he is holding up well, Gardiner thinks.

"Now, Major Reno, let me ensure that we have understood these movements. Is it correct——"

"I object. He's leading the witness," Jacobson says from his chair, softly but distinctly. Schofield raises his eyebrows at Gardiner, who lifts his arms.

"I am reviewing testimony," he says. "If and when I proceed into undiscovered country, as it were, I would expect an objection against me to be sustained."

"I will overrule." Schofield sighs. "Please, Major Gardiner, may we continue?"

Gardiner nods toward Jacobson, who smiles and nods back.

"Now is this correct? The number of hostiles in the valley was so enormous——"

"He never did say enormous," Jacobson says, still in his seat. "He said great and very large, but he did not say enormous."

"Mr. Jacobson, the patience of this court——" Schofield starts. Jacobson waves his hand and nods. Beside him, Custer glances back at Libby and they exchange a smile. She brushes one hand across her breast, and Custer looks down at his coat. It has come open at the top and he fastens it, his fingers lingering on the large brass button while he looks at the witness again, a faint smile still evident under his moustache.

"The number of Indians was so . . . great you halted your charge and fought for a while on foot. Then, feeling your command was in danger of complete destruction, you ordered it back across the river to the bluffs?"

"Yes, sir, that was my meaning," Reno says quietly.

"And arriving there you were joined by Captain Benteen and his battalion—coming over from the left or south—and together you developed a position for defense."

"Well, part of the command went forward to the north before we could——"

"Yes, yes, I understand," Gardiner cuts in. "That will be brought out, Major Reno, but I am trying here to review your testimony."

"Yes, well, Benteen came up and we joined forces," Reno says.

"No more questions," Gardiner says. He is halfway into his seat when Jacobson speaks.

"A very bad job of coaching your witness, Mr. Gardiner."

The trial judge advocate, still irritated with Jacobson's refusal to use his military rank, turns red and starts from his chair again.

Jacobson waves his hands, laughing. "I apologize, I apologize," he says. "I am so unaccustomed to the formality of military proceedings."

"Very well, Mr. Jacobson, very well," Schofield says. Gardiner, half suspended between standing and sitting, finally sits.

"Let's see, Major," Jacobson starts. "Will you tell us once more what your last orders were from . . . this man?" He turns and points to Custer. Custer appears to lift himself higher in his seat as all eyes follow Jacobson's hand and look at him. Under his sloping chin his Adam's apple is pronounced.

"The adjutant came to me——"

"Yes, yes, Major, the adjutant officially speaks for the commander, does he not?"

"Yes, sir, he does."

"Very well then, the adjutant—let's see, what was his name? Cooke—yes, Cooke comes to you and what did he tell you General Custer wanted you to do?"

On his feet, Gardiner interrupts. "I thought we had agreed to use the ranks as posted last year in the frontier Army, not the temporary ones of the Civil War."

With a bow toward the trial judge advocate, Jacobson says, "Of course, a slip of the tongue, Mr. Gardiner. Now, Major Reno, what did Colonel Custer want you to do——"

"Lieutenant Colonel." Gardiner still on his feet.

"What did Lieutenant Colonel Custer want you to do?" Jacobson says, and he turns and smiles at his client and at Libby. Most of the spectators smile back at him.

"To the best of my recollection——"

"*Major Reno,*" Jacobson shouts, and General McDowell starts as though suddenly awakened. "Why do you say to the best of your recollection? We *all* testify according to the best of our recollection."

"Mr. President, I object to this constant interruption of the witness," Gardiner says.

"Of course I interrupt him," Jacobson snaps, and now he is not smiling. "The witness is addled."

Gardiner's voice goes up as he objects again, red-faced.

"Gentlemen." Schofield's voice cuts across the room. "Keep your voice down, Major Gardiner. And Mr. Jacobson, please be careful not to intimidate the witness." He taps the billiard ball lightly.

"Mr. President," Jacobson protests, "I am not trying to——" Schofield slams down the ivory ball.

"I said be *careful*, Mr. Jacobson."

The defense counsel scratches his chin, head down. When he

turns to Reno again, the witness is even tenser. Sweat is
beginning to stain his collar.

"Just tell us your last orders
from Custer, Major."

"To the best of my recollection," Reno says, and Jacobson
shakes his head and smiles.
"Lieutenant Cooke said . . .
uh . . . General Custer directs
you to take as rapid a gait as
you think prudent and charge
the village afterward and you
will be supported by the whole
outfit."

MAJ. MARCUS A. RENO

"And what did you take the word *afterward* to imply?"

"I took it to mean that after I'd crossed the river and seen the
Indian village, I was to charge it."

"You are a man of much experience, Major Reno. When you
charge something—let's say a trench or a battery position—what
does that mean?"

"Well . . . uh . . . it means that you ride over it."

"Ah, you ride *over* it. Why on earth do you do such a thing?"

"Because cavalry's greatest effectiveness is in shock. Bringing the
horses and riders onto the enemy position, the shock of a charge——"

"But isn't it true that you *stopped*, Major Reno?" Jacobson cuts
in harshly. "That you didn't come *close* to the village which Custer
had told you to charge?"

"Well, we were close all right."

"Did you charge the village? Did you deliver the *shock* your
commander had asked you to deliver? *Did you, Major?*"

"No, I've already said——"

"You've already said, Major, that you *failed* to do what Custer
ordered—*ordered*—you to do. That he was expecting you to take
certain actions which you failed to take and therefore you may
well have caused his whole plan——"

"Are you making a closing statement, for God's sake?" Gardiner
shouts.

The billiard ball comes down with a crack. Everyone looks at Schofield. "Mr. Jacobson, please make your points here from testimony of witnesses. You know the rules."

Jacobson makes a small bow to the court. He is happy to let it go and strides back to his table. But he holds up one hand and everyone knows he is not finished. Reno is shaken by the exchange and he wipes at his face with a handkerchief he has held clutched in one fist throughout his testimony.

Custer squirms in his chair, looking back through the courtroom. He nods at the press gallery and most of them nod back. He scratches under his coat, beneath his arm. He looks toward the other side of the room and sees a strikingly handsome woman a few rows back of Gardiner's chair. He smiles, his teeth even and bright against his sunburned face. He continues to watch the woman, who pretends to be unaware of his glance. Libby looks toward the woman, too, lifts her eyebrows, then takes no further notice.

Jacobson is ready once more and he confronts Reno. "Major Reno, when you arrived on the bluffs and Captain Benteen came up, what was your condition?"

"As I have said, we had suffered heavily and the men and horses were——"

"No, no, no," Jacobson cuts in. "Not the condition of the command, Major Reno. Your own personal condition."

"I . . . I don't know what you mean."

"Were you excited?"

"Yes."

"Were you tired . . . physically tired?"

"Yes, very tired."

"Were you distraught?"

"I . . . I don't know if I would categorize it——"

"Isn't it true, Major Reno, that you found the need for a stimulant?"

Gardiner is on his feet. That same hint had been in the newspapers for months now—that Reno had been drunk, incapable of leading his battalion after they had reached the bluffs. Maybe even before. But Gardiner has no opportunity to object to the question. Schofield is looking directly at him and he knows it will do no good.

"I . . . uh . . . I beg your pardon?" Reno stammers. His face is blotched and wet.

"Isn't it true that you carry a small—oh, let's say a pint-sized—metal flask in your saddlebags?"

Reno looks at Gardiner, but the trial judge advocate's eyes are on his fingers drumming rapidly on the table before him. Reno wipes his mouth with the handkerchief.

"I often do," Reno says.

"In fact, isn't it well known on Army posts that you are addicted to alcohol?"

"I object," Gardiner snaps.

"Sustained," Schofield says.

"Very well, the flask. In the saddlebags. What do you have in it usually?"

"Well . . ."

Reno hesitates so long that Schofield starts a light, almost inaudible tapping with his billiard ball.

"Sometimes brandy, sometimes whiskey," Reno says.

"And on June 25, 1876. What was in your flask that day?"

"Brandy, I think."

"Yes."

"I was not drunk, sir!" Reno shouts. Then his voice suddenly lowers. "I was not. I was not drunk."

Jacobson lets it sink into the court's awareness, going to his table to ruffle through papers which Gardiner knows is only an act. Goddamn him, Gardiner thinks. Finally Jacobson resumes. "Major Reno, from the time you rode into that valley, and in fact from the time you last saw Custer, did you ever, at any time, consider riding to his aid?"

"I had no notion where he was and he had given me no instructions about——"

"Of course you didn't know where he was. And wouldn't that in itself have indicated he might be in trouble—at least to any officer still in full possession of his faculties?"

"We were beaten——"

Cutting in again, and moving in close to Reno: "With Benteen up? Fresh troops? They hadn't seen any action, had they? *Had they?*"

Reno shakes his head and wipes his face again. His collar is now black with wet. He seems to be pulling his head down into his chest like a tortoise.

"Reporter, indicate a negative answer to that," Schofield says.

Jacobson presses. "Had you not lost command of your faculties, Major Reno?"

"I don't understand."

"Weren't you incapable of command?" Jacobson shouts, slapping his hands directly under Reno's face. Reno stares fixedly at the defense counsel's mouth. "Isn't it true that you lost all ability to command in those trees by the river, where you first dismounted?"

"I object, Mr. President," Gardiner says, rising, but he sinks back quickly.

"I'm going to take this, Major," Schofield says.

"Thank you, Mr. President. Now, Major Reno, *please*, weren't those moments—even hours—so confused in your mind that you cannot relate what happened even now?"

"I . . . it was an overwhelming experience." Reno senses that Gardiner can no longer help him and his eyes dart to the court and then to Custer. Custer smiles slightly, still fondling his buttons.

"But, Major Reno," Jacobson says softly now, "you were in command." His hands clap again and the court jumps, but Reno only presses back deeper into the witness chair. "*You were in shock,*" Jacobson shouts. "*You were incapable of command, were you not?*"

"It was a terrifying experience," Reno says. God, I hope he isn't going to cry, Gardiner thinks.

"Afraid," Jacobson says, backing away as though Reno is diseased. "Afraid? A leader of men in battle—*afraid?*"

"It was a terrible experience."

Jacobson wheels toward Custer and points to him. "And *this* man is being tried——" Jacobson stops, looks back toward Reno. Then quickly he moves behind his table, reaching out to place a hand on Custer's shoulder as he sits down.

"I have no more for this . . . this . . . *officer*," he sneers.

Every face in the room turns to Gardiner, who is trying to control his anger. After a moment the president of the court breaks the deep silence.

"Recross?"

Gardiner rises but he remains behind his table, a good distance from the witness. He speaks loudly and slowly. "Major Reno. I want you to answer questions clearly and carefully." Reno's eyes fix on the trial judge advocate. His damp hair streams across his forehead.

"I realize this may be difficult for you, Major Reno, but recall if you will what happened in the valley when you—how did you phrase it?—when you felt overwhelmed."

Reno stares at him a long time, flicking his tongue across his lips. His tightly fitted uniform heaves up and down with his breathing.

"Was it the general violence and confusion of the fight?" Gardiner prompts him, and Reno seems to realize he is expected to answer.

"No . . . no. It wasn't that. Although the fight was a violent one."

His voice is low and General McDowell has to lean forward and cup one ear with his hand.

"I had given the command to move back to a defensive position on the bluffs—across the river. I was about to mount when one of the new men—I didn't know his name—was hit badly in the stomach. He threw his arms around my legs as he fell and almost dragged me down. Bloody Knife was beside me and pulled me free, helping me mount——"

"Who is Bloody Knife, sir?"

"What? Oh . . . yes . . . he was my best Ree scout. He mounted too and I was trying to find out from him if there were any Sioux between us and the river. He was leaning toward me, very close. And . . . suddenly his face . . . his face disintegrated. I couldn't see for a long time. . . ."

The court is deathly still. The heavy breathing of General McDowell can be heard clearly in the back of the room. Reno sags on the stand, his mouth open, his eyes glazed as he sees that faraway battlefield.

Gardiner remains behind his table but leans forward and urges his witness gently. "You couldn't see, Major Reno?"

"No. . . . I couldn't see. Bloody Knife was close to me . . . trying to tell me something, when . . . a bullet struck his head. His . . . his brains splattered into my face. . . . I had to wipe my eyes to see . . . and my mouth——" Reno gags and quickly covers his face with the handkerchief. His retching is the only sound in the room. It is soon over.

Gardiner straightens, then slowly settles in his chair. "No more questions."

Jacobson is shaking his head. Beside him Custer's fingers are still on his buttons, and directly behind, Libby stares straight ahead. A small muscle in her jaw twitches.

Schofield says, "The witness is excused."

Reno bolts from the witness chair and stands stiffly before the court, salutes, wheels, and marches down the aisle and out of the still silent courtroom.

The room seems to deflate on Reno's exit, the crowd letting out a long breath, muttering softly as the tension is suddenly released. Members of the court take glasses of water and speak softly to one another. Pope leans to his left and holding a hand over his mouth whispers to Augur, whose flared white muttonchops look like a goat's whiskers. Augur holds an unlighted cigar between his teeth.

Gardiner bends to Beakin and says, "Do you have a copy of that petition?"

For an instant Beakin does not understand, then he nods. "In my quarters."

"Get it. Quickly." Gardiner faces the court. "The government calls James Foster."

As the young man is brought in, Beakin hurries out past the provost guard. The day has turned clear and warm for November, and he leaves the building without his hat, running toward the sally port and the main compound of Fort Columbus.

On the witness stand, the young man is nervous and embarrassed. He wears an ill-fitting civilian suit just purchased from some mail-order house. The left sleeve is empty, folded neatly across the front and held in place by a large shiny safety pin. His hair hangs straight and corn-silk fine across a high forehead. His eyes are blue, his face freckled. Along his left cheek is a deep, brutal scar which disfigures his face, pulling his lip up into an unnatural, constant sneer.

"I was a private with Company A on the Little Bighorn, sir," he says, looking only at Gardiner as though afraid to let his eyes wander elsewhere. "When we crossed the river it was a bad time. There was some quicksand at the crossings and I was afraid of getting into it. I wasn't very good at controlling my mount."

"Mr. Foster, did you see Major Reno after the command rode into the valley?"

"Yes, sir, right after we crossed the river and we could see Indians riding out, he called me over—I was on orderly duty that day with the battalion commander. Captain Moylan had detailed me. Major Reno, he called me over. He told me to take a message to General Custer back on the other side—of the river."

The boy's eyes dart toward Custer and then away. Gardiner waits but the boy sits staring at him.

"What was the message?"

"Major Reno said, 'Tell General Custer—the Indians were not running but were coming on.' "

"Do you recall those words exactly?"

"Yes, sir. 'Tell General Custer the Indians were not running but were coming on.' "

Gardiner waits again.

"I could see they were, too. I remember thinking what I might do because I had never been in an Indian scrap before."

"What did you do, Mr. Foster?"

"I ran my horse back to the ford and across and I rode up to high ground and started north. I struck back away from the river a ways and then I found General Custer's trail. I crossed some high ground and saw his battalion strung out about a mile off. I caught up to them on the hill where we finally ended up—I mean where Major Reno's battalion finally ended up."

"Could you see the river from there?" Gardiner asks, walking over to the large map and staring at it.

"No, sir, we was back a ways from the bluffs over the river."

Gardiner points at the southernmost high ground indicated on the map. "About here, then. All right, Mr. Foster, what happened then?"

"General Custer's adjutant saw me as I was riding up and I went over to him with the message. He knew I was a messenger because when the 7th detailed a soldier for messenger, they had these red arm bands you put on——"

"A brassard."

"Yes, sir, that's it. When Captain Cooke saw me with that on he knew I was from Major Reno. I said to him, 'Major Reno says tell General Custer the Indians are not running, they are coming on.' He asked me to say it all again and I did."

"Did he give you any answer for Major Reno, any instructions?"

"No, sir, he just said I should rejoin my command, and so I did."

Gardiner walks away, pauses a moment, and looks back at the witness.

"When were you wounded, young man?"

"Coming up the bluffs. After I got back to Major Reno we tried a stand in some trees but had to get out. When we were riding back one of them got right alongside me. My pistol was empty and I'd lost my carbine. He swung a hatchet at me and he sure knocked out some teeth." He laughs shortly, shaking his head. His eyes are brittle bright with the memory of it, an unnatural brightness. "Then a minute later a ball hit my elbow. I was halfway up the bluff before I fell off my mount, but Lieutenant Varnum grabbed me and dragged me on up to the position."

"Do you recall anything of the fight on the bluff?"

"No, sir, not after Lieutenant Varnum dragged me up. He was dismounted, too, and he had a Colt in both hands, and he was crying and swearing like I never heard anybody swear and shooting at the Indians. On the bluff somebody else got me and all I recall is how thirsty I was."

"And now you are released from the Army with an invalid's pension?"

"Yes, sir, they told me they would give me five dollars a month."

Once more Gardiner starts for his table, glancing back toward the door. He looks at Custer; the cavalryman has pulled his cape around his shoulders and sits slumped in his chair as though cold.

"How old are you, young man?"

"Eighteen."

Gardiner turns and looks at the empty sleeve. "Did you like the Army?"

"Sometimes. I liked it at Fort Lincoln, where they had started to teach us how to ride, and other things I liked, too. The officers would have dances—they'd last until midnight. We would stay out on the barracks' verandas listening to the music across the parade ground. It would be dark and cool and we'd smoke. Next day would be Sunday and late stable call. Then when the ball was over the officers and their ladies would come out and stand in the moonlight and all the soldiers would sing 'Auld Lang Syne' and they would stand there and listen. . . ."

The room has become still again, with only the muttering of the stoves and the sound of the harbor wind whispering against the high windowpanes.

"Were you proud to be a part of the 7th Cavalry?"

"I most surely was, yes, sir." He smiles crookedly, his mouth toothless where the hatchet struck.

"And you trusted your regimental commander, didn't you?"

"Mr. President," Jacobson cuts in softly but insistently.

"Yes, Major Gardiner, I would agree, unless you can show——"

"No, General Schofield, it is all right." Gardiner waves his hand and smiles slightly as Beakin comes in and hurries down the aisle with a sheet of paper. The document is entered into evidence as prosecution exhibit D, and once it is so marked by the reporter Gardiner hands it to the witness.

"Do you recognize this, Mr. Foster?"

"Yes, sir, it's a petition the men signed right after the battle. I signed it at the Fort Lincoln hospital."

"What is the gist of it?"

"I beg your pardon, sir?"

"What does the petition ask?"

"It asks the President of the United States to make Major Reno the lieutenant colonel of the 7th Cavalry, what with General Custer being hurt and laid up with serious wounds."

"And this was signed by enlisted men of the 7th?"

"Yes, sir."

"How many of them signed it?"

"I'd have to count——"

"That won't be necessary," Gardiner says, taking the paper and depositing it in front of Jacobson at the defense table. "We have already counted for you, Mr. Foster. Your name is number 187, Private James Foster, Company A, 7th Cavalry. Exactly 235 of your comrades signed it with you. No more questions."

"I have nothing for this witness," Jacobson mutters, scowling. "I see no earthly purpose to be served in introducing this."

"Please reserve comments for the proper time, Mr. Jacobson," Schofield says, and he excuses the witness.

First Sergeant John M. Ryan is a burly man with a handlebar moustache, typical of the non-commissioned officers of the frontier Army—tough, leathery skin tanned and wrinkled by dust and wind, sun and rain. He identifies himself as the top soldier of Company M.

"In the valley with Major Reno it was hard to see from where I was in the line. The red devils was stirrin' up a fearful dust, to what purpose I don't know. But there was a goodly number of them visible to us from time to time. The major had ordered us into a trot, and the horses was tired and hard to handle. Private James Turley, who was a recruit in the company, lost a-hold of his reins, and his horse charged right into a big bunch of the Sioux —with Turley still on him. We found his head later in one of the abandoned tepees after General Terry came up. It was tied to another head nobody could identify. They was tied together with rawhide strips."

Elizabeth Custer holds a small, lacy handkerchief to her mouth and she is pale. Directly in front of her Custer grinds his teeth, his jaw muscles rippling. He has slipped his cape off now and sits drumming his fingers on his thigh, the diamond glinting like a white-hot coal.

"Sergeant Ryan, what were your orders that day?"

"The company commander—Captain French—he was always good at passin' on orders. But that day he said he didn't have any to pass because Major Reno didn't have any. We were just going to ride down there and bust up anything we found. We found a-plenty, too. I saw Lieutenant McIntosh waving his hat when we broke into a gallop towards the Sioux, and he was yellin' that whoever got the first scalp would get a ten-day furlough."

"And who got the first scalp, Sergeant?"

"I have no idea, sir. Most of us don't take scalps—some do. But any one of us would have liked a furlough. It didn't matter, though. A little later we tried to stand in the trees—there was too many to charge—but that was too hot as well, so we had to get out of the valley. There were some stragglers left behind. Lieutenant Mc-

Intosh went back to help 'em. I saw his mount go down, but he caught up another loose one—horses was runnin' all over the valley, wild and scared. He was a little ways behind us when about a dozen Sioux rode right around him. I think he may have killed one of them before they got him with lances and clubs. They was mostly naked and painted black. Lieutenant McIntosh was a brave man. But he never got to furlough anybody."

Gardiner paces a moment, well aware of the effect these battle-field stories have on the court and the press. Everyone watches the witness intently, trying to imagine him on that bloody field. This is good, Gardiner thinks. Nobody has such solid credibility as a good Irish first soldier.

"How bad did it get in the valley, Sergeant?"

"Bad, sir. The word went around when we was in the trees that the Sioux might be flankin' us, so we ran for it. It was a good thing we did. Gettin' across the river was bad too. I was pushing along a line of young troopers, whipping their mounts with a stick so they wouldn't fall behind. Halfway up the slope we was all a-scramble and I dismounted 'em there and we started shootin' at the Sioux below. Some we couldn't get a bead on because they was right in amongst our own boys. I saw Lieutenant Hare almost caught, but he pointed his .45 right in this big buck's face and let go. I heard Lieutenant Hare say later we got hell beat out of us down in that valley."

"Were you expecting help?"

"The whole time. Only thing Captain French had told us was that no matter what happened, the rest of the regiment would support us. But it went on and on. And the rest of the regiment didn't come. By the time we got to the bluff, some of us had started thinkin' maybe it was another Washita."

"What does that mean, Sergeant Ryan?"

"At the Washita——"

"I object," Jacobson says. "What does Washita have to do with this campaign?"

"No, I'll take this," Schofield says. "You can answer that question, Sergeant."

"Yes, sir, General. At the Washita in Indian Territory back in the winter of '68, the 7th tied into a big Cheyenne village in the snow. But we had one group out on a flank away from the rest. It was commanded by Major Elliott—Major Joel Elliott"—he glares at Custer, as close as he has ever come to insubordination —"as fine an officer and gentleman as ever I seen. The main body tied into the village and cleaned it out. It was messy. Their women and kids fought like cornered wolves and a lot of them we shot. When it was over a lot of warriors were coming downstream at us. We had tied into the tail end of a big village. We'd just hit the lower end of it. So we pulled out. Only thing was we left Major Elliott behind, along with his men—about a dozen I recall. We found their bodies over a month later when the 7th was back patrolling that area. We buried what little we could find of 'em. There wasn't much."

"And you suspected the main body had ridden off again and left you there on the bluff above the Little Bighorn?"

"Yes, sir, a number of us talked about it that evening and all night. Almost everybody in the regiment knew the Washita story. We tried to keep still about it around the younger soldiers."

Gardiner takes his seat and Jacobson moves in on the witness, who looks at the clubfooted man with obvious suspicion.

"Sergeant Ryan, is it? Very well, then, Sergeant Ryan. Let's recall the valley once more—before your Major Reno made his heroic dash for the hills—did you see any casualties as the troops raced their mounts toward the enemy village?"

"There was Private Turley, whose horse——"

"Yes, yes, yes, but I mean casualties from enemy fire?"

"No, sir, I did not see any casualties from hostile fire."

"The first casualties you suffered came after you *stopped*, isn't that true?"

"Yes, sir."

Jacobson smiles and looks at his client, who is obviously very angry—as he has been since the Washita testimony. "Sergeant, this Washita business. Isn't the real truth that Major Elliott and his patrol blundered into some of those Indians coming down the valley and were killed before they could get free?"

"No, sir, and General Custer never even looked for the major.

We went up river a ways with the band playin' 'Garry Owen' to put the scare into those red devils comin' down toward us, then we turned and tucked tail and ran and left the major——".

"Sergeant," Jacobson cuts in harshly. "What is the largest unit you have ever commanded in combat?"

For an instant Sergeant Ryan looks balefully at the defense counsel. When he answers, his words come clipped through clenched teeth.

"I am a non-commissioned officer, sir, and I have never commanded a battalion or a company, but I know——"

"Thank you, Sergeant Ryan, that will be all."

Gardiner lets the witness go without further questioning. The points were either made or not, and he sees no point in drawing it out.

Schofield, there being no objection, recesses the court for twenty minutes to allow everyone—especially the members of the court—to stretch his legs. The room quickly empties except for a few newspaper reporters who talk softly together and watch as the artist from *Harper's Weekly* remains in his chair, sketching Sergeant Ryan as he appeared on the witness stand.

Gardiner moves quickly away from his colleagues and walks toward the sally port, enjoying the sunlight and the salt breeze. He lights a cigar. On the gravel walk in front of the court building he sees the Custer party, surrounded by press reporters. It puzzles him that both Custers have cooperated so long in keeping their own stories out of the newspapers. It is unusual behavior for both of them.

Gardiner pauses in the sally port and leans against the cold masonry, enjoying his cigar and watching the wind ruffle the surface of the harbor. A young officer and his lady smile a greeting and stop to talk.

"I thought Major Reno's testimony was devastating," she says, smiling gaily. Her hands are before her, buried in a sealskin muff.

"Yes, ma'am," Gardiner says, holding his lighted cigar behind him until the lady departs.

"But that scalping by our own men. Surely a joke. . . ."

"One does strange things under the stress of combat, ma'am," he says, knowing it is true, although he has had little experience with it.

"It was dreadful about those heads, wasn't it? Why do those savages do such things?"

"In the heat of the moment, I suppose," Gardiner says, now ignoring good manners to puff his stogie. "Or perhaps to gain new courage or even as a trophy of some sort."

"Such barbarians! Hacking away at our soldiers."

"Well, much of the mutilation is performed on the dead."

"How horrible! Disgusting, to be so uncivilized."

"You must recall, madam, that our immediate forebears once hacked off the hands of thieves—not too long ago, either." Gardiner puffs away happily at the expression on their faces.

"Well, it's still . . . just dreadful."

"Yes, and remember the heretics," Gardiner says. "Burned at the stake. And of course they were roasted alive. I should think having a finger chopped off after one is dead would be much nicer than being burned alive."

The officer—whom Gardiner has already been careful to note he out-ranks—quickly takes the woman's arm and they turn away, flushing.

"Good day, madam," Gardiner calls after them.

Striding back to the courtroom, he is only a little ashamed of his conduct. These damned spectators, he thinks. Schofield should close the court to them and to the press . . . well, no, not the press. We need them for the work here. If the court will not do the work needed on Yellow Hair, then perhaps we can arrange it so the newspapers will. So far, he thinks, they have done splendidly, reporting the testimony verbatim—and of course already reaching their own verdicts. As it was expected they would. The *Herald*, Custer's traditional champion, remains his staunch supporter, and the *Tribune*, that Republican stronghold, has rather taken to the Democrat Boy General, too. Strange.

As the court is about to reconvene, an enlisted man hurries down the aisle and locates Beakin, handing him a folded note. The young officer passes it to Gardiner, who is about to call his next witness. Gardiner frowns as he reads, then passes the paper to Schofield. As Schofield reads, he frowns as well.

"He was to have been your witness?"

"No, sir," Gardiner says. "I think Mr. Jacobson was going to call him."

Schofield raps the bench with the billiard ball. "I have an announcement to make, ladies and gentlemen. A sad announcement. Just a few hours ago, Captain Thomas Weir, commander of Company D of the 7th Cavalry—who I think was to have appeared here later—suffered a stroke at Fort Hamilton in Brooklyn and has just a short time ago expired. I understand his family is at Fort Hamilton for those interested—I know he had many close friends." He looks directly at Custer. "My deepest sympathy to all of them."

Shock shows on Custer's face and Libby is clutching her breast, mouth agape. Jacobson hurries around the table and the three of them whisper. Gardiner hears Libby sob once, very softly. Jacobson faces the court.

"General Schofield, as you may know, this comes as a great blow to my client and his wife. May we hope for a recess in order that they might go to Fort Hamilton and comfort the widow? They were close. . . ."

"Most certainly, Mr. Jacobson," Schofield says. "I will recess until tomorrow morning."

"What does it mean?" Sommers says to Gardiner as they stand watching the Custer party hurrying out of the room, spectators crowding about them, reaching out to touch their shoulders, whispering their condolences.

"I think it means Jacobson has lost one hell of a fine defense witness," Gardiner says. "But somehow I don't think it's going to help us very much."

12

In time he would be a general officer, and already as a young lieutenant of cavalry he shows all the marks of a distinguished leader. He holds his head high, shoulders back. His white-gloved hands rest on his thighs as he sits in the witness chair, relaxed and confident. His hair, thick and waving, is parted on the left. His moustache is close-cropped above a firm mouth with full lips. His eyes, wide apart and clear, are laugh-wrinkled but set above unmarked cheeks. He is Winfield Scott Edgerly, second in command of Company D, 7th United States Cavalry.

As a preamble to his testimony he expresses his shock and sorrow over the death of Captain Weir, his company commander. He then details the march of Benteen's battalion. Benteen had complained bitterly about being sent off "valley hunting," with no instructions except to "tie into anything you may find." After more than two hours, stumbling about in broken ground far to the south of the rest of the regiment, Benteen had decided to turn back north—disgusted and making no pains to hide it—completely unaware of where the rest of the regiment might be by that time.

"We came to the trail of the regiment at about three-thirty in the afternoon," Edgerly says, "and found there what was left of a lone Indian tepee. It was smoldering, apparently having been burned by someone of the main body. Inside we could see, wrapped in

LT. WINFIELD SCOTT EDGERLY

smoking blankets, the body of a dead Indian. Near here was a bog— a small swampy area—and Captain Benteen watered our animals. While we were there the pack trains caught up to us and some of the mules were so thirsty they ran directly into the water and got themselves bogged in the mud."

"Had you any word of Custer?" Gardiner asks.

"Not at that moment. As we began to follow Custer's trail—we found out later it was his trail, not Reno's—a sergeant came riding back with a message to bring up the packs. Captain Benteen, not being in charge of the packs, sent him back to the pack train which we knew was following some miles behind. The man had no information about Custer except that he had ridden to the north—which we already knew by then from the trail.

"Then a second man came riding up, a Private Martin, a bugler, I think, who could hardly speak English at all. He was shouting that the Indians were running—I think he said 'skedaddling'—and that Custer was charging through their village. His horse had been hit a number of times and was bleeding badly. There were still two feathered arrows stuck in its rump."

"Did this man have any message from Custer?"

"Yes, a written one. Captain Benteen read it and called Captain Weir and me over and showed it to us. He seemed very skeptical about the soldier's comments that Custer was charging through the village."

"Had you seen the village at this time?"

"No, I had not, we were still some distance, but Captain Benteen was constantly riding far ahead of his column with his scouts. He always threw scouts far out to the front to avoid being surprised. He may have seen some portion of it by then."

"Now, Lieutenant Edgerly, back to the message. What did it say?"

"I can read it," Edgerly says, pulling a tattered paper from an inside pocket. It is obviously a sheet torn from the pages of a notebook. "Afterward, I asked Captain Benteen if I might have it as a memento and he gave it to me. I would appreciate having it back."

"Of course, of course, but allow me to introduce it."

After the reporter marks it prosecution exhibit E, Gardiner passes it to Jacobson, who scans it with a frown. Once more the witness has it in his hands.

"Please read it, Lieutenant Edgerly."

"Yes, sir. 'Benteen—Come on—Big Village. Bring Packs!' Then it is signed by Cooke. He adds 'P.S. Bring Pacs.' He misspelled packs the second time."

"Does the note suggest peril to you?"

"At the time we first read it, it hardly did," Edgerly says.

Edgerly outlines how the Benteen battalion moved on toward the river, bearing north all the while, until at last they saw the valley where the last of Reno's command was making its fight. Crow scouts soon found them and beckoned them on to the high ground where Reno's battalion was struggling up and into a defensive position. Edgerly leaves little doubt that, although Reno was senior, once Benteen arrived on the hill he was the actual commander of the situation. Soon they were joined by the pack trains and Company B, the unit detailed to guard them. Reno's men began to distribute ammunition from the pack mules.

"Some of us had seen a part of the village in the valley below and were greatly impressed. It was striking, too, the difference in attitudes—some of Reno's men seemed beaten, drugged, completely whipped. Others—well, I saw one of his troopers coming up the bank on foot, covered with blood, but laughing and waving a freshly taken Indian scalp. When others saw it they cheered. Reno and Lieutenant Varnum were highly agitated, firing their pistols at the Sioux in the valley, who were obviously far out of range."

Edgerly explains that they heard firing, some close by, other shots far downstream. Captain Weir was concerned that Custer might be in a fight. He rode over to Reno and Benteen, and in a moment Edgerly saw him start toward the north. Edgerly concluded instructions had been given to move to Custer's aid, and he ordered the company into a column pointing downstream. Soon the other companies of Benteen's command were following.

"It was General Custer's greatest battle axiom, 'Ride to the sound of firing,' " he says with a small smile.

"How far north did you ride?"

"To the next prominent high ground—Weir Point."

Edgerly says this was about 5 P.M. As they came up to Weir Point they could see, just beyond, a deep draw called Medicine Tail Coulee, leading down to the river. About three miles beyond that was a high knoll—Custer Hill. There was dust and scattered firing, and they could see riders milling about. Edgerly says they appeared to be firing into the ground. He indicates that the general impression was that there had been a fight but that Custer had gone on to meet Terry.

Soon hostile riders were swarming into Medicine Tail Coulee and up the slopes around Weir Point. By then Benteen had come up, and he ordered the command back to Reno Hill where the defensive positions were much better.

"Once you had begun your march north, why did you not continue until you came up with Custer?" Gardiner asks.

Edgerly looks at him a long time. Then he smiles and shakes his head. "We were quickly being surrounded. Had we lined out north, the Sioux would have butchered us!"

As Gardiner releases his witness, Jacobson is across the room in a few bounds.

"You say you could see no fighting on Custer Hill?"

"That is correct."

"Isn't it true, Lieutenant, that you *wanted* to think any fight was over, and you therefore convinced yourself it was so?"

"Sir, we saw——"

"Isn't it true, Lieutenant, that your mind conceived this little scene *after the fact,* so that you might with clear conscience not have to explain to yourself why you left General Custer and all those men to die?"

"It is *not* true," Edgerly snaps, his temper under control by great effort.

"You saw shooting into the ground and made no assumption? What magnificent eyesight but what dismal perception!"

"Objection," Gardiner says.

"To what do you object, Major Gardiner?" Jacobson snaps, wheeling on the trial counsel. "Do you, too, object to all these people stopping when they should have carried on? First Reno, now these——"

Gardiner is up and around the table almost onto Jacobson, his face contorted. "I object to your sly observations being insinuated as opinions of my witnesses——"

"*Gentlemen!*" Schofield shouts, banging the bench. Gardiner and Jacobson stand for a moment toe-to-toe, glaring at one another—like bulls in the bull ring, Sommers thinks. As suddenly as he came out Gardiner turns back to his chair as Schofield sustains the objection and Jacobson, brows still bristling, stalks across the room, seeming to dare everyone. At least he finally called me by my rank, Gardiner thinks.

"I have nothing else, Mr. President, we can drop it on that pleasant point," Jacobson says. Gardiner lets it go.

Everyone turns to watch as the next witness walks in, for other than Custer himself, he is likely the most famous soldier of the 7th Cavalry. Captain Frederick W. Benteen was a Virginian and during the war the only one of his family to decide for the Union. Because of that—because he is a Southerner—and because he is not a West Point man, he has long been convinced that men of lesser ability have been promoted over him. His reputation is as a combat leader and his every move emphasizes it—he is hot-tempered, headstrong, and pugnacious.

Benteen is a large man, his great head making him appear even larger. His hair, full but beginning to gray, waves back over his ears. He is clean-shaven, with a fat nose and pale, malevolent blue eyes in puffy sockets. His mouth is full-lipped, and as he takes the stand he holds an unlighted pipe which he will suck on from time to time, making a moist gurgling sound. Like the other men, he does not smoke out of deference to the ladies in the room.

He quickly confirms all of Edgerly's testimony about the march to the left and about rejoining the regiment.

"I had no orders except to valley-hunt. I soon discovered it to be useless. No, there were no instructions to coordinate with anyone. I had no idea where Reno was, where Custer was, or what they were doing."

There is a charge in the room, not evident before, as the witness looks at the defendant, and the glance is returned with equal heat. On this day Custer is much tenser for it is the first day Elizabeth has been absent—she is staying with the Weir family at Fort Hamilton. Gardiner knows it has come as a bit of luck, for all the officers of the 7th Cavalry have been careful not to criticize Custer too strongly out of respect for her feelings. Now, with Benteen on the stand, she has chosen the best possible day to be away.

"There was no plan of any kind that I was informed of," Benteen says.

"When you had the messages from Custer—particularly the written one—what were your reactions?"

"To begin with I was not in charge of the trains. But the note was addressed to me. So I sent Lieutenant Hare, one of the officers we found with Reno on the bluffs, back to hurry the mule train on. We gave him a fresh horse for the job. At this time we had come onto Reno and we saw what a mauling he had taken in the valley."

"Did the messenger say Custer was in the village, charging?"

"Yes, but he didn't know what he was talking about. It was obvious. He was so excited he was very nearly hysterical."

"From what you saw, how many hostiles were opposing Reno in the valley?"

"When we rode up, about nine hundred, but that number was growing rapidly."

"What was Reno's personal condition?" Although this is supposed to be a star prosecution witness, Gardiner has an uneasy feeling about Benteen.

"He was under great strain, but holding up. We talked about where Custer was, what we might be expected to do. And then there was some firing—increased firing, I should say—somewhere off to the northwest. I paid little attention. Captain Weir, rest his soul, came over and was talking to Reno. Then in a great show of bravado Weir rode his company north. There was little to do but follow. Weir had no orders to march. He did it on his own. Luckily, he stopped on the high ground you have labeled Weir Point, two miles from Reno's bluff."

"Why do you say luckily?" Gardiner asks.

"Beyond that to the north was great trouble. At the Medicine Tail Coulee we could see just how big this village was. At the time I thought eighteen hundred tepees, but since then I've revised that estimate upwards by about a thousand. There were Sioux riders in the valley, and they had seen us. We'd been getting fire, increasing in intensity, from the moment I rode up."

"What was in the distance, Captain Benteen?"

"About three miles—high ground with a great deal of dust and riders. They seemed to be riding about aimlessly."

"Did you detect shooting from there?"

"A little. Not very much."

"Did you give the order to move back to Reno Hill?"

"I did."

"Why?"

"The point was a bad position. The Reno position was defensible, with a place to corral horses and set up the hospital facility. As the pressure on us increased from the hostiles coming up the coulee, I realized we needed the best defensive ground we could find. I ordered Godfrey to use Company K as a rear guard to cover us into the position."

"Where was Major Reno at the time?"

"I don't know. Still on the bluff, I imagine."

"Was there any discussion about going on north to find Custer?"

"No. It was useless. We would have been butchered in column. I suspected he had had a brush with them and had gone on to Terry."

"You succeeded in regaining Reno Hill, then?"

"Yes. We formed a defensive position shaped like a 'U' with the open end south. Moylan and Varnum were weeping. But it was from anger, I suppose. There was no breakdown in the command. I told Lieutenant Wallace to take Company G and place it in such-and-such a position and he said he didn't have a company, only three men. I told him to put his three men there, and he did and held it well. Fire was getting very heavy there by dark. At that time there were about two thousand immediately around us, shooting. Another two thousand were on the ridges out of range, watching, waiting their turn, I suppose." Benteen laughs a long, bellowing laugh. "In the valley were another two thousand, watching, milling about, yammering like wild dogs."

"Quickly, Captain Benteen, describe that evening and the next day."

"We were under siege. Water was the worst problem. Some men slipped down to the river during the night. Twice I led forays—small counterattacks to drive the Indians back so we could reach the water. Worst were the horses. They were half mad with thirst. We had some wounded who were trampled by stampeding horses, maddened with thirst.

"Horses killed early in the fight had begun to turn bad, too, and by the middle of the next day—the 26th—the smell was enough to gag a man. And it did many. The Sioux and Cheyenne made a number of attacks but we beat them back. We dug little trenches with our hands—we put up sacks of bacon and bread as breastworks.

"Toward evening the camp below began to break up, and a great parade began—travois, pony herds, children, and dogs running along. The thing stretched for miles as it strung out in the direction of the Bighorn Mountains off to the southwest. They kept the pressure on us as their people moved off—until after dark."

"How many warriors would you say . . ."

"I have thought about it a great deal—how it looked moving away from us, a column two miles wide, I don't know how long—and I have come to think there were about six to eight thousand warriors."

Gardiner walks back to his table, letting the effect last. Glancing at the court he thinks, remember Reno and those pitiful few who rode down into the valley! It cannot fail to have an impact. One can hardly imagine eight thousand Indians. He turns back to his witness.

"Where did you suppose Custer was all this time?"

"General Schofield, that calls for an opinion," Jacobson objects. "Which, I must add, most of this testimony is."

"Overruled. It goes directly to the question."

"I supposed he had gone on to Terry," Benteen says. "I could suppose nothing else. We all hoped he would appear again."

Custer leans forward in his chair as though about to spring up. Gardiner moves over to stand between them, so that Benteen cannot glare at the accused.

"Did you discuss it with Major Reno?"

"Of course, and he was of the same mind, even though I have never had a particularly high regard for Reno's opinions."

Jacobson sits up straight in his chair and blinks and then scribbles furiously on a yellow pad. Gardiner clenches his teeth. This Irish bastard is going to botch it all, he thinks. Before he can collect his thoughts, Benteen has started again.

"I recall a bugle call during the night. It was a depressing, lonely sound, coming across that place where we had lost so much. A great many of the men thought it was Custer come back to rescue us. I knew better. I ordered their cheering stopped before it revealed their positions. I knew it was some buck out there, blowing a bugle picked up from a dead trumpeter or given to him perhaps as a gift from the Indian Bureau."

There is nervous laughter that dies quickly. Gardiner is ready to proceed with his witness, but thinks better of it. I would rather let him go now, he thinks, and hope they remember the bugle story and not the part about Reno. But there was one other thing.

"Captain Benteen, did you say anything to anyone about the deployment of the regiment on 25 June?"

"I did. I mentioned it to a number of officers when we were on the hill. Scattering the regiment as Custer had showed no general-ship at all."

"You have commanded regimental-sized units, have you not?"

"Absolutely. Brigade-sized units." He pauses. "I was sent off on a wild chase, and according to all the instruction I had, could still be marching—clear to Fort Benton. And once back in contact primarily through my *own* initiative, the only orders I got were to bring on the socks and blankets."

"Your witness," Gardiner says.

"Yes, I have been looking forward to this, Captain Benteen," Jacobson says, spitting his cud into the cuspidor, shuffling toward Gardiner's table. He knows how to manipulate that foot for any effect, Gardiner thinks.

CAPT. FREDERICK W. BENTEEN

"It interests me, Captain Benteen, that you hold such a low opinion of Major Reno. How long has this gone on?"

Benteen pauses before answering, sucking on his dead pipe.

"Since I first knew him. We have never been what might be termed close friends."

"Is it true that once in a trader's store near Fort Lincoln you slapped Major Reno's face in the presence of other officers and asked him to step outside?"

The members of the court are now alert, and Gardiner can sense a quiet hostility.

"I did. Reno said——"

"That's all right what he said," Jacobson cuts in. "We are not concerned here with that."

Benteen's face begins to redden.

"Captain, you saw a part of Major Reno's withdrawal from the valley the evening of June 25, did you not?"

"Yes, we came up and saw one group of about twelve being overrun as they tried to make the creek. And we saw a number of the men as they finally reached the top of the bluffs."

"How would you describe Major Reno's retreat—in a word?"

"I would call it a rout."

"Yes, of course, and, Captain, when you joined Reno on the bluff, you in fact assumed command, did you not?"

"Of course not, he was senior——"

"You conferred, but *you* made the decisions. It was to you the young officers looked."

"I suppose so. . . ."

"Of course, because Major Reno was drunk and incapable——"

"I object." Gardiner is on his feet, slamming the table with his fist. "A conclusion no one has arrived at but defense counsel."

"Sustained," Schofield snaps. "But, Major, you have no need to be vehement, your remarks will be heard if made calmly."

"All right, Captain Benteen, why *did* you assume command—or at least the appearance of it?"

"I suppose . . . because Major Reno is a rather weak leader. Some-one needed to be direct and strong on the hill."

Jacobson paces back to the far side of the room. He scratches his chin, smiling as he turns to look at Benteen. "Captain Benteen, could Reno have continued his charge on the village or did this weakness prevent it? Did he have to stop in those trees and then retreat to the bluffs?"

"Once he had stopped he had to retreat, but as to his stopping in the first place——"

Gardiner stands, almost resigned at this point but trying to salvage what he can. "Mr. President, I object and move the answer be stricken from the record."

"Mr. President," Jacobson says, equally calmly. "We have heard one opinion after another admitted for prosecution because a witness is a soldier of much experience. You reminded me, General Scho-field, that the members of this court are capable of placing such expert opinion in proper perspective, that you are each capable of determining competence. That is all I ask here."

Schofield frowns, fingering his muttonchops, rolling the ball ever so slightly under his palm. "I am going to overrule your objection, Major. I will allow it." He has asked no opinion from other mem-bers, but they raise no objection.

"Thank you, Mr. President." Jacobson smiles. "But we need not embarrass trial judge advocate further. Captain Benteen, let us turn now to another subject." As he speaks he opens a large pocketknife and cuts a chew from a plug which has been lying among his docu-ments. "You have a reputation for intolerance, don't you?"

Benteen's face darkens and his teeth show as they clamp loudly against the pipe stem.

"After the Washita, did you not write for public print an article critical of General Custer's conduct there?"

"I did," Benteen blurts. "At the Washita he was——"

"When the regiment was a part of the Yellowstone expedition under Colonel David Stanley, did you not verbally abuse General Custer before another group of officers, claiming he had falsely accused you of grumbling constantly?"

"I gave him every opportunity to defend his honor."

"None of the histrionics, Captain, just yes or no."

"Yes," Benteen snarls.

Jacobson has stopped before Custer, who sits as though ready to spring from his chair. Jacobson points at Custer. "Captain, tell us, please, have you not often voiced in public your opinion of this man, your superior officer, haven't you often said what you thought of him, how little you respected him?"

Benteen and Custer stare at one another for an instant. Benteen's jaw tightens and he slowly takes the pipe from his mouth.

"Yes. I am proud to count myself foremost among the many who despise him."

There is a murmur in the courtroom and Schofield raps for order. It is Jacobson's turn again to allow a point slowly to sink in, and he does so, glancing with a smile at the press gallery and nodding slightly. He slips the cud into his cheek, the jackknife still open in his hand. As he resumes he points it like a bayonet at the witness.

"Is that why you failed to go to his aid when you rode up to Weir Point and saw the dust on the far slope?"

"Absolutely not," Benteen snorts, his face livid.

"Isn't it true that you did not *want* to go to Custer's aid? Because you so despised him, and your so-called superior officer on the scene despised him too—and was addled besides with either whiskey or shock? Isn't it true, Captain, that at Weir Point you *convinced* yourself that there was no way to aid General Custer and you turned your back and left him to be slaughtered?"

Jacobson's voice rises as he speaks, then drops on the last phrase almost to a sob.

"General Schofield, for heaven's sake," Gardiner says. His own voice rises too. "For heaven's *sake!*"

"I will answer that, allow me to answer that," Benteen yells from the stand. "I would never desert a comrade on the field, no matter who he might be. . . . The fight on Custer Hill had to be ended by the time we saw it. . . . We could not even recognize it as a fight."

"All right, Captain Benteen!" Schofield shouts as well, to be heard. "Let the court make a decision on the objection of trial judge advocate. I think the objection is well taken. But I feel, too, that your own witness has led himself into this area. I am going to let him answer for the record—well, he already has. Let it stand."

"I can't believe . . ." Gardiner stops. He sits down and slumps in his chair.

"Thank you, General Schofield," Jacobson says. He is stirred by the direction the answers have taken—or the direction his own thinking has taken him. He stares at Benteen a long time, then shakes his head and returns to his seat. "I am finished with him."

Gardiner is up at once. "Captain Benteen, did you think at the time you rode to Weir Point there had been a fight on Custer Hill?"

"Somewhere along the line a skirmish or a brush with them, but no real fight. I couldn't bring myself to believe a serious fight had been made yet. I thought ours was the big fight. I was sure Custer had ridden to General Terry."

"It was only later that you realized there had been a fight?"

"Yes. When we arrived at Weir Point, Custer had passed that way at least two hours before. From there his ride to Custer Hill could hardly have taken over an hour. Once on Custer Hill, his fight there could not have lasted over thirty minutes. That means that at a minimum, when we arrived at Weir Point, Custer's fight had been over for a half hour. And we certainly saw nothing that looked like a fight from the point."

Gardiner is back at his table, glancing through notes made during the cross-examination. When he turns he points his pencil much as Jacobson had pointed his knife.

"There have been comments here on your relationships with the accused, but no attempt has been made to determine the basis of that relationship. Can you tell us why you feel as you do about Custer?"

"When the regiment was on campaign, Custer had a great deal of latitude as to where he could hold the unit to be ready for whatever service might be directed next. For obvious reasons, usually he would position the regiment near a military post."

"Captain Benteen, please state those reasons."

"Why, to be near the communications offered by a post and its hospital, blacksmith shops—this kind of thing. Now on these posts there were sutlers—civilian traders who made their living selling commodities to the soldiers. Extra socks, tobacco, spirits, candy. Custer would demand special privileges from these sutlers, else he would threaten to place their establishment off limits and march the regiment to some other post when he paid the troops. This blackmail——"

"I object, I object to that, it has no bearing on this case." Jacobson is waving the still-open knife.

"No, Mr. Jacobson," Schofield says. "Now it is the turn of the defense. It was you who opened this line and we took it on the record. So we are going to take this. And please close that knife before you slice off somebody's ear."

The remark brings a burst of laughter. The sound startles Schofield, who looks around and blinks owlishly—then smiles himself and blushes. But Jacobson is not smiling, nor is Gardiner as he moves to the stand and continues.

"Can you tell us more exactly——"

Benteen breaks in, not waiting for the question to be finished. "At Camp Supply in Indian Territory, in 1869, the paymaster joined the regiment, but we immediately marched elsewhere to pay the men because the sutler at Camp Supply had refused to cooperate with the Custer gang, . . . and they didn't want him to benefit——"

"I object most strongly, Mr. President."

"Captain Benteen, these are serious accusations. What is the basis for such statements?"

"General Schofield, it was a matter of common knowledge among the troops. They had a saying. 'I hope we can find a post soon where the trader has paid off Custer or we'll wander about on the empty Plains forever, our pockets stuffed with money.'"

"Mr. President——" Jacobson starts, but Schofield waves him to silence.

"Captain Benteen, you are treading on dangerous ground here."

"There were a number of officers who openly admitted procuring favors for the regiment through this practice. Often we got supplies the government couldn't issue. We even got ammunition on some occasions for practice. But usually it was hunting ammunition for Custer and his friends. His brother Tom and Cooke and Smith and Calhoun——"

"All dead on the Little Bighorn," Jacobson shouts. "All dead and unable to defend themselves from these slanders."

Benteen's face turns a deeper red and he shouts back. "I will give you a name of one not dead, by God. He was a lieutenant of Custer's right after the regiment was first formed. It was his duty to ride into the posts and make a deal with the sutler or post trader. Provide this commodity or that, or when the paymaster arrives we'll ride off. We would never pay near that post again. The man bragged about it. His name was Lieutenant George Wallingford. And I'll spell that for you——"

"And where might he be found?" Jacobson sputters, angry as he has been at no other time.

"In the Kansas State Penitentiary. Sent there for horse stealing."

"All right, this has gone far enough," Schofield says sharply. "Captain Benteen, I hope you are aware——"

"I am, General. And I will make the charge openly at some later time when I am not under privilege of my oath and after it will not affect the deliberations of this court. I will make the charges and if they are lies, then let Custer bring suit for slander or libel," Benteen says, glaring directly at Schofield, completely unawed by his rank.

"I must admire his gall," Jacobson mutters as he moves into his chair.

"Have you any more for this witness, Major?" Gardiner shakes his head. "Very well, I excuse you, Captain Benteen."

Pausing a moment, Schofield glances around the courtroom, then leans back and pockets his cue ball. "Gentlemen," he says, "I feel we may need at this time more than the usual respite. There are aspects of this trial that become almost unbearable at times. There being no objection, I am going to recess until Monday morning. I have been informed that there is to be a polo game at Fort

Hamilton tomorrow afternoon. It is late in the season, but a number of officers in New York for this uh—uh—hearing have requested that the Fort Hamilton riders give a game. At any rate, I announce it to you in the hopes that it might be restful."

As the spectators file out, talking softly, Gardiner sits slumped, rubbing his eyes. Sommers and Beakin move up and settle down beside him.

"Mighty good so far, boss," Sommers says, but when Gardiner does not respond he adds, "sir."

Gardiner laughs. He shakes his head. "He is tearing me to bits," he says. "The old bastard is a fine lawyer. God, he's got everyone in the room nodding and smiling like a bunch of . . . well, that's the way it's played."

"I thought we were doing pretty well," Sommers says.

"No matter," Beakin says, grinning. "What we all need now is some of Ned Stokes's Bavarian beer." They all nod and with mention of the name, Gardiner pulls a fistful of cigars from his pocket and hands one to each.

Sommers whistles as he sees the band. "Our lady of the saloon painting. My wife would never believe it."

"You gentlemen go on tonight," Gardiner says, striking a heavy sulfur match and lighting up. "I'm going home. Just a few buckets of cool beer and a plate of corned beef. I feel tight as a screw."

Gardiner takes his time pulling his material together and getting it into his briefcase. He considers stopping at the Fort Columbus officers' mess for a brandy, but decides against it. He has seen enough Army blue for the day.

There is still a streak of orange light in the western sky, a solid band along the horizon which fades upward into pale blue, purple, and then black, arching into the vault of the sky and sprinkled there with stars. The land beneath is black too. Now and then, standing up from it, a man is silhouetted for an instant before he drops once more into the darkness.

The wounded horses have all been killed, but some of the men mutter for water, and now and then one cries out loudly, heard over the whole position. There is everywhere the smell of old blood and horse sweat, mingled from time to time, now that the wind is dying, with the faint aroma of sage. The breeze is sporadic, blowing in from the Bighorns, cool and fresh after the hot sun of afternoon, coming with the sharp hint of the snow still lying in the high, sheltered valleys. Grit is so thick on everything that a finger groping in the dark can feel the trace of a furrow marked on a carbine stock, a saddlebag, a cheek bone.

Now and then, still, a single shot snaps out. One strains to see a muzzle flash and waits for it in the night, but it never comes. There is only the flat, hollow cough of a shot, then without echo it is gone.

They are breaking out the bacon and eating it in the dark—raw. It is rancid, the taste pure salt. Chewing coffee beans with it kills the taste but makes the thirst afterwards even worse.

Lying flat on top of the bluffs, one cannot see the floor of the valley at the base of the sharp slope. But when the south breeze dies, the sounds come up. The drumming, low and insistent, like the hum of an insect caught in mesh, the chanting voices quavering. It goes on and on until it becomes something other than sound. It becomes a part of the night. A part of the past. A part of the centuries. It grows louder, then fades, and then is back, stronger than ever, thrilling out of the bristling darkness.

Now and then, too, along the stream at the foot of the bluffs is the call of a whippoorwill, like a caress against the back of the neck that makes the hair stand up, because everyone knows it is not a whippoorwill.

Gunmetal grows cold under the hands, the fingers numbing as they grip too long, too hard. From far up along the divide a coyote begins to yammer, and soon there are more of them. Some may be wolves as well.

There is a sudden swift scurrying, so close the flesh crawls. It stops, then begins again, right at the muzzle of the carbine. Then even closer, creeping over the hard-baked ground under stiff prairie grasses—coming for the smell of bacon. They are furry plains mice, large-eyed and large-eared, silver gray and bringing the surface of the hill alive with their tiny rushing feet.

Then the bugle starts. It is only a short distance down the ridge. The sound is clear and carries well over the rolling swell of ground.

A brass bugle. Bought in some Indian trader's store or given as a present to a naked, paint-daubed Plainsman. There is no recognized call, only notes blown at random. It comes closer, then stops abruptly. Sleep begins to creep in, forcing heavy eyelids down. The bugle blasts again, so close the air can be heard rushing through the tubing. It creates fear. Fear of the darkness and what it hides. Again the bugle and someone screams aloud. . . .

Gardiner is sitting bolt upright in his bed, drenched with sweat. Below, on 33rd Street, a taxi horn is being squeezed again and again until someone shouts from one of the buildings. Gardiner sits a moment, eyes still gummed with sleep, struggling to recognize the shape of his window and the light on his ceiling reflected from the gas jets in the street. He is shivering. He tosses off the covers and stumbles to the window, looking out toward the river. He begins finally to reassure himself that the noise from the saloon is not Sioux chanting and that the Hudson is not the Little Bighorn. Still shivering, he turns back to his bed and crawls between the sheets once more, finding a dry spot. As he closes his eyes he tries not to see that bleak Montana field, not to smell the rotting blood or taste the uncooked bacon—tries not to hear men beg for water in the night— beg quietly, for fear some terrible destruction may find them in the darkness.

13

Fort Hamilton is a quiet post, set among the huge elms at the tip of Brooklyn, its streets and walkways overhung with branches bare now in November. Many of the fallen leaves, sheltered in brown windrows beneath the squat cedar shrubs, elude the lines of soldiers who parade each morning "policing." The cobblestones seem to shine here, unlike those of the city outside the gates, where the un-attended passage of many horses makes for a constant hazard to polished boots and buttoned shoes. Here the common horse drop-ping reaches its loftiest purpose, being swept up carefully and trans-ported to the rose bushes around the sturdy red brick houses along officers' row. In anticipation of the coming frost, the roses are wrapped now in burlap—but they are fed each day, just the same.

The sun is bright. Warm as it can only be in New York on a late fall afternoon, Gardiner thinks. He had come in the forenoon from Manhattan, lunched in the officers' mess, going unnoticed as he ate his calf's liver and onions. Then to the polo field, best in the country. The crowd is large and has settled itself around the field on small folding campstools or blankets spread on the ground. Tubs of cold fried chicken and potato salad have been located at various places around the field, and to one side, discreetly hidden behind a canvas wall, the beer kegs. Carriages have been drawn up close behind the crowd, and in many of them the ladies remain with their escorts to watch the play from upholstered seats. Parasols make colorful pastel blooms along each side mark. Some of the officers are in blues and brass, but most wear their walking costumes—jodphur boots, striped pants, thigh-length fawn coats, and top hat or derby.

Gardiner has looked through the crowd, seeing a number of members of the court—in fact, Colonel MacKenzie was preparing to ride in the game. He has avoided them all. He strolls now toward the seawall, his light topcoat flapping against the dark plaid trousers that match his soft Scotch cap. Between his clenched teeth he holds an unlighted cigar. The streets are wide and stretch away like lacy tunnels, canopied with the delicate branches of the elms. In some of the yards he passes children playing on swings or on brightly colored wooden tricycles.

Near the seawall the salt air strikes his face, a cold, refreshing jolt. He moves across the last street that surrounds the built-up area of the fort, out from beneath the trees, and into the bare sunlight of the stone and cement parapets. He walks casually, noting the heavy structure of the revetments, the casements, the gun ports, and the deep, circular, rifle pits, where heavy naval guns crouch like monstrous black beetles under tied-down canvas. At the seawall he stops and looks across the Narrows, trying a number of times unsuccessfully to light his cigar in the wind.

The water is choppy, the crests of the waves reproducing the sun's blinding brilliance like a hundred million tiny windowpanes. The sky is clear except for a low bank of gray-white clouds far down on the horizon behind Staten Island. There are a number of large vessels moving into the harbor or setting out to sea. Some are old square-riggers, sails white against the dim background of the far shore. But most are steamers, looking somehow clumsy and out of place on the water, their tall stacks boiling out a thick, greasy smoke.

Gardiner turns and walks back along the gun positions, pauses a second time to light his stogie, fails, and tosses it away. It is then that he sees a man standing some distance off, watching him. He is a tall, rangy man wearing a long coat and a hat of broad brim, much like some that Gardiner has seen during his Dakota trips, worn by men who work in the hot sun and rain. Even at this distance

Gardiner can see the man wears a black patch over his left eye. He has the feeling he has seen the man somewhere before.

He continues his stroll but the man comes on quickly, and Gardiner stops and faces him as he walks up. His face is weathered. He has bony cheeks and nose, is clean-shaven, and the one eye which stares at Gardiner is a yellowish gray.

"Major Gardiner, sir, beggin' your pardon," he says, touching his hat in a military salute. "I saw you walkin' here."

Gardiner waits but the man says nothing more. "Well, sir, you know me but I don't think I know you," Gardiner says.

"Jefferson Quinton, sir, at your service. An old soldier. I was with the 3rd Arkansas in the war."

"A Rebel regiment, I seem to recall," Gardiner says.

"That's it, sir."

"Then you might be interested to know," Gardiner says, sweeping his hand to indicate the parapets, "these emplacements were designed by Robert E. Lee."

"You don't say! I never knew that. I guess he was a Yankee before the war and I got to be one after. I was recruited at Fort Lincoln in '75, you see. Served with the 7th Cavalry, I did."

Gardiner's interest now becomes apparent and he studies the man from head to foot. The hands are bony and hard-used, yet are now well manicured. The clothes fit as though tailored, the boots show a high polish, and the coat is silk-lined. Only the hat appears to have been long in service.

"I lost this at Little Bighorn," Quinton says, and he lifts the patch hiding his left eye. The empty socket is an ugly, swollen wound, inflamed and moist. Gardiner quickly turns his face away.

"A Sioux bullet, almost spent. Very painful at the time, and you know, sir, sometimes when I close my good eye, I can still see out of the one that ain't there." Quinton laughs harshly.

"There are ways you might have it mended that might be an improvement. . . ."

The man laughs again, positioning the patch over the socket. "Oh blazes, sir, I could see no better from one of them little colored marbles they make out of glass. Now, a milk-eye agate would be nice."

"You appear to be doing well, Mr. Quinton."

"Oh, yes, sir, a body can always find means." When Quinton smiles his wide mouth pulls back tautly over teeth the size, color, and texture of pin oak acorns.

"How can I serve you?" Gardiner says.

"Well, sir, I know you are the officer trying General Custer," Quinton says. "I may well have some information—some items—that might be useful to one making a case against him."

For a long moment Gardiner looks at the man, but the single yellow eye looks back, unblinking.

"You said you served in the 7th," Gardiner says. "In what unit?"

"Company B, sir."

Gardiner frowns, thinking before he answers. "That was the company guarding the pack train. . . ."

"Yes, sir, that it was. Captain McDougall, Thomas McDougall, a fine man. He was killed, you know, same place I was hit on the bluffs after we joined up with Reno and Benteen."

"Yes, I recall his name on the casualty list."

"A fine gentleman, sir, although I had little time to serve him. At Fort Lincoln I was posted to the Custers. That's how I come by this information I have."

"Posted to the Custers? What does that mean?"

"I was their quarters orderly. I was surprised they let me join my company when the regiment moved out to the Yellowstone. You see, right after my enlistment, I got into the spirit of things one night and into an awful row with some of the boys—we re-fit the Battle of Sharpsburg, where the old 3rd Arkansas whaled hell out of a passel of Yankees, no disrespect, sir—but I was outnumbered again, so they not only battered me around good, they court-martialed me for bein' drunk. Which was true. General Custer, he took me on parole to stoke the fires in his house. I just stayed on there because I work good and General Custer, he liked teasing me about being a whipped Rebel carrying coal now for the U.S. Cavalry. Miz Libby, she was always nice to me, and sometimes she'd scold the general like she was his mama."

Gardiner is uneasy at being forced to a curtain which has been drawn aside to reveal intimacies he is not sure he is prepared to witness. But his interest is intense, and there is no question of breaking off the conversation. Besides, he thinks, this man has said he may have something valuable for me.

"No disrespect to General Custer, he was a brave one all right. But they'd play these parlor games. Just the two of 'em, rompin' and tearin' around like two kids, breakin' up furniture. I swear I never saw two grown people act like that."

Gardiner turns and walks along the revetments. Quinton follows, gesturing with both hands, laughing from time to time, his acorn teeth showing as he speaks. Gardiner is listening closely, but he finds it difficult to look at the man.

"Custer had this racetrack built at Fort Lincoln. Him and his friends—not all the officers were invited—his brother and his brother-in-law. You know Lieutenant Calhoun married General Custer's sister?"

"Yes. Yes, I knew that."

"He was killed——"

"Yes, I know that, too," Gardiner cuts in impatiently, ashamed that this gossip fascinates him.

"They would have horse races. And picnics. Or go shoot on the range. General Custer always had these big wolfhounds around. They'd ask people out from Bismarck. Important people. Mr. Lounsberry, who owns the *Bismarck Tribune*, he was always there. And lots of ladies. The postmistress in Bismarck, now there was a looker. Mrs. Slaughter her name was. The ladies all liked the general. They had a birthday party once, and after they'd cut the cake, and General Custer opened presents, why then he said he had a present for all the ladies. So he cut off a lock of his hair for each one of them."

Gardiner stops and stares at Quinton and the tall man grins.

"It's true. They did some strange things, some mighty queer things. They'd have parties and do charades. Or sometimes they'd have a party and the general wouldn't even come out—stay in his room, he would, and now and then Miz Libby would go in there, then she'd come back and nobody would see him all evenin'. They'd dance in there, all by theirselves."

"Mr. Quinton . . ." Gardiner begins. The man nods and reaches inside his coat and produces a packet of papers tied with twine. Gardiner sees they are letters.

Quinton hands them to Gardiner. As he does so, he continues to talk. "General Custer sure liked to tease. He teased his brother Tom all the time about them two Medals of Honor he got in the war. Tom always wore 'em, too, like for spite. The general may have been a mite jealous, don't you think, Major?"

"I'm sure I don't know."

There are about two dozen letters. More than half are in the hand Gardiner immediately recognizes as Custer's. The others show a delicate script and he knows they are Elizabeth's. He hears Quinton saying that in all the stacks and stacks of letters they have written one another, saving each one, they could hardly miss these few. A hard knot begins to grow in the pit of Gardiner's stomach. It would be dishonorable, he thinks, an invasion of privacy to look at the letters. And yet . . . it is a duty, a duty to do what must be done and if there is evidence here, then I should . . . he slips the string off the packet.

They come from their envelopes stubbornly, as though resisting this invasion. Gardiner reads quickly. Quinton still talks, but Gardiner no longer hears him.

"My Darling Standby: I arrived in New York last night at seven. A good-looking lady boarded the train at Syracuse, occupied the seat next to mine. . . ."

Again in another: "A friend has taken a box at the Academy of Music and invited me to take the seat whenever I choose. Miss Gertrude Kellog, the beautiful actress, always expects me behind the scenes later. . . ."

And: "The old Irish servant who takes care of my rooms looks at me with suspicion when I return home each morning, my bed not having been touched. I think she believes I do not spend my nights in the most reputable manner and circumstances are against me."

He stares out across the water for a moment, drawing his breath deeply. Can this really be true? He studies the penmanship once more. There appears to be no doubt. It is Custer's. Incomprehensible, he thinks. The self-adulation, the women. Is it a test of faith and trust or something else?

"Dearest Standby: There is a beautiful girl, eighteen or nineteen, who has walked past the hotel several times trying to attract my attention. Twice, for sport, I followed her. . . ."

The women who adore him are always beautiful. The men who admire him are always famous. Generals, publishers, bankers, actors. Each of these letters was written when he was in some city—usually New York—and Libby back at some dismal post. His eyes scan one of her letters.

". . . the only active thing at this post is a pig that from time to time wanders across the parade. . . . "

Old Standby indeed! What a ghastly name for her. I have heard men call their wives Pumpkin and Pigeon and Cutie and Kitty Cat. But Standby? It is more like the name for a locomotive. Or at best a cavalry horse.

"Precious Standby: Last evening Mr. Osborn took your boy to Wallack's theater, where he had a box, and we met three ladies. . . . One of the young women has apparently taken a strong fancy to Your Bo!"

And she calls him Autie. As Gardiner's fingers clutch her letters, they seem to have a sudden warmth. But he can endure only a few words—enough to see her love for Custer and her devotion to him and what she perceives as his greatness. Even in the strong sea breeze there is a faint perfume about the letters, not of cinnamon, but sweet and cloying. He lifts them to his nose.

Quinton is grinning. "She is a fine lady," he says. "Very refined. But she dyes her hair, you know. She's only thirty-five, but she dyes it, yes, sir."

"Keep still," Gardiner says. He strides along the parapet away from the tall man, who follows, but slowly. Another of Custer's letters is open in his hand.

"Dear Little Standby: I was at a dinner party, one I can never forget for the talented and distinguished men there. It was for representatives of the press. Your Boy was the only outsider. On the right of the presiding officer sat Mr. Horace Greeley and Your Bo next to him. On my right, Mr. Bayard Taylor, and next to him, Whitelaw Reid. Opposite, Mr. Charles Dana of the *Sun*, and the poet Stedman next to him. Mr. Stedman said he had sought an introduction to me. He said that during the war and since, I have been to him and to most people their *Beau Ideal*, knight without stain and above reproach, unrivaled as the young American hero. Had I not had some experience at such things, I would have been overwhelmed . . ."

Gardiner stares at it a long time, noting the date. He re-reads the lines about the young American hero. Quinton is beside him once more.

"The general had card games. Oh, he was a gambler. He knew cards, too. Every lieutenant in his regiment owed him money."

Gardiner laughs. The young American hero. Quinton stands beside him, staring at him. Gardiner replaces the letters in their envelopes, wrinkling them, tearing a few. They are worthless to me, he thinks, they have nothing to do with the trial. . . . Well, perhaps ambition does shine through them, but how could I introduce them without showing the court what an unhealthy curiosity took hold of me. Like a thief breaking the lock of some private locker and peeking in, with heart pounding and palms damp. He turns on Quinton so quickly that the man backs away a step, his hand going quickly under his coat. The bastard is armed, Gardiner thinks.

"Take them," he says, thrusting the packet toward Quinton. "I must tell you, Mr. Quinton, I think you are a common thief and a blackmailer. If you come to me again in any capacity I will have you arrested."

It affects Quinton not at all. He slowly grins, taking the letters and slipping them into a pocket inside his coat.

"Oh now, Major, sir, a body has to do with the opportunities that present theirselves. We all of us steal a little along the line somewhere—or maybe covet a wee mite here and there, huh, Major?"

Quinton's smile grows broader.

"But now, Major. Blackmail! That's a hard word. And you must recall, sir, that I asked nothing for these"—he touches his breast—"but I was only tryin' to see justice done."

Gardiner turns and walks away, back toward the tree-lined streets of the post and the security of the solid brick buildings. This time Quinton does not follow. Looking back once, Gardiner sees him standing on the revetment above the water, watching as Gardiner walks away. His coat whips about his legs. His face under the broad-brimmed hat is pale, the black patch clearly visible, like the empty eye socket in a bleached skull.

Luckily for his purpose, the custodian of the *Tribune* morgue is still in his dingy basement office when Gardiner gets there, having hired a two-man rowboat to ferry him across the East River from Brooklyn. The *Tribune* morgue is a collection of clips and notes, facts and figures, secreted in tall file cabinets, available to the newspaper writer who comes down from the upper floors of the building by a narrow, ill-lit staircase. But at the rear of the large room are shelves of old newspapers, musty, dirty, rat-gnawed, stacked according to date of issue and available at half-price—one penny—to anyone willing to look for the one he wants.

After almost an hour, Gardiner comes away with issues for the first ten days of December 1871. On the cross-town trolley he resists the urge to start through them. He hurries the last block to his flat, then bounds up the stairs three at a time, fumbling impatiently with his keys.

He is standing before his library table, his coat still on, when he finds the headline. "*Mr. Greeley Excellence Awards.*" Gardiner yanks off his coat and drags up a chair. He reads rapidly, then goes over the article again more slowly. The occasion was an annual dinner that Horace Greeley had initiated before the war to honor New York journalists who he felt deserved recognition. The guests are named and Gardiner carefully reads down the list, his finger guiding his eye. There is Reid, Dana, Stedman, Greeley himself—all those Custer had mentioned in his letter plus many more. There is no representative from the *Herald*. Gardiner suspects, too, that these men are all Republicans. He reads the names again and cannot find a single recognizable Democrat.

The award that year went to a man Gardiner has never heard of —for developing a Sunday newspaper. The account is thorough, listing the menu, the wines, and what a number of dignitaries wore. The affair had been held in the Green Briar Tavern just off Union Square.

"Mr. Greeley, who was candidate for President on the Republican ticket in the election of 1868, made the principal address, praising the work of many others not honored by formal award, and telling all present that the New York press leads the world in honesty, initiative, and enterprise."

Gardiner sits for a long time, looking at the faded copy, the room growing dark around him. Strange, how one could be removed in time and place. . . . On the night he said those words, Greeley had less than a year to live.

Bending close to the page, Gardiner reads it once more. There can be no mistake. In the long, detailed account—in the endless list of the famous, infamous, and unknown—the name of George Armstrong Custer does not appear.

14

Monday morning. And Gardiner is still disturbed over the letters. He is more convinced than ever that the Army must somehow rid itself of George Custer, but it is distressing to him that someone is willing to use such things as the letters to help the process along. Over a long, cold Sunday he has stayed in his room, reading, lashing himself from time to time for not having taken the letters so he could burn them.

Now, as Elizabeth Custer re-enters the courtroom for the first time since Weir's death, he looks at her closely. Her hair is waved back over each ear, a neat bun at the back, over which perches a dainty fur-trimmed hat. Does she really dye it?

His eyes linger too long on the Custers—they now march down the aisle together, George no longer making the dramatic, solitary entrance of the first day. Standby and Autie!

"Well, Major," Schofield says loudly.

Gardiner wheels around. "Sir, all parties to the trial present when the court was recessed are now present."

"Carry on, please."

"I call Colonel John Gibbon."

Gibbon is a handsome man, his face is angular with hair swept back across a high brow, clear, well-set eyes, and a generally pleasant expression to his lips, visible between moustache and chin whiskers which, unlike the hair on his head, have begun to turn white. His cheeks are clean-shaven. He wears the uniform of colonel, although during the war he had attained the rank of brigadier general and had won renown as commander of the Iron Brigade. He identifies himself as commander now of the 7th Infantry Regiment, stationed at Fort Shaw, Montana Territory. The members of the court attend his words carefully, for he is a highly respected officer throughout the Army.

"On June 25 my column and General Terry's arrived at the mouth of the Little Bighorn and started our march south. On the 27th we came into the broad valley where the fight had occurred, although we didn't know it at the time." Gibbon sits comfortably, his hands laced across his flat belly. His testimony is unhurried and he gazes about the room confidently. "Our scouts told us there was a large encampment ahead. In a broad, open valley. Before we could arrive there, our scouts brought in some Crows who had been with Custer. We thought they had been sent by General Custer to communicate with us, but we soon found that not to be the case. They told a horrible story—wild in the extreme, it seemed to us—that General Custer and his entire regiment had been butchered by Sioux and Cheyenne. General Terry and I asked them many questions. We could hardly believe such a tale. But there was great apprehension. We had seen clouds of smoke up ahead and our Indians were acting scary. Finally, as we marched into the valley, we could see evidence of a large village. But all the Sioux had fled."

Gibbon pauses, brushing down the ends of his moustache with his fingertips. Custer sits with a fur-lined cape pulled up around his shoulders. He appears to be suffering from lack of sleep. As he blinks, with the fur about his face, eyes bright and feverish, he reminds Gardiner of a fox peering cautiously from its burrow. The suntan has begun to wane and his nose continues to peel dead skin. He looks sickly, and his limp as he walked into the courtroom had been most pronounced.

"Colonel Gibbon, when Custer's scouts came to you with this story of massacre, did they indicate the size of the hostile force?"

"They claimed it was huge—too large for us to believe. But they certainly were afraid. They wouldn't ride with my leading elements. In fact, they infected my own scouts with fear. I sent them to the rear. We moved on into the valley—to the area where the great village had stood. I assumed that the hostiles, in trying to elude my column, had fired the prairie. It was still smoldering. The entire area except along the creek bank, where grass was too green to burn, lay barren and blackened. We found the circular marks on the ground where the tepees had stood. We saw a number of dead Indians—gunshot wounds, all of them. Apparently lying in state. We assumed the survivors had run off in a hurry because they generally do not leave their dead to be mutilated by their enemies. There was scattered about all the gear found in an Indian village— a few of the tepees were intact. These usually had dead inside. Lodge poles, bits of clothing, pots, a few items of Plains Indian households, scrapers, awls, other bone tools, a dead horse here and there.

"Then some of our men found two items of great significance. A buckskin shirt with a clean bullet hole in it. We identified it as the one worn by Lieutenant Porter when the 7th marched up the Rosebud. Lieutenant James Porter, I believe, of Company I."

Gibbon pauses a moment at the recollection and Gardiner urges him on.

"And the other item?"

"Yes. A pair of underdrawers, soaked with blood. They had a laundry stencil on them—'Sturgis, 7th Cavalry.' That would be Colonel Sturgis's son."

"Yes, sir, it would," Gardiner said, "Lieutenant James Sturgis, he was serving in Company E. The body of neither was ever found— or at least never identified. Please continue, sir."

"With these finds, we began to have some foreboding and dread. We had seen riders on the high bluffs to the south. Only a few. We could not identify them. We supposed them to be hostiles. They came closer, but very cautiously. About this same time, too, we saw something else that troubled us. Strange objects—foreign objects— on the hill directly across the river from where we were inspecting the village site—well, actually, it was back to the north slightly. The crest was almost two miles away. Some said these objects were dead horses, perhaps Indian ponies slaughtered to prevent our catching them. There were light-colored objects as well. It disturbed me that a number of buzzards and crows were in that area. A huge flock—or whatever you call a group of crows—a rook? Well, at any rate, we looked with glasses and couldn't tell. It looked like dressed-out buffalo carcasses, but General Terry and I both found it strange that, even fleeing, the Sioux would have left behind something as valuable."

"Could you show on the map where this high ground was?"

"Yes, there, on the high ground to the extreme north of your chart—the one you have marked Custer Hill."

"And you were directly west of that—or perhaps a little south of west." Gardiner points with a yardstick Sommers has provided. "In the center of the village site."

"That is an adequate approximation," Gibbon says. "We sent a scout of mounted infantry across the river to investigate, under the command of Lieutenant J. H. Bradley. Then, as we waited for his report, we moved on south down the valley. Before we left the village site we began to discover white bodies. Badly mutilated— heads smashed in, arms and feet severed, the private parts . . . slashed. One of these we identified as Lieutenant McIntosh. The rest were unidentifiable."

"How near the village were these bodies, sir?"

"Some actually in the village. I suspect they had been dragged there. Others were in a copse of trees south of the village but very near it. While we were investigating these remains, the horse-men we had seen on the bluffs drew nearer and someone shouted that they were white men. The boys let off a cheer and the riders came in to us. They were 7th Cavalry—Lieutenants Godfrey and Wallace, I recall, and some men. They said Reno and Benteen were forted-up in the bluffs—that they had had a bad scrap on the 25th and a siege since then on the bluffs."

"What did they say about Custer?"

"They asked if he was with General Terry and me."

"Did they intimate Custer had been in a fight?"

"No, they did not. They appeared confused, they said they had no hint of where General Custer might be. But it was soon re-solved—a courier from Lieutenant Bradley arrived with the worst possible news. He said the Bradley scout had gone to the high ground east of the river and had counted over 195 bodies there. I asked if they were white men, and the courier replied in the affirmative. He was crying and was visibly shaken."

There is a long pause in the testimony, but everyone seems willing to wait. Gardiner stands quietly beside his table, arms folded. Jacobson, chewing slowly, sits slouched at his place, doodling with a pencil on a yellow legal tablet.

Custer suddenly rises, glaring about the room. He tugs his cape tight about his shoulders. His eyes fix first on one, then another of the uniformed officers in the room. When he speaks, his voice is high-pitched and harsh. "Get Keogh up here!"

Elizabeth is partly out of her seat, a hand reaching toward Custer as he seems to shudder. He looks around, his face reddening, then he sits down. Schofield stares incredulously. Jacobson moves quickly from his place and bends over his client. The room is absolutely still. Gardiner waits, watching as Elizabeth and Jacobson whisper for a moment.

"Mr. Jacobson," Schofield says, "is there some reason for this interruption?"

The defense attorney faces the court. He smiles and bows. "No, Mr. President, please excuse us. I think now we are ready to continue."

Schofield appears uncertain as he looks from Custer to the civilian attorney. Elizabeth has settled back in her seat once more and smiles at Schofield. The president of the court looks inquiringly at Gardiner, who lifts his shoulders slightly.

"Very well, then. Colonel Gibbon, you may continue."

"General Terry and I conferred and agreed that we should first go to the bluffs where there were men still alive. The dreadful business of identifying the men on the hill farther north should be done by officers and men of the 7th Cavalry, anyway. I left instructions with my men to encamp near that woods and to drag off the dead horses and bury the men who had fallen there—it was becoming unpleasant. Then General Terry and I, with a few couriers, rode to find Reno, guided by the detachment that had found us. Lieutenants Wallace and Godfrey seemed shocked beyond words at what we all knew now for almost a certainty—that Custer and his battalion had been destroyed."

"Colonel, on the size of the village. How many lodges would you estimate there were?"

"I had them counted—we may have missed some—but we counted 2,143 of those circular patterns on the ground."

Gardiner pauses long enough to be sure the press people have the number in their notes. "As a campaigner of extensive experience, would you have sent three companies against such a village— or against any village before you determined its size and whether or not the hostiles were going to stand or flee?"

"I object," Jacobson says quietly. "Speculative opinion, and I suspect irrelevant."

"I suspect it is none of that," Gardiner says. "But I will withdraw the question." Let the court ponder the answer they all know Gibbon would have given, he thinks.

"Colonel, other than the very size of the village, were you surprised that Custer had made a fight?"

"Yes, I was. General Terry had been specific in his orders. No one expected Custer to engage until the 26th."

Jacobson takes the witness carefully, standing and bowing with great respect from behind his table. He remains there as he speaks. "Colonel Gibbon, sir. I would ask only one question, I think, simply to make clear in my own mind . . ."

Here it comes, thinks Gardiner.

"Very well, sir," Gibbon says.

"You say, sir, that General Custer—let me see now, I want to get this straight—I believe you indicated General Custer attacked one day early, is that true?"

"Yes, it is."

"He should have attacked on the 26th? Not a day early?"

"Yes, sir."

"But, sir . . . isn't it true . . . that *you* arrived one day *late?*"

Gibbon's face reddens. "I was ordered to the mouth of the Little Bighorn, and from there I was supposed to march south and I did."

"Yes, sir, but you did not arrive at the battlefield until the 27th— a day *after* you say there was supposed to be a coordinated effort. Thank you, Colonel Gibbon, thank you so much."

Well, let it go, Gardiner thinks, making no redirect. If the court thinks he was in supporting distance on the 26th—anyway, perhaps they will remember the mutilations. That seemed to wake McDowell, at any rate.

Lieutenant James Bradley, 7th Infantry, takes the stand and relates that he had a mounted infantry patrol on scouting detail on June 27 and had generally operated east of the Little Bighorn until the command had entered the wide valley. He had then crossed to the west bank, but was dispatched back to the east side again to investigate the objects spotted there on the high ground. A short distance from the stream he discovered a group of dead horses.

"Cavalry or Indian horses?" Gardiner asks.

"They were stripped of all gear, but they were heavy, grain-fed, and branded. They also wore steel shoes. They were cavalry mounts."

Bradley is young, unlike many lieutenants of the post–Civil War era who are much too old for their grade. Unfortunately for the many, the higher grades are filled with former generals and colonels from the war, and junior officers find themselves serving as lieutenants for fifteen years or more before promotion. There is no mark of financial pinch on Bradley, whose uniform is new and neatly brushed.

"We began to see dead bodies almost a mile from the top of the hill. There was a long hog-back running up toward the knoll. We followed that to the top, counting bodies. They were scattered generally, but in a long line. We saw four or five horses dead in a bunch, no men around them. Then a little farther along, the same number of dead soldiers. We assumed they had been going for the high ground and had had their horses shot from under them, then as they went on afoot were caught and killed too. We saw this a number of times. Toward the top of the hill the bodies were much closer together. Finally on the knoll were about forty dead troopers and officers. We found Custer there."

Everyone in the court leans forward except Custer, who still sits slumped in his chair. He seems to smile now, but Gardiner cannot be sure because Custer's mouth is hidden in the fur collar of his cape.

"You recognized him at once?"

"Yes, sir. He was sitting there against a dead horse as composed as could be. I could see he was alive. He was unconscious, but he did not have that fishy white color of the dead and we could see he was not bloated and . . . starting to decompose as the others were."

There is a low muttering in the room and Schofield raps for silence.

"He had not been scalped. He seemed peaceful. There was a group of men around him, in the form of a crescent—about twice as long as that table." He points toward the bench. "The dead horse was in the center and General Custer was leaning against it. As though someone had carefully undressed him after the fight and placed him there against the horse."

"How do you explain that, Lieutenant?"

"Sir, I can't. Some of the newspapers printed stories that an Indian recognized General Custer—or maybe a woman did after the fight when they came out to pick over the battlefield. I don't believe that. There weren't that many of them knew General Custer. He was wearing buckskin like all his officers, no rank insignia. He'd even had his hair cut for the campaign. I don't believe it was intentional. It was just strange."

"You saw his wounds, then?"

"Yes, a bad swelling in the thigh. Just a small, ragged puncture, but debris had been blown into his leg. Then a very nasty head wound. A bullet had creased his skull. The slug hadn't entered his head. I washed his wounds and got some water down him. Beside him I found a canteen—about three-quarters empty. He was rather cold. He showed no signs of life. He was badly sunburned. We wrapped him in saddle blankets and started making a horse litter. While we were working a company of the 7th Cavalry rode up with Captain Benteen. They had been sent by General Terry to identify their dead and bury them. They helped with the litter. Benteen dispatched an officer—I don't know who he was—and a group of men to carry General Custer back to the mouth of the Little Bighorn where the steamboat was waiting. General Terry was evacuating Major Reno's wounded there too. I sent two of my men as guides on our back-trail to the boat."

"Lieutenant Bradley, let's talk about the battle position. Can you describe it?"

"Yes, sir, I can," Bradley says, looking at the large map.

LT. JAMES BRADLEY

"If you would, please, just indicate to us on the chart what you found."

Bradley moves from the witness chair to the map and stares intently at it for a moment. He places a finger on the place marked Custer Hill, turns toward the court, and continues. "It wasn't much of a battle position. The only stand had been made at the knoll, around General Custer. That was the northernmost point of the fight. From there the position of the bodies formed an inverted 'V,' the knoll being the apex. The eastern portion was a long ridge running almost due south. There we found Company I and Captain Myles Keogh. That company might have been in a battle line—but there were no horse holders to the rear. On south along the ridge we found Lieutenant Calhoun, almost alone. Then south of him, his company, badly scattered and obviously hit from all sides when they were in column."

Gardiner interrupts Bradley to ask him if he will mark on the map the position of each company as Bradley's men found it. Bradley agrees, accepts the pencil Gardiner offers him, and continues his description.

"Along the western leg of the 'V' we found Companies F, C, and E—in that order from the knoll; they were in column, too, apparently running for the top. It was bad ground, and where we found the bodies was lower than surrounding ridges mostly. The officers who commanded these companies were not with their units. We found them around Custer at the top. Tom Custer was there—near the general. I recognized him at once, too, although his face had been badly smashed. They had stripped him, too, and disemboweled him—and his genitals had been severed. . . ."

From the corner of his eye, Gardiner catches a sudden movement at the front of the rows of spectators and turns in time to see Elizabeth Custer sliding slowly from her chair to the floor. A woman shrieks and a number of men in the room swear. Jacobson and Major Winthrop are there at once, and although he starts in that direction, Gardiner stops. Custer hears the gentle thump behind him and turns. He throws off his cape and moves back to kneel beside his wife. They lift her shoulders and her eyes flutter open, vacantly. The spectators and press gang gawk, standing for the most part, whispering loudly.

"What is the trouble, what happened here?" Schofield demands. He is standing, as are all the members of the court, watching with concern. Colonel MacKenzie comes around the bench and goes to the group kneeling on the floor. After a moment he turns to Schofield.

"General, I would suggest a short recess. Mrs. Custer seems to have fainted."

Schofield recesses the court. He instructs the provost guard to prepare a place for her in the guard room and to summon a post surgeon. It soon appears to be unnecessary. Custer has found smelling salts in his wife's purse and she is now on her feet. They help her down the aisle toward the anteroom. Schofield calls to the provost sergeant to send for hot tea. Bradley watches it all from the witness stand.

As he passes back to the bench, MacKenzie pauses and looks at Gardiner, who still stands leaning against his table. "You should caution your witnesses to be careful of such testimony," he says in a rasping voice. His eyes are pale blue, his nose long and sharp. As he stands there, Gardiner knows MacKenzie is probably the best cavalry commander in the Army. What he does not know is that within a few years MacKenzie will be medically retired from the Army, hopelessly insane.

"Sir, I had no idea he was going to mention Tom Custer," Gardiner says.

Bradley has resumed his place in the witness chair, embarrassed that his testimony has created such a commotion in the courtroom. Gardiner tries to reassure him with a look and a nod.

Custer returns without Libby. He walks with his head back, his ringlets flowing. In his chair, he slumps once more into his great cape. Schofield has the proceedings quickly underway.

"Almost all the men had been scalped," Bradley says. "But not too many had been mutilated further. We supposed that was because this was farther from the village than the fight in the valley, and the old women and dogs had less chance at the bodies before the village moved. The buzzards were not as bad as one might imagine, but the crows were thick. We found Mr. Mark Kellogg, the newspaper correspondent, some distance off the hill. He was among the dozen or so we found who had not been undressed completely. He must have been hit early and must have fallen into the brush—the Sioux never came back for him. His notebook was there and pencils were scattered over the ground where he lay. The battlefield was littered with dead horses. But we saw only two Indian ponies among them. There was the usual trash. Clothing too bloody even for the scavengers. There were no weapons or ammunition, of course, but a great many brass cartridges around Keogh and the Custer group. A strange thing—blowing about the battlefield were a great many greenbacks—money. The place was all aflutter with the stuff. Of course the Sioux know the uses of money, but they missed a great deal of it. I learned later that the regiment had been given three months' pay after they marched out of Fort Lincoln."

"Why would Custer pay his men after they left Lincoln?"

"Because if they'd had their pay at Fort Lincoln, some would have jumped the fence. So he waited until he was two days out . . . into country where a man would be a mite nervous over leaving the regiment."

"Such a fine regiment as Custer's? Would there be a desertion problem there?"

Bradley laughs. He glances over at Custer. "The 7th Cavalry is one of the worst outfits in the Army for desertions. In 1867 they had more desertions than any other regiment. And it's never gotten much better."

"I object. What has this to do with the charges in hearing?" Jacobson says heatedly. "I move that answer be stricken from the record."

"Overruled, but trial judge advocate will pursue it no further," Schofield says.

"Thank you, Mr. President," Gardiner says. "With the court's permission, I would like to introduce this document."

He takes a paper from the table, Schofield glances at it, hands it to the reporter.

"Prosecution exhibit F, marked for identification," the reporter says. Gardiner hands it to Jacobson and as the defense counsel reads it, he says to the witness, "You mentioned finding a Mr. Kellogg on the battlefield?"

"Yes, sir, he was a reporter from Bismarck. The *Bismarck Tribune*, I think the paper is called."

"Thank you, Lieutenant Bradley," Gardiner says, taking the document from Jacobson. "I would like to read this, with the permission of the court."

"Do so, Major," Schofield says.

"It is a wire addressed to General Terry from General Sherman. The purpose of this wire is to restore Custer to command of the 7th Cavalry for the expedition against the Sioux and Cheyenne. And I call your attention to the last sentence. General Sherman wrote, 'Advise Custer to be prudent, not to take along any newspaper men, who always make mischief.'"

Gardiner glances toward Jacobson, but the defense counsel is writing on his yellow pad and makes no move to object.

"I am finished with this witness, sir."

"The witness is excused."

MacKenzie breaks in. "General, may I have a question?"

"Of course."

"Just a moment." Jacobson is on his feet. "Meaning no disrespect, Colonel, but what kind of procedure is this, when anybody who wants to may ask questions?"

"It is a procedure well established in military courts," Schofield says. "Members of a court may question witnesses at any time to clarify or, in fact, to introduce new evidence."

Jacobson is obviously grumbling as he takes his seat. He shakes his head as MacKenzie begins.

"Lieutenant, was there any system of defense—any organized defense on Custer Hill?"

"I should think not, sir. It looked like a panic. Men dying right with the horses in most places, because there had been no time to organize the holders or the ground—only at the knoll was there anything like a stand."

"Examining the terrain, could you tell whether the battalion was moving toward the village or away from it?"

"Away from it, sir."

"From tracks and other evidence, could you tell whether the battalion had ever threatened the village?"

"Not really, sir, but I think——"

"I object now most emphatically, Mr. President," Jacobson says. "Is this an expert witness who comes with these kinds of opinions?"

"The objection is sustained." Schofield looks at MacKenzie.

"That's all I have," MacKenzie says.

It is time for the mid-morning recess, and Gardiner sends Sommers for their next witness, who has been waiting in the quarters of the commanding officer of Fort Columbus.

Brigadier General Alfred Terry was once the gamecock of Union generals. Dressed always as though on parade, his neatly clipped beard has become frayed and his middle has begun to press visibly against his belt. He is short, ramrod straight, and when he comes into the courtroom, each member of the court, including Schofield, nods and smiles a silent greeting. Terry identifies himself as Commanding General, Department of Dakota, and immediate superior to Custer on the Montana expedition.

"General Terry, we will not detain you here with any detailed account of the campaign. That is not necessary," Gardiner says. "But there are a few particulars only you can provide."

"I will be happy to do so."

"Good, sir. Now in order that there be no misrepresentation, who charged Custer and how did it come about?"

"I charged him. After the campaign, both General Sheridan and General Sherman agreed he should be charged. As his commander, it was my duty to bring charges. I did so."

Gardiner shows Terry the document he has just introduced.

"Do you recognize this, sir?"

"I do. It was the last instruction I received from General Sherman concerning Colonel Custer. It restored Colonel Custer to the command of his regiment."

"Was Custer aware of this dispatch?"

"He was. I showed it to him."

"Then he knew of the Commanding General's instructions not to take newspaper correspondents with him?"

"He did."

"Who dispatched Mr. Kellogg, a correspondent from the *Bismarck Tribune*, with Custer's column?"

"Nobody did. Mr. Kellogg was with my headquarters as per arrangement of long standing. He simply marched out with Custer and I was not aware of it until some time after the regiment had departed."

"Thank you, General Terry. Now, would you explain to the court your general plan for the campaign and how it was eventually carried out."

"I was concerned with the Indians' escaping into the mountains. I planned to place a strong force on either side of them. Expecting to find them in the Little Bighorn valley, I planned to have Gibbon move on their northern flank. Custer on the southern. Faced with troops on either side, I hoped with a minimum of fighting to get them back to their reservations." Terry speaks in short, clipped sentences with traces of a New England accent. He sounds like a court clerk reading back testimony—in fact, he once had been a court clerk.

"How did your plan develop, General Terry?"

"It could have worked well. However, Colonel Custer did not follow instructions. He attacked a day early. This failed to allow for any coordination and cooperation with the other column."

"General Terry, I refer you to what we have marked here as prosecution exhibit A." Gardiner takes a copy of the document from his table and hands it to Terry.

"Yes. It is the written order Captain Smith drafted for me aboard the *Far West*."

"Is it not discretionary, General?"

"In tactics only. In grand design, no. Until he was in contact, Colonel Custer was to have followed orders. Otherwise the plan must fail. Once engaged, the local commander has the initiative. Until then, he must obey."

"Then you do not believe he was engaged on June 24, when he turned west at once when the Indian trail did?"

"Of course he was not engaged. His instructions clearly indicated he was to push farther up the Rosebud before turning west."

"Then you feel he disobeyed orders?"

"Nothing has happened to make me change my mind since I signed the charge sheets. The spirit of the order was disobeyed. I believe the letter of the order was disobeyed as well." Although his tones are sharp and his words short, Terry's warmth is felt as he speaks. He looks frequently at Custer with something like compassion. Despite his apparent composure, he appears deeply disturbed at the part he is playing.

"I thank you, General Terry," Gardiner says, not unaware of Terry's feelings.

Jacobson comes across the room, gliding, his customary cud of tobacco missing. He smiles graciously at Terry.

"It is indeed an honor, General Terry, to meet you after having admired your work for your country throughout the recent war and beyond," he says. Terry nods, watching Jacobson closely.

"General, just a few questions, please. No more than trial judge advocate do I wish to detain you. I believe you have stated that there was some concern with the hostiles' escaping?"

"Yes, sir. If they broke into the rough country the job of getting them back onto the reservations would be much harder."

"That was, I understand, a universal fear among military men, was it not, including General Sheridan?"

"I would say so."

"Then if General Custer thought he was discovered and the Indians were running, he should have tried to stop them, isn't that true, General?" Jacobson still smiles, standing in the center of the bull ring, leaning forward slightly at the waist.

"But they would not have discovered him had he not turned west too soon," Terry says.

"Please, General, this is conjecture, isn't it? Think a moment. You are in the field. There to catch the hostiles before they escape.

Now, they are running. Someone must stop them. Don't you agree?"

Terry looks directly into Jacobson's eyes. "But they were not running."

"*Ahhh!*" Jacobson shouts, pointing one finger straight up. "They were *not running*. But how was General Custer to *know* that? You, General Terry, and everyone else, for *weeks* had been harping, yes *harping* on the Indians' running. *Harping* on the necessity for not allowing them to escape, isn't that true?"

Terry stares at the defense lawyer.

"Come, come, General, I have telegrams and letters to prove it. You can save us so much time...."

"Yes, it was true."

Jacsobson wheels and starts for his table, grinning at Gardiner as he goes. He inspects some of his notes, his back to the court. When he turns, he is no longer smiling. "General Terry, you wrote two reports of this action within a short period, isn't that true?"

"It is."

THE HON. ALLAN JACOBSON

"The first was in no way critical of General Custer."

"I wrote such a report."

"But the second, introduced here as prosecution exhibit B, written only a few days later, *was* critical of General Custer's conduct in the campaign and in fact was the first hint from any source of any such criticism. Is that correct?"

"I wrote a second report critical of him, yes."

"Why did you write two reports, one uncritical, one critical?"

"My first message to General Sheridan was delayed. A fact I was

unaware of at the time. My second report was confidential. It was longer, written on reflection. It reached the East before the first one did. It was made public. I had no intention of ever making it public."

"You mean, General, that you had an officer who had done these bad things, yet you intended to hide it from everyone except certain officers in the Army?"

"I hadn't really . . . it had not been my intention to hide it. But at that time I had not determined that charges should be made."

"Isn't it true, General Terry, that you made the second report— the critical one—after you had had time to realize that someone had to be made to appear at fault, else *you* would be blamed?"

BRIG. GEN. ALFRED TERRY

"I object to any such accusation against this officer," Gardiner says. Schofield is obviously upset, yet he takes a long time to make his ruling.

"Mr. Jacobson, General Terry is not on trial here."

Jacobson throws his hands up and turns to his seat, speaking loudly enough for all to hear. "Well, maybe he should be!"

Gardiner is already on his feet, in front of the witness stand.

"General Terry, sir, did Custer disobey your order when he followed immediately the Indian trail as it turned west from the Rosebud?"

"Yes!"

"Now once he had disobeyed that order—perhaps you can assist us here, General—once he had moved west and thought he was discovered, why did he enter that valley without trying to determine what it was he was facing, and perhaps more important—if he thought he was discovered, why did he not slam into that valley with his forces intact, for if discovered his chance of surprise was gone—so why did he, thinking the Indians had already seen him, split his regiment into four widely divergent forces?"

Terry looks at Custer and slowly shakes his head. "If my life depended on it, Major Gardiner, I could not explain it."

"Thank you, General, I have no further questions."

"I have one," Jacobson says. He remains seated. "General Terry, can anyone say what decisions a commander should have made on a field of combat, unless he was on that field himself?"

"I cannot say. I truly cannot say whether that is true or not."

As Terry is excused and salutes the president of the court, Schofield says to him, "Thank you, Alfred, for doing what I know you feel a distasteful duty."

"You're most welcome, John," General Terry murmurs, and then retires up the aisle.

"You needn't put any of that in the record, Lieutenant," Schofield says to the reporter. Gardiner glances at Custer. The Golden Cavalier is slumped in his cape, eyes hooded as though almost asleep.

15

"Yes, I have known Colonel Custer and served with him at various times and places since the war." The witness is Colonel William Ludlow, Corps of Engineers, presently attached to Terry's Dakota Department with headquarters in St. Paul. "What happened in Montana was not a great surprise to me. Those of us serving near but outside the 7th Cavalry were well aware of the split in sentiment among the officers of that outfit. One group was strongly attached to their leader. The other was not what you would call friendly toward him."

"Now, Colonel," Gardiner says, "tell us of your experience with the accused which made the disaster at the Little Bighorn unsurprising to you."

"Yes, yes of course," Ludlow says. "I was at Fort Leavenworth in 1867 when General Hancock went into the Plains with an expedition to calm the Cheyenne. At one point he ordered the 7th —Custer commanding—away from the main body, after some marauders of some sort. Colonel Custer rode away and stayed away for almost two months. Partly due to Custer's belligerence, what had been a relatively peaceful area turned into a major theater of war. It was a disastrous war for the United States—nothing like the Little Bighorn, of course. There was a grand total of 11 Indians killed. During the same period, 147 whites were killed, another

426 were carried off for ransom of various sorts, and very nearly 1,000 head of stock were stolen. Then, when Colonel David Stanley led an expedition into the Yellowstone country—let me see, that was in '74, I think—Custer moved away from him as well, operating independently."

"Colonel Ludlow, were you associated in any way with the Little Bighorn campaign?"

"Yes, I was in General Terry's headquarters while the expedition was being formed, but I did not accompany it. Colonel Custer had originally been scheduled to command that expedition. However, due to instructions from Washington, he had been taken from that post and General Terry himself was going to take it. Custer arrived in St. Paul, asking General Terry to intercede with the President in his behalf, so that he might at least go on the expedition as commander of his regiment. General Terry did so, through General Sheridan, of course, who sent the message through General Sherman, who . . ."

There are giggles in the courtroom and Schofield is annoyed, rapping with his ball.

". . . and the reply to that message was not long in coming. Colonel Custer had made an impassioned plea. He had tears in his eyes. And apparently General Terry was persuasive as well. Permission was given and Custer was naturally elated about it."

"How did Custer indicate his elation to you?"

"I saw him later in the day—he was preparing to leave for Fort Lincoln—and he said to me that his first purpose would be to swing clear of Terry just as he had of Stanley on the Yellowstone. He said he had done it with Stanley and he would be able to do it with Terry, too. He was overjoyed, laughing—slapping my back."

"What does that mean, to swing clear?"

"Why, to ride free of the main body and operate independently."

"Mr. President," Jacobson says. "I have been listening to all of this with great amusement. This is hearsay and not admissible."

Schofield turns to Gardiner. "Major Gardiner. I am sure you are as aware as anyone in this room about the rule of hearsay—the evidence you have just introduced is admissible only to show that such a thing was said, not as proof that such a course of action was taken."

"Yes, General, but it may be admissible to indicate intent, I feel sure, especially when it shows a pattern of behavior," Gardiner says. "I would point out that Custer's actions in Kansas in 1867 and on the Yellowstone with Stanley are not matters of hearsay. Nor is the fact that he boasted of it and claimed he would repeat that performance."

Schofield frowns, his fingers nervously caressing the cue ball. He glances to either side but neither McDowell nor Pope seems inclined to help.

"I will let it stand, but the court in its deliberations will have to take great care in considering it."

"Of course, Mr. President, I would expect that, and thank you."

Jacobson heaves an explosive sigh and sits down.

"Sir, were you associated with Custer at any other time?"

"Yes, 1874, on the Black Hills expedition. There had been rumors of gold in the Black Hills and after a sudden spate of newspaper stories about it had appeared, white men were going in there and some were getting killed. The territory had been ceded to the Sioux by the Laramie Treaty of—well, some years before, I can't recall the date."

"It doesn't matter, Colonel Ludlow. What was the purpose of the 1874 expedition?"

"The 7th Cavalry was sent in there to—well, the public explanation was that we were exploring a military road from northwest Nebraska into the Powder River basin. Actually, we were a show of force to quiet the Sioux. But we also were looking for gold—to see if, indeed, there was any."

"Was there, Colonel?"

"There was evidence of gold, but most of it was hard to get out. It would take a great investment in machinery and so on. A prospector with a pan and a jackass could hardly expect to get rich. However, we had two newspaper people with us. And Colonel Custer wrote a long report about gold being in the grass under the horses' hooves, and he showed it to the newspaper people before he forwarded it."

"Was it published?"

"Of course. I recall a Chicago headline that day. 'A Belt of Gold Thirty Miles Wide.'"

"Were the reports that came from that expedition exaggerated?"

"Very much so."

As he strides around his table, Gardiner says loudly enough for the court to hear, "Such an irony. Custer involved in starting the war that would destroy his own regiment."

"I object to these summations," Jacobson says, glowering at the trial judge advocate.

"You know as well as I," Gardiner shouts, wheeling and pointing toward Custer, "that the Black Hills gold rush was the very basis of this war, a war in which we are still involved at great public expense."

"All right, gentlemen, all right," Schofield says, and for some reason he is amused at the two men standing, glaring at one another from across the room. "Major Gardiner, the witness?"

"I am finished with him," Gardiner snaps. "Sir."

Once again, MacKenzie wants a question. "Sir, did you actually see this report of gold that Colonel Custer gave the press?"

"I did. I was near Colonel Custer throughout much of this period. I hunted with him. One occasion I will never forget. We had sighted this great elk and Custer was about to fire when there was a shot from a nearby wood and the animal dropped dead. Two of Custer's soldiers rode out from the woods, laughing and gesturing, completely unaware of our presence. Colonel Custer was furious. He drew his rifle to his shoulder and fired a shot over the soldiers' heads. They dove from their horses and lay on the ground and he fired over them again."

"I object, this is absolutely absurd," Jacobson shouts, running out into the bull ring, waving his arms. Schofield is infected with his own laughter and has to struggle to control himself as he taps the bench with the cue ball.

"Yes, sustained," he chokes. "That will be all, Colonel Ludlow."

"I thought it was a fine story!" MacKenzie grins.

Schofield finally regains control of himself. "Major Gardiner, it's getting on in the day. How much longer are you going to take with your case?"

"Sir, I have one more witness." Actually, he has seven. But if my points haven't been made, he thinks, they never will be. Now for

Custer's ambition. Damn! Why did Billy Dunn put that charge in, anyway?

The last prosecution witness causes a stir among the newspaper correspondents. He is R. L. Meeker, *New York Herald* correspondent renowned in journalism circles as one of James Gordon Bennett's best hatchet men and a leading character in the recent *Herald* campaign against the Grant administration. He is a rather small man with a great handlebar moustache and fluffy sideburns beneath a bald pate. He wears a suit too light for the season with a red rose in the lapel. He has gold caps on his front teeth, which he shows in a constant smile. He started his newspaper career as a typesetter, and it appears that since that time he has never bothered to clean the printer's ink from beneath his fingernails.

Meeker explains that by the mid-seventies, the *Herald* had become involved in a new kind of journalism—crusading. Chief among their targets were the Grant administration and the corruption of government officials during that period. Not only was young Bennett a Democrat, he was violently opposed to a third term for the aging soldier in the White House—and there had been talk of such a thing among Republicans.

"Mr. Bennett and General Custer got on well together. On one occasion that General Custer was in New York, he suggested to Mr. Bennett that an exposé be made of corruption in handling post and Indian traderships on the frontier. He offered to assist. In fact, he offered to lead such an investigation."

"Why would a man like Mr. Bennett entertain such an idea? That an Army officer help him in a crusade?"

"General Custer had frequently written for the paper. He wrote a great many things, of course. Published in various places. Mr. Bennett said to me that we should take advantage of the general's fame in order to . . . well, to attain our ends."

"And did you use his fame?"

"Not at first. His part was secret. But later we would bring him out into view. Mr. Bennett told me that General Custer had aspired to high office for a long time, and it was common gossip at the *Herald* that he was our Boy Candidate—old Mr. Bennett had given him the name Boy General during the war."

"We are not here for gossip," Jacobson says loudly. He is still fuming over the last witness.

"I will sustain what I assume is an objection," Schofield says.

"Very well, Mr. Meeker, did this investigation take place?"

"Yes, it did. General Custer was indeed the principal in it. I was able to move about the area of Fort Lincoln as a trader. There were only two other people who knew my purpose or who I was. They were Emmit Lounsberry, editor of the *Bismarck Tribune*, and Mrs. Linda Slaughter, postmistress at Bismarck. We would all meet at General Custer's quarters and plan the people I should see and the places I should go. In order to keep my identity secret, we didn't use the telegraph in Bismarck to file stories. General Custer allowed me to use the Army's telegraph system to Chicago."

"You were using the Army's facilities to get your stories to the *Herald?*"

"Yes, sir. I have no idea how much Mr. Bennett paid General Custer——"

"Just a minute." Jacobson is on his feet, furious. "I will not have these guesswork accusations made against my client. Here we have a self-admitted sneak, and he is accusing a brave soldier of——"

"All right, Mr. Jacobson." Schofield raps him down. "Major Gardiner?"

Gardiner produces a slip of paper which he hands to General Schofield. "If it please the court, I would introduce this document."

Schofield reads, glances at Custer, and has the paper marked prosecution exhibit G.

"Mr. President," Jacobson protests, "this document has no bearing whatsoever on the case in hearing."

"The court will determine that, Mr. Jacobson."

"This is a request of a certain Robert Seip, a banker of Bismarck, Dakota Territory, to cash a check. It reads as follows: 'Friday, October 8, 1875. Mr. Seip, can you let me have the money on the enclosed draft from Mr. James Gordon Bennett? If so, please return by bearer, and oblige. G. A. Custer.' This is a copy of the original certified by Mr. Irwin B. Linton of the War Department. Mr. Meeker, are you familiar with such transactions?"

The witness looks at the paper and smiles broadly.

"Oh, yes, in fact I recall this one. Mr. Bennett, to protect my identity, always sent my pay through General Custer. On this date General Custer cashed the draft and gave me one hundred dollars."

"Did you see the draft?"

"Yes, but not the amount. General Custer handed me a hundred dollars and said, 'This is your share.' I assumed by that he had a share as well."

"Major Gardiner," Schofield says, "where is this leading? I can see little direct connection between this and any of the charges."

"I am finished with it, sir." Gardiner places the paper on his table and continues. "Mr. Meeker, what exactly were you looking for in your investigation?"

"Traders who had bought their licenses. Or those who issued only part of the supplies to the Indians and then sold the rest."

"What does that mean, bought their licenses?" Gardiner asks.

"Well, say there is a post tradership available. A post tradership can mean a great deal of money, selling goods to troops or Indians. So along comes a man willing to pay for the appointment. He gives the politician a bribe. The politician exerts influence to have this man appointed post trader at some fort. Sometimes, there have even been agreements that a trader would share his profits with the politician responsible for getting him the appointment."

"Did you find such things actually existed?"

"We found a good deal of smoke but not much fire." Meeker laughs. The courtroom remains silent. "Nobody was ever convicted in a court of law with evidence we found."

"But you wrote the stories making the accusations?"

"Yes. We filed a total of eight stories. I wrote six of them and Custer wrote two."

"Primarily as a result of these stories, you were called before the Clymer Congressional Committee, were you not? The committee looking into impeachment of various officials?"

"Yes, General Custer and I were called. We rode east on the same train together. It was all out in the open then, and General Custer got on the stand and accused Orvil Grant—that was General Grant's brother——"

"General Grant who was then President."

"Yes, and he also accused Secretary of War Belknap of all sorts of wrongdoing."

"And this was all printed in the *Herald*, with Custer's name prominently displayed."

"Of course. Mr. Bennett was delighted to have one of our best-known soldiers speaking against the President. He was not so happy about the nature of General Custer's testimony."

"But why not?"

"It was all hearsay. The committee was disappointed, too. I had warned Mr. Bennett it would be that way, but I don't think he believed me."

"How could Custer do that, knowing he was making accusations against what amounted to his superiors—and all nothing but hearsay?"

"General Custer seemed to ignore all that. Mr. Bennett said he would. Mr. Bennett said General Custer would do almost anything just to keep his name in the newspapers."

"I object. It is pure opinion, and secondhand at that," Jacobson says.

"Sustained."

"Mr. Meeker, have you ever heard Custer speak of his political ambitions?"

"Yes, often he has spoken about public officials and how they must bend to public opinion and how he is suited to that, having spent much of his life dealing with superiors who have no mind of their own and who——"

"Mr. President," Jacobson shouts, banging his table with a clenched fist. "I protest most vigorously."

"Mr. President, what a man says about his political ambitions is more than hearsay. It is a statement of intent. When a man stands for election, he does so by stating that fact—that he is running. I submit such a statement is admissible as an indication of intent."

"That may be, Major Gardiner, but I heard no statement of the accused to that effect in the last testimony of the witness."

"May I rephrase?"

"I think you must do so, and even then I may sustain Mr. Jacobson's objection."

Gardiner turns to Meeker and bends close to him. "Mr. Meeker, did Custer ever confide in you?"

"Yes, many times. We spoke of politics often. He asked me if it was not true that the *Herald* would support him against a Republican in 1876. I had to hedge my answer because I knew Mr. Bennett had little interest in supporting Custer for the presidency, because he had told me once that we had had all the soldiers in the White House we could possibly afford."

"How did Custer take that?"

"I can be very diplomatic. I told him how brave and good he was. And of course, he is a brave man. But a great liar——"

"That is bald, bloody perjury, sir," Jacobson rages, on his feet, his arms waving again.

MRS. CUSTER

"Very well, Mr. Jacobson," Schofield warns. "Major?"

"Allow me to continue, Mr. President, and I will show the comment is not perjury," Gardiner says. Schofield nods and the TJA turns back to Meeker. "Explain to the court your statement that Custer is a liar."

"During the Clymer Committee testimony, he said that former Secretary of War Belknap visited his post once, but that he and his officers snubbed the Secretary because of his corruption. In actual fact, as everyone in Bismarck knows, Custer met the Secretary, escorted him about the post, entertained him in his quarters." Meeker looks at Elizabeth Custer, who has resumed her seat and she is staring back coldly. "Mrs. Custer showed him about the place and served tea and cakes."

Gardiner takes a thick folder from Sommers and holds it up. "If defense insists, I have here the transcript of the Clymer hearings, I have depositions of persons who were in the Custer home at the time former Secretary Belknap was entertained there, I have——"

"All right, very well," Jacobson says, and sits down suddenly. "It isn't important anyway."

"Did you see Custer after the Clymer hearings?"

"Yes, sir, he had been relieved of his command. There was a story in the *World*—the rumor was all over town that Custer had written it—to the effect that General Grant had relieved Custer of his command because of his testimony. Nobody really knew who wrote the story, not even the people at the *World*. They got it in the mail from Washington. Anyway, a few days later General Custer came through New York on his way back west. He had not been reinstated but he told me he would get himself back into that expedition one way or another. He told me he had to establish his good name. He said he had to prove to the country he was still second only to Sheridan as a cavalry leader."

As Gardiner releases the witness, Jacobson waits a long time at his table, working his new cud and scribbling on his yellow pad. Finally he rises and comes across the bull ring, his foot dragging loudly on the boards.

"Sir, you have said the *Herald* wanted to use General Custer's name in order to attract attention to its crusade, isn't that right?"

"Well, I'm not sure I used those exact words, but that seems a fair statement of Mr. Bennett's intentions."

"Have you heard—and I assume you have, because you have said little here that was not something you *heard*—have you heard that General Custer used the press for his own ambitions?"

"Yes, everyone has heard that."

"But in your own experience—we are not speaking now of what you have *heard* but what you *know*—in your own experience with General Custer and the *Herald*, who was using whom, Mr. Meeker?"

Meeker glances about the room, his smile growing broader to expose more gold than at any time before. "Nobody ever uses a Bennett for long, sir. The *Herald* was using General Custer, of course. The *Herald* was using Custer."

"To attract readers?"

"Well, in this case to impeach government officials."

"But to attract readers as well?"

"Yes, of course, that's what a newspaper is for, to attract readers and make money."

"And is it not true, Mr. Meeker, that the *Herald* is *still* using General Custer to attract readers?"

"I don't know, I've left the *Herald*. . . ."

"I have nothing more for this man," Jacobson says. As he shuffles back across the bull ring, he looks at Gardiner. "Now if you want to introduce that file, go ahead. I doubt it will do you much more good than all the hearsay this witness has been spouting."

Schofield is expecting an objection from Gardiner, but the trial judge advocate is tired and he shows it.

"Sir, the government rests."

PART FOUR

The Press

16

John Schofield is not unaware of how the press of New York functions, nor of its politics. But on this windy morning of Tuesday, November 13, he is puzzled—not to say flabbergasted—at what is in the newspapers.

He frowns as he stands in his flannel underwear before a full-length mirror, shaving his delicate chin with a finely honed German straight razor presented him as a gift by a group of Prussian officers visiting West Point earlier in the year. His orderly sergeant—whom he brought with him from West Point—moves about the large bedroom behind him, laying out the day's uniform on the four-poster bed, which has already been made.

These spacious quarters have been provided by General Hancock. They had in fact been the post commander's quarters before the new ones were built on the east side of the island in 1867. The windows open onto the west sally port, and beyond that is the cold expanse of the harbor, whipped up now by the weather. As he scrapes away carefully beneath his flared muttonchops, he can hear the wind, turned viciously cold overnight, sending bits of icy snow against the windowpanes.

The shave finished, Schofield wipes his face with a dry towel, looking down at the newspapers lying on the dressing table beside his washstand. They are the *Tribune* and the *Herald*, both of which he has delivered each morning by the first ferry from Manhattan. He has the uneasy feeling that were he to lift them to his nose he would find they reeked of battlefield decay. For they have, as always, reported in minute detail the testimony of the court-martial, and on the front pages he can see the description of that scene on the Greasy Grass—the stiff-limbed horses, the naked human bodies, white and bloating in the sun.

I swore I could hear crows at dawn this morning, Schofield thinks. Perhaps they flew over from Brooklyn. There are a great many there, among all those old trees.

He has obtained yet a third newspaper, the *New York Daily News* of the evening before. Established in 1855, the *Daily News* has devoted itself largely to a readership among the new immigrants of the city. Begun in the era of sensationalism, it competed accordingly, but as the other newspapers matured, the *News* continued to concentrate on stories of crime and sex. Even so, Schofield knows the appeal of the *News* reaches far beyond the immigrant ghettos, and its circulation compares favorably with that of the *Tribune* and the *Herald*. On this day, the *News* has surpassed itself.

On the front page, in both outside columns, are stories that provide an intimate and unflattering glimpse into the private lives of George and Elizabeth Custer. On the left is the headline "Custer Picnics on the Prairie—Libby Complains of Dogs in Bed." It is a long account of the home life of the Custers at Fort Lincoln—the outings, the elaborate festivities, the favors shown to certain friends, the hunting parties, the horse racing, the childish pranks. And the wolfhounds sleeping in the couple's bed.

"The following information," the story begins, "comes to the *News* through the hand of a gentleman of unquestioned credibility and is surprising proof that the hard and lonely life on the Plains is often both lively and lacking in hardship if one has enough soldiers handy to do the toting and hauling and cleaning. Most inhabitants of the tenements on the Lower East Side would indeed be happy to change places with such 'Hardy Pioneers'! The gentleman in question graciously allowed an interview, the results of which you may read only in the *News*."

Little of it is damaging, only irritating, except for one item to the effect that Custer appeared at various times during the war wearing a pair of golden spurs which had belonged to Santa Ana and sub-sequently to a cadet at West Point—Custer's roommate. The story claims those same golden spurs continue to grace Custer's boots, and that the true owner, a former Confederate officer, has asked for their return—in vain.

In the opposite column, personal letters from Custer to his wife are printed under the headline "Cavalier in High Society—'Your Boy' Not Lonesome in City."

"Through the good offices of a friend of the *News*, a number of letters have come before us. As a matter of public interest, they are reprinted here, for they were written by G. A. C., now under court-martial charge at the Governor's Island Army station."

When he first read them, Schofield, a man not taken to senti-mental expression or self-aggrandizement, was stunned. But as he studies them, the contents of the letters come to surprise him less. As he rereads some of them, he cannot suppress a low chuckle. That disturbs him. During the past few sessions of the trial he has been finding entirely too much that is funny in a business that is completely serious. At least in his quarters he does not have to struggle to control his laughter.

"Darling Standby: My letters, like immense riches, perhaps are less enjoyed because they leave nothing to be desired."

They are not all so amusing. In one letter Custer writes of a lady who has had an abortion. In another he reports seeing a certain married general—whose name the newspaper leaves blank—going into a fashionable hotel with an attractive young woman not his wife, although he registers as Mr. and Mrs.

The *Herald* and the *Tribune* have reacted violently to the stories in the *News*. Half, Schofield suspects, out of jealousy. Both castigate the *News* in editorials and neither of them has reprinted any of the stories or the letters, which surprises Schofield.

The *Tribune* shrieks that the whole thing is a government ploy to influence the court by publication of near-scurrilous materials which could not possibly be introduced into evidence in the trial. It is clearly the cry of a champion defending a fallen hero, and it has all the hysterical morality that one might expect Greeley himself to telegraph from the grave.

Schofield wonders about the *Tribune's* use of the word *scurrilous*.

The letters are perhaps risqué, but the language is impeccable. It may be, he thinks, that they know more than they are printing. In one of the letters, Custer had written, ". . . I know you enjoy rereading Your Bo's letters, but you must be careful, Standby. Some of the things I write to you when I am carried away with longing are for your eyes alone and could embarrass us among the staid and the wretched, and we are certainly surrounded by these. You should burn such letters much as I know how you hate to. . . ."

To Schofield, the *Herald's* accusation is more serious. Bennett's editors see a Republican conspiracy to destroy the man who had courage enough to speak out against the corruption of the Grant administration, with sinister overtones that Grant's old military cronies are involved as well, regardless of party, and that the former President is in Europe in order to be away when the "crime against Custer" is committed.

But what disturbs Schofield most is the last paragraph of the *Herald's* front-page story: "Who would have access to such material? Who would profit by its publication? Unimpeachable evidence points to the fact that Major Asa B. Gardiner, the trial judge advocate—is he prosecutor or persecutor?—had access. And who profits by their publication? The former intimates of a corrupt regime, of course! The real culprit of the battle of Little Bighorn, General Terry, of course! And Major Asa B. Gardiner, of course, who stands to earn a star for his crown by bringing to bay this country's greatest military hero, through shrewd and calculating courtroom maneuvers and now the publication of the Your Boy letters."

Reading it, concerned or not, Schofield cannot keep from smiling. No matter their moralizing, the *Herald* could not resist the temptation to call them the "Your Boy" letters.

I must reserve judgment until I can learn more, Schofield thinks. My position requires it. But I know Cump Sherman, and if he's made up his mind to destroy Custer. . . . Well, the question is whether that young Army lawyer is really involved in something that goes on outside the courtroom. If not, fine. We can try this case the way a case is supposed to be tried, without any involvement of anyone in authority—even Sherman. If Gardiner is shilly-shally . . . we'll have to face that when we come to it. Unfortunately, the *Herald* story may be closer to the truth than we'd like to suppose.

PROVOST GUARD

But if Gardiner isn't involved in something, then I must force this court to consider only what we are presented in evidence and nothing more. I'm not sure McDowell has heard any of it.

He slips into his pants and Sergeant Hill fastens his rear galluses. Red flannel shirt, slip-on pumps, white cardboard collar with black tie, waistcoat with a single row of brass buttons down the front, greatcoat with fur collar, and high shako with plume, red braid, and a large brass eagle on the front. He glances into the mirror one last time and allows just a pinch of the red flannel to show.

The crowd of press people and spectators waiting for the trial to reconvene are trying to take shelter on the warehouse veranda, but the veranda affords limited protection. Schofield is aware of their discomfort as he walks to the back of the court building. Opening the door, the provost sergeant leans forward, Schofield pauses, and they speak together. The Custers are in the guard room. With double sentries at the courtroom doors, perhaps the crowd could be allowed into the anteroom, out of the weather. Schofield agrees.

The usual pot of coffee is steaming on the single stove in the center of the room. Members of the court stand about with heavy white china cups in their hands. They speak softly and nod at Schofield as he glances around the room. He takes the three newspapers from his greatcoat pocket, hangs the coat on one of the clothes trees at the back of the room, and clears his throat. Everyone watches him.

"Gentlemen, I suspect you have read these," he says, holding up the newspapers. "I have some questions concerning the stories. . . . I propose to ask them in closed session. Shall we proceed?"

Gardiner stands before the bench, a newspaper in one hand.

"General, when I read last night's *News* I was greatly distressed they would print such things. This morning I was flabbergasted that the *Herald* would accuse the government of some connivance in the matter."

"We are not concerned with what the newspaper printed, Major Gardiner. We are obliged to ask you certain questions." Schofield leans forward on his elbows, his fingers laced before him. The other members of the court are watching Gardiner intently. From the defense table, Jacobson and Major Winthrop watch as well. Jacobson chews slowly—like a cow, Schofield thinks, waiting for its milking time.

"Would you want me to take the oath, sir?" Gardiner says.

"Not at all. Not at all." Schofield indicates the newspaper open before him on the bench. "The *Herald* indicates that you had access to all these materials printed in the *News*. Is that true?"

Gardiner admits that it is true and tells about the Fort Hamilton meeting with Jefferson Quinton. He is obviously upset, but he speaks clearly and coolly, not hesitating to look members of the court in the eye. It is somewhat reassuring, I suppose, Schofield thinks.

When Gardiner finishes he stands, waiting, and everyone is silent as Schofield rubs his chin, frowning deeply. The room is so quiet they can hear the stoves drawing with gusty coughs and sputters. The sleet rattles against the south windows, blown in across the Narrows.

"Major, why did you allow such a thing to pass without warning the court that someone had such materials? That they were ready to use them against—that they were ready to use them to try to prejudice the case against the accused?"

"But they were irrelevant."

"All the more reason. Had they been relevant, you would have taken them and used them, wouldn't you?"

"I doubt it seriously, sir. The nature of those letters . . ."

"But you determined not to report your encounter with this— what was it, Quinton?"

"I saw no purpose to be served. I had no idea this would happen." He lifts the newspaper. "I wished a thousand times I had taken the stuff and burned it."

"Had you ever seen this man before?"

Gardiner says he has not, insofar as he can recall.

"Was the eye patch a disguise?" General Augur asks. After a week of trial, it is the first comment Schofield can recall his making.

"No, sir, he was missing an eye. He showed me."

"He showed you?" Augur's voice trails off.

"And he is out of the Army only recently?" MacKenzie says.

"Yes, sir. We might locate him. He is a pensioner. But if we did, the Army has no jurisdiction over him now."

"Hell, he hasn't broken any law yet," Jacobson says from his chair.

"He asked for no money, you say," MacKenzie says.

Gardiner shakes his head. "I accused him of being a blackmailer but he laughed at that, and as Mr. Jacobson has said, he did nothing wrong. He offered me the materials."

"Major Gardiner, a more serious question. How would the *Herald* have known you had seen this material?" Schofield asks.

"I haven't the faintest notion, General."

They all sit—except Gardiner—Schofield tapping his pencil, watching the tip bounce on the hard surface of the bench. Finally he looks up at Gardiner, then across to Jacobson. "Mr. Jacobson, how does all of this affect your case?"

"Not at all that I can see," Jacobson says.

"I think I can assure you the court will make decisions based on evidence presented here and not on what appears elsewhere."

"I have no doubt, General. But as Major Gardiner has said, nothing the newspapers have printed bears on the case."

"Very well. Major Gardiner, I must admonish you, please, if any such thing happens again, inform the court immediately. I am still at a loss as to why you did not do so in this instance." Schofield taps the bench with his fingers, thinking carefully about his next words. "I am going to recess the court until tomorrow morning. I must get into Manhattan and obtain whatever other information I can about this business. It is something I think must be done. I must satisfy myself about it. Mr. Jacobson, I am sorry for the inconvenience to your client. But after all, we have been indulgent in not having him under arrest."

"I understand your position, General, and I am sure General Custer will as well."

As the others move from the courtroom, MacKenzie sidles over to Schofield, who is studying the notes he has scribbled.

"General, would you like me to accompany you?"

Schofield gives a small start and stares at MacKenzie a moment before answering. He shakes his head, smiling slightly, and indicates a chair.

"No. This is a touchy situation, Ranald—political overtones. I must admit I am fearful for my own future in the Army, but that's only a part of it. One simply doesn't know what forces are at work."

"Of course, sir."

"We need to be extremely careful. The press will surely—well, part of the press anyway—will find fault with whatever we do here. Put a political connotation on it. We can't let politics get involved in any way."

"Custer has always been very outspoken. How can we help but be accused?"

"Yes, yes, yes." Schofield touches MacKenzie's arm gently. "Of course we will be accused. But the record must stand in history. That's what concerns me. After the politics of today are forgotten. You and I know Custer is not being tried on how he and Elizabeth run a household or correspond with one another. We must constantly remind ourselves of what he *is* being tried for."

"I would be happy to accompany you, General."

"Not at all necessary." Schofield pauses, his brow furrowed. "It is something I must do. I'm not sure if I am supposed to do it. But I know I must. I must see if Gardiner is clear of this thing. If not— well, we may have to call a mistrial, although I've never heard of such a thing in a court-martial. But hoping he is clear, then perhaps we can proceed to a fair verdict that will do us and the Army credit. I have no less feeling of affection for the Army than any man alive—including Cump Sherman, who I suspect would garrote his own mother if it would help the Army. You see, the Army must not suffer from this, no matter what our verdict. And I'm afraid it will if we have a trial judge advocate involved."

"Where will you go, General?"

"The *Herald*, of course. If Gardiner had told us about this when it happened, I don't think I'd have to go anywhere. But he didn't. And that plus the *Herald's knowing* he had, well, at least seen that stuff. I have to be a man of suspicious nature on such a thing. God, if only Sam Grant hadn't flown off the handle and sacked Custer because of that Congressional committee testimony! It threw the whole mess into politics."

"If I'd been General Grant, I would have done the same."

"So would I!" Schofield laughs bitterly. "That's the thing giving all of this the flavor of Greek tragedy. Everyone involved did the wrong things, leading straight to this"—he waves his hands. "And even the Indians lost. After the Little Bighorn, we were bound to go after them hammer and tongs. Congress loosened the purse strings. . . ."

"It's a pity that we couldn't have won that battle, isn't it?"

"I'm not at all sure, Ranald. Perhaps it's all for the best—if we had won, who might be in the White House right now?"

They stare at each other a moment and each knows that the other, because they are sitting in judgment, is trying not to show what he really feels. But MacKenzie cannot control a small shudder. Schofield pats his knee and smiles.

PART FIVE

The Defense

17

Allan Jacobson sits before his hotel window in a heavy dressing gown, gazing out at Fifth Avenue. The street lamps and the trolley car lights make halos of yellow gauze on the windowpane. The effect comes from a thick layer of dust on the glass, and the fact that the windows are dirty bothers Jacobson not at all. He has chosen the Clarendon Hotel because it is the only respectable hostelry in New York where the dining room is served by waitresses rather than the customary tail-coated men, white towels draped on their forearms. To him, the Harvey railroad restaurants in the West, with their white-organdy-pinafored waitresses, are the grandest contribution the frontier has made to nineteenth-century culture.

He muses on the hotels of New York and how one can make a fair estimate of the man by the accommodations he seeks. Custer, of course, had never developed any sensitivity to such things. As a result, it had taken three days of arguing and cajoling to keep him out of the Metropolitan—a Democratic party stronghold. The last thing Jacobson wanted to emphasize was Custer's politics. But in the end it had been Elizabeth, with a few quiet words, who had dissuaded her Autie from doing what he damned well pleased, regardless of what anyone thought.

Her Autie, indeed! Jacobson bends forward and sprays a jet of tobacco juice toward the cuspidor near his feet, striking home with a little over half of it. They had finally gotten the Golden Cavalier to accept lodgings in the Grand Central, primarily because the Wintergarden Theater was in the same building, and Custer could visualize himself consorting with all the actors and actresses. Which, of course, he had done.

I had thought the Brevoort Hotel on Fifth Avenue and 8th Street staid enough not to attract attention. George and Libby would have made such a good impression chatting calmly under the portraits of Queen Victoria and the Prince Consort. But of course, unless he was sitting for a photographer, one could never get Custer to be still, much less look calm. He would dash about, his curls flying, sputtering in his rather rasping voice. Well, the Grand Central is just as well, I suppose. It keeps them well away from me except when absolutely necessary.

There should be some kind of guilt, Jacobson thinks, about this repugnance I have always felt toward the Boy General. My old association with Elizabeth's father . . . her entire family, in fact. But George is the kind of man I actively avoid. It's sometimes a mystery to me why I accepted this case. Except for the challenge it presents. Of course, I've defended many men I did not care for— with whom I would no more associate socially than I would with a rutting hog. One might be tempted to accuse me of hypocrisy. But I've never made any show of affection for him. He is well aware of our relationship. We've made a rather uneasy peace for the time being, and with the help of Elizabeth it may work out— although I lost the fight to keep him off the witness stand. One might know the great strutter would insist on that bit of the limelight. Such a damned play-actor, always treading the boards in his greasepaint, worse than one of those howling savages who almost finished him.

And Libby. Certainly there would be no George as I know him without Libby. Charming, intelligent, beautiful. But a conniving bitch. Since she was ten years old, when she began to realize there was a difference between boys and girls and she could use the difference like a deadly weapon.

He lifts the heavy book in his lap and begins to read. It is Plutarch's *Parallel Lives* and he is on number seventeen of the twenty-three pairs of ancients. It irritates him that he is not further along. He has been reading it since he took the Custer case, expecting to finish before the trial was over, but now it is obvious he will not. He reads it in the original Greek. Some of the book's pages are stained with amber droplets.

But the words have no power to reach him this day and he finally places the book aside and turns down the lamp, sitting in the dark room and watching the traffic on the street below. He thinks once more of his case—which he will present tomorrow.

At least twenty witnesses. Even more, perhaps. But I shall strike them hard, in a bunch, he thinks. Economy of force and employment of mass, I think the military call it. Sharp and decisive, I would hope. If Nelson Miles is as good as he says he is . . . Perhaps I can do with as few as six. No need to muddle the members of the court. No need to bury them under too many.

Those damned Your Boy letters are enough to muddle anyone! Not what George wrote, of course. The prattlings of an adolescent boy showing off for mama! But the very idea that someone out there is ready to discredit the prosecutor in the case just for the sake of showing a little of George's infantile, self-centered prancing. It was good the way Schofield handled it. It may not be entirely legal for a judge to go around looking under rocks outside the courtroom, but it was damned well morally right! I've seen no trace in Gardiner's character of the kind of meanness a man would need to be involved in such shenanigans. What a shame if some gossip monger were the instrument of his ruin. But, not now— not yet, anyway, thanks to Schofield. That man runs a good court. He runs it his own way, his own two-star way, but I like it.

Jacobson rises in the darkened room and moves to his bed. He will retire now, take ten hours sleep, rise at 4 A.M., and go through his notes again before the trip to Governor's Island. He has the mental discipline to sleep when he wants to sleep and to wake without an alarm within a few minutes of the time he desires. He is in bed and almost asleep before he realizes that he still has the sodden cud in his cheek.

His sleep is dreamless as usual. When he wakes, he dresses hurriedly in the dark, lights a lamp to make his toilet, then goes downstairs for breakfast.

It is November 14, 1877. A cold, wintry Wednesday in New York, with heavy snow flurries. Through the pre-dawn half-light in a world already shrouded in tones of white and gray, the early risers of the city hurry toward their work, heads bent against the harsh blast that blows across the Hudson from the Jersey flats. Jacobson stands at the window in the main dining room of the Clarendon Hotel. I could stand and watch these New York streets for hours, he thinks.

He has bought a *Herald*, and before he begins his own chilly trip to Governor's Island, he sits in one of the lobby's overstuffed chairs and glances through the newspaper. At the bottom of the front page is a small barb that comes as a result of Schofield's visit to the *Herald* the day before, although Jacobson does not know this. The story catches his eye and brings a smile to his face.

"The Great Have Served Us" the headline bleats.

In the multitude of servants who have from time to time served the *Herald*, it is difficult to remember whether General Custer was among them, as hinted in various spoutings of the kangaroo court now sitting on Governor's Island. But even if true, he was only one of a distinguished company. Kings and emperors, as well as presidents and cabinet ministers, congressmen and military leaders, have enrolled themselves among our contributors. Is every man who ever wrote for the *Herald* touching on public affairs to be investigated in some drumhead court?

18

Schofield taps the crowd to order and Gardiner announces that all are present.

"I have intentionally waited until the court was open," Schofield announces, "to say anything about the statements made recently in New York newspapers implicating parties to the trial. At the outset, let me say that the court discounts any significance of these stories insofar as the charges are concerned. The stories will be ignored in all the court's deliberations."

Gardiner sits stiffly, his hands clenched over his stack of documents on the table before him.

"It has been my duty to this court, and to the members thereof, that I satisfy myself that no party to this trial was in any way responsible for the appearance of the information in the newspapers. I have, by personal visit to the newspapers involved, so assured myself. Therefore the trial may now proceed without any cloud of suspicion over any officer attendant to it."

Gardiner's breath comes out loud enough for everyone to hear. Jacobson smiles. Schofield glances at the trial judge advocate and continues.

"I must add for myself that I abhor any policy of the press that encourages publishing or using in any way to attract their readers material such as this, which is private, personal, and intimate." He turns and looks toward the court reporter. "And I want all that in the record, Ben."

Schofield proceeds to the business at hand, but Jacobson waives opening statement and calls the first defense witness. Everyone in the court—except Elizabeth Custer, but including her husband—turns to watch as Mrs. Linda Slaughter comes into the room. She is a woman in her mid-thirties, dressed brightly in street gown and matching hat. As she passes Custer, he stands and bows and she smiles at him. He remains on his feet until she is sworn and takes her place on the witness chair. She arranges her skirt so that it falls well down on her ankles, exposing only the toes of dainty, fur-trimmed galoshes.

"You were acquainted with General Custer in Dakota Territory while you were postmistress of Bismarck," Jacobson begins. He has cut himself a plug but it remains on the table, along with the open jackknife.

"Yes, I was. We were both concerned——"

General McDowell has leaned forward, cupping his ear with one hand. Schofield breaks in gently. "Mrs. Slaughter, could you speak more loudly please?"

"Oh! Yes, of course, I'm sorry, gentlemen. I knew General Custer in Bismarck, and we were both concerned with corruption in post and Indian traderships—men in political office taking bribes to influence their decisions in appointing people to these traderships. And men, once appointed, cheating the troops and the Indians, and often sharing their illegal profits with their friends in high office."

"Were you involved with General Custer in exposing these crimes?"

"I was. General Custer, Mr. Emmit Lounsberry, who is editor of our newspaper, and I were the only persons who knew the *New York Herald* was sending a man to investigate. General Custer had always been deeply concerned with the treatment of the Indians. It upset him that traders raised prices or cheated on weights. Or sometimes they would issue only part of the government provisions to the tribes and sell the rest."

"Yes, Mrs. Slaughter, now you say your involvement was a secret arrangement?"

"Yes, it was secret."

"Why did you feel it important to keep it secret?"

"I was afraid of reprisal. My position was in the nature of a political appointment."

"But later it became known that you were involved?" Jacobson stands directly in front of Schofield and close enough to the bench to touch it. Mrs. Slaughter can look at him and still appear to be addressing the court. He has told her to look only at him. He is not sure he can depend on her testimony if her attention wanders even for a moment.

"During the Congressional committee hearings, it all came out."

"With what result?"

"I was dismissed from my post."

"From where did this dismissal originate?"

"From the highest level. As with my appointment. The territorial governor recommended me, and I was made postmistress by presidential appointment."

"Who actually informed you of the dismissal?"

"The Postmaster General, Mr. James Tyner."

"And who, Mrs. Slaughter, was appointed in your place?"

"A certain Mr. A. L. Bonnafon."

Jacobson frowns and appears to ponder, scratching his chin. He pauses a long moment before continuing, well aware that everyone is waiting expectantly.

"Bonnafon? The Philadelphia Bonnafon?"

"Yes. His father is the businessman of Philadelphia."

"What do you know of this family?"

"Only that for years the Bonnafons have been intimate friends with Orvil Grant."

Jacobson smiles, turning away from his witness and cutting his glance toward Gardiner. But the trial judge advocate makes no objection. Winthrop hands Jacobson a yellow pad and he looks at it closely for a moment, then resumes his place before Schofield, allowing his crippled foot to drag noticeably.

"Mrs. Slaughter, in addition to yourself, was political reprisal taken against others who were involved in exposing corruption in the Grant administration?"

Gardiner is up now and Jacobson waits patiently as the objection is made. "There has been no evidence presented here showing that

MRS. SLAUGHTER

corruption existed, nor has anyone proved that this woman's dismissal was politically inspired."

Before Schofield can respond, Jacobson shrugs and speaks, looking at each member of the court. "Well, I shall withdraw that question then." His eyes linger on McDowell and he smiles. If the implication is not clear enough, even for the victim of Bull Run, then it is not worth pursuing.

"Mrs. Slaughter, I assume you are well acqainted with Mr. Emmit Lounsberry?"

"Yes. Very well indeed."

"Were you aware that he was planning to accompany the expedition to the Yellowstone?"

"Of course. Everyone knew that. He was a very close friend of General Terry. When the general was in Bismarck, he often had refreshments at the Lounsberrys'. I was there on a number of these occasions. General Terry himself had agreed that Mr. Lounsberry would accompany the expedition."

"Why, then, did he not?"

"The expedition lagged far behind schedule, and when it did go, Mr. Lounsberry had sickness in his family and asked if he might substitute another representative of his newspaper. A Mr. Mark Kellogg."

"Then it was a well-known fact in Bismarck that General Terry had authorized a newspaper correspondent on the campaign."

"Absolutely, and he had the freedom of the march as he explained to me——"

"Object. That last is hearsay."

"Of course, and I withdraw it. Mrs. Slaughter, once more, just answer the question in a straightforward manner. You and others knew that General Terry had authorized a newspaper correspondent to accompany the campaign?"

"Yes."

"Thank you." Jacobson extends an arm toward Gardiner. "The charming lady is your witness, sir."

"Madam, were you aware of the relationship that existed between Custer and Mark Kellogg?"

She tosses her head. Like an unbroken mare, Jacobson thinks.

"They were acquainted. Mr. Kellogg often served as General Custer's telegrapher."

"Then Custer would recognize Mr. Kellogg as a newspaper correspondent for the *Bismarck Tribune?*"

"Of course."

Jacobson pops the chew into his mouth.

"Madam, the conspiracy of which you were a part—this so-called exposure of wickedness being carried out by the *New York Herald* —did you read everything that was published as a result?"

"I think so," Mrs. Slaughter answers haughtily, but the color in her cheeks has risen.

"Did you believe everything charged by the *Herald?*"

She looks at Jacobson and he shrugs. He doubts if half the members get the implication of Gardiner's line of questioning anyway.

"No, not all of it."

Gardiner turns and walks away from the witness stand. He looks at Custer, pauses at his chair, turns, and continues in a loud voice. "Madam, were you ever a guest in the Custer home at Fort Lincoln?"

"Yes, a number of times."

Jacobson is alert now, sitting up straight, watching the trial judge advocate.

"And has he ever been a guest in your home?"

"Yes," she says, her face pink.

"Please speak up, Mrs. Slaughter," Schofield says.

"And, madam, on these visits, was Mrs. Custer always present?"

Jacobson is up, charging out into the bull ring, no hint of a limp in his stride now.

"*I object!*" he shouts. "I resent, Mr. President, the foul implications made against the fine woman who has come here all the way from the Dakota Territory to testify. . . ."

"Mr. Jacobson, Mr. Jacobson, calm yourself," Schofield says. "Major Gardiner, I think the court requires some explanation of where you are taking the witness."

"I am simply trying to show, sir, that this witness has more interest in the case than the facts might indicate, as well as a profound concern with its outcome."

"I resent that implication most deeply."

"Please, Mr. Jacobson, calm yourself. I am going to sustain your objection."

Jacobson subsides and clumps back toward his chair. Before he can reach his seat, Gardiner's next question brings him around, furious.

"Madam, has General Custer ever given you a lock of his hair?"

"*Mr. President!*"

"Yes, I agree, Major Gardiner, you are in danger here. The court will ignore that question and it will be stricken from the record."

Gardiner shakes his head and starts to speak.

Schofield raps his cue ball. "No, I will not permit it. The question has no bearing on the charges in this case." As Gardiner retreats behind his table, Schofield looks at Jacobson, who is still glaring about and puffing loudly. "Please take a seat, Mr. Jacobson."

"Mr. President, I object to trial counsel addressing the witness as he does. He knows her name."

Gardiner turns toward him and smiles wickedly, as the newspapers will report. Jacobson damns himself for losing control.

"Why, sir, 'madam' is a perfectly normal and polite form of address. Unless, of course, you place some other meaning to the word in the case of this witness."

There is barely suppressed laughter among the spectators as Mrs. Slaughter sits red-faced, glaring at Gardiner.

"I cannot believe this is happening," Schofield says, looking first at one then the other. "I am embarrassed for the witness and would ask you to continue, Major Gardiner, and we will all pretend this last little exchange never happened." He glares at Lieutenant Jones. "None of that on the record, Ben."

"Very well, now, madam . . ." Jacobson clenches his teeth, but he knows he can do little except make the situation worse. "You have said Custer is a compassionate man, concerned with the welfare of the Indians."

"Yes."

"Do you know of the Battle of the Washita?"

"Of course, it was one of General Custer's greatest victories."

"Well, if you choose to call it that . . . no matter. Do you know that Custer claimed to have killed 103 Cheyenne warriors there?"

"I have no idea of the numbers in such a ghastly business."

"And were you aware that in the official reports it was revealed that Custer had actually killed about twenty warriors at the Washita—the rest were women and children?"

Custer sits with his teeth bared, no longer smiling at Mrs. Slaughter as he has since she came in, but glaring at the flag on the wall behind Schofield. Jacobson leans forward, ready to protect his witness when he can.

"Is that what you call compassionate?"

Jacobson breaks in, but he speaks coldly now, directly to Schofield.

"This is absurd, Mr. President. Trial counsel is speaking of a battle situation in which we all know innocent people are often caught, and he tries to make this appear a deliberate act."

"I am finished, she needn't answer any further," Gardiner shouts, and he sits down. Schofield watches, astonished.

"Major Gardiner, I will tell you once more. I am embarrassed for your conduct with this witness."

Well, the harm is already done, Jacobson thinks. Why did I ever call her? I got less than Gardiner did on this one.

But there is no time to labor it. Major Winthrop has called the next defense witness and there is a loud stir in the courtroom as everyone, including the court itself, seems to stiffen, awaiting the entrance of the Army's second highest ranking general, Philip Sheridan. Custer rises, standing at attention, facing the rear of the room. Libby is up, too, beside her husband. She places one hand on his arm as they both watch the provost sergeant swing open the door.

Forty-six years old, Sheridan is the only lieutenant general in the Army, and the three stars on his shoulder boards look large as goose eggs when he marches down the aisle. He is short, conveying an impression of mental and physical stubbornness. His head is close-cropped and his eyes are startling—slanted and puffed. His uniform is pressed and spotless, the buttons shining down the front.

As Sheridan nears the front of the room, the court rises, but Jacobson observes that Schofield does so reluctantly. For himself, the defense counsel remains in his seat.

Sheridan wheels across the front of the room, the first military witness who has not saluted the president of the court. Jacobson notices that, too, and scowls. He knows there may be some competition between Sheridan and Schofield, but whether there is or not, such an act of disrespect cannot help but irritate. At least, Jacobson thinks, he is Phil Sheridan and there is no other like him in the Army.

Everyone knows that soon old Cump Sherman will be leaving active life and that Sheridan will most assuredly be his successor as Commanding General. The war-horse with his hair thinning, his stubble beard whiter by the day, replaced by this bantam rooster of a man, a powder keg of energy and temper. Every uniformed man in the room is aware of this and senses the power, no less so the members of the court than the two wide-eyed lieutenants sitting behind Gardiner's table.

As Gardiner completes the oath, Sheridan sits in the witness chair as though it were the saddle of a cavalry horse, his legs wide apart. He glances around the room, dismissing all of it except the Custers, whom he now acknowledges for the first time with a curt nod and a small smile. Apparently having been waiting for that, Custer once more settles into his chair, Libby arranging the collar of his cape about his neck before she takes her place as well.

"General, in order that there be no misunderstanding concerning your appearance here, would you explain to the court why you have responded to defense request to appear?" Jacobson says. He has stationed himself as far from the witness as he can—on the side of the room near the court reporter—in order not to distract from the very presence of Sheridan as he speaks.

"At the outset, I was aware of this court's being convened and in fact had agreed that it should sit. A court-martial is an excellent means of laying to rest rumors and vague accusations. Or it can determine if wrong has been done and punish for it. I felt then as I do now—let the truth out and let the court decide." He speaks in sharp staccato bursts, like a rapidly cranked Gatling gun. As each of Sheridan's words erupt on the room, General Pope nods emphatically.

"But I have agreed to come here on petition of Mr. Jacobson because I feel I may add to the truth. I am concerned that General Custer have a fair hearing. What with various newspapers calling for his head—even though others ask for his immediate acquittal—I am interested that there be no mistake about the truth. I doubt most of the newspapers have access to much of the truth before they arrive at their verdicts." He laughs a hard, metallic cackle that is gone as suddenly as it came, changing his expression not at all.

Most members of the press gallery smile ruefully, and there is enough mutter of protest among them to catch Schofield's attention. He shakes the cue ball in their direction and they immediately become silent.

"General Sheridan, what is ambition?"

"The desire to better one's self in one's profession."

"And in what profession is General Custer engaged?"

"Why, the profession of arms, of course."

"And is ambition in the profession of arms unusual?"

"It is common. I would not have around me subordinates who are not vitally interested in bettering themselves as soldiers."

"And what of political ambition, sir?"

"It is a bug which from time to time bores into the brain of many intelligent men, doing little harm if they control it." He bursts out laughing again, and a number of spectators join him.

"Is it debilitating?"

"Of course not. It is healthy, if controlled."

"General Sheridan, think back to last spring. Just before the Dakota column left Fort Lincoln. Would you say General Custer was politically ambitious at that time?"

"Certainly not. Politics was the last thing on his mind. It was his career which concerned him. His military career."

"Could you explain that for us, General?"

"Custer had involved himself in the Congressional hearings on impeachment of certain parties. It was ill advised. But there was some thought that he should remain in Washington City for the duration of those hearings and perhaps for possible trials as well. Grant indicated to Sherman that Custer should remain where he was and not return to command the Dakota column as had been planned. Terry would take command instead."

"Excuse me, General, but wasn't it true that General Custer was actually relieved of command because he had offended President Grant by accusing certain members of the administration of corruption?"

"I cannot speak for Grant," Sheridan says. Jacobson finds himself wishing his witness would call the man General Grant or former President Grant or even Sam. "I can only say that Custer was ordered from the list as commander of the column. Custer went to see Grant but Grant wouldn't see Custer. Custer waited all day. He went to Sherman and was told the order stood. As he explained to me later, Custer began to realize his entire military career was in balance because he had incurred the wrath of Grant."

"Then he had incurred the wrath of the President?"

"Custer came to Chicago to see me. He asked that I intercede with Sherman. I told him I would not. He was frantic about his career. He left Chicago for St. Paul, and only a few hours afterward I got a wire from Sherman telling me to hold Custer if he came to my headquarters because he had left Washington against orders. I then realized the depth of Custer's concern. He had violated Sherman's instructions in order to regain a place in the expedition."

Jacobson hands Sheridan a glass of water, and for a moment the room is completely silent as he drinks. Custer turns and whispers something to Libby and she smiles and pats his shoulder.

"Then Terry wired that he thought Custer should go along and command his own regiment. Terry said he could think of no one else who could do it as well—Reno was too junior, others did not know the unit. I forwarded the request to Sherman. He saw Grant, and the President agreed to let Custer take his regiment into the field."

"At the time the expedition moved out, you believed that Custer was capable and not influenced by motives other than those of leading his regiment?"

"I was convinced then and I am now."

"I object to that as an opinion," Gardiner says. Everyone in the room, intently watching Sheridan, now looks at Gardiner, many in amazement that he challenges Sheridan's opinion. Sheridan glares at him.

"I believe the court can take expert opinion of a commander, Major Gardiner," Schofield says. There is no heat in his voice and he looks at the trial counsel with something like sympathy.

"Thank you, Mr. President," Jacobson says, and he turns to his witness, who is still glaring at Gardiner. "Now, General, can you tell us, as overall commander of the campaign of 1876, why did it fail?"

"I will not address details of tactics. Others will be here, I expect, for that purpose. I will give you the major reason as I saw it, which foreshadowed anything else that might have happened. The Army was misled. Estimates of the number of hostiles given us were completely in error. We were given the job of getting hostiles back onto reservations in February because the Bureau of Indian Affairs could not handle their Indians. They never can. So the Army must do it for them. Based on the estimates the Bureau gave us, we expected between five hundred and eight hundred warriors in the field. There were that many thousand. I suspect the Bureau was ashamed to tell us how many of their people actually *had* jumped the reservations." He laughs again, and many are so intent on his words that they laugh, too, automatically. But Gardiner sits frowning, his fingers silently tapping the table before him.

"General, I want to express my appreciation for your coming here and providing this important testimony," Jacobson says. "I will not take any more of your valuable time."

"I shall take some, however, General," Gardiner says, moving quickly to stand directly in front of Sheridan and only a few feet away. As he goes back to his place, Jacobson realizes that some of Gardiner's gruffness may be a deliberate attempt to stir Sheridan's hair-trigger temper. But for a relatively junior Army officer to bait the powerful Sheridan . . . Jacobson shakes his head and spits.

"General, if a commander precipitates headlong battle prematurely, does it matter whether he does so for military or political motives?"

"I do not accept that battle was precipitated headlong."

"But, sir, you have stated that you agreed this court-martial should sit."

"Major"—with an angry rasp in his voice—"I have stated as well why I felt that way."

"Very well, sir. If a man does wrong as a result of overriding ambition, does it matter whether it is political or military?"

"I do not accept that there was overriding ambition."

Gardiner and the witness stare at each other for a moment. Schofield appears fascinated with what is happening, for, no less so than Jacobson, he is aware of Gardiner's danger.

"To another subject you discussed, General," Gardiner says. "When you are estimating the size of a hostile camp in preparation for battle, and your scouts can count the lodges, how many warriors do you usually assume will be present for each lodge counted?"

"I fail to see what that has to do with any of this. But, if you want the answer, I would say perhaps three or four warriors for each tepee."

"General, I have here a copy of a dispatch sent you by General Terry on March 4, last year. With the court's permission . . ."

"Let me see that," Schofield says. He reads the dispatch, frowns, passes it on to the other members of the court. "Mark it court exhibit A, Lieutenant Jones."

After the paper is marked, Gardiner takes it and smiles at Jacobson.

"Very well, Major Gardiner, you may read it," Schofield breaks in.

"The dispatch is marked 'Letters Received, Headquarters, Division of the Missouri'—your command, General Sheridan—dated March 4, 1876, and it reads: 'The most trustworthy scout on the Missouri recently in hostile camps reports not less than two thousand lodges and that the Indians are loaded down with ammunition.' It is signed by Terry." Gardiner stands, facing Sheridan, the paper at his side. The general's face is blotched with purple and a vein stands out on his neck. "Let me see . . ." Gardiner looks up at the ceiling, pretending to calculate. "Using your own estimate, General, that would mean about six thousand warriors."

"I could only assume it was an error in estimation." Sheridan is livid, his words sputtering now.

"You assumed *then*, General, or you assume *now* that you are confronted with this dispatch once more?"

LT. GEN. PHILIP H. SHERIDAN

Sheridan half rises from his chair, his hands white-knuckled on the arms as he lifts himself.

"Major." It is a squeaking sound that bursts from Sheridan's lips. He seems unable to say more.

Gardiner wheels from the witness, saying over his shoulder to the court, "In view of the witness's distress, I will withdraw that last question."

He spends a great deal of time at the table, his back to Sheridan, giving the general time to compose himself. Jacobson does not understand that. Sheridan had almost gone out of control, and if it had been me, Jacobson thinks, I would have torn in. . . . I wonder if it's true what I've heard . . . that in battle Sheridan sometimes screamed and ranted and foamed at the mouth?

"General Sheridan," Gardiner says, turning back to him with a newspaper clipping in his hand. "Immediately after President Grant relieved Custer from command of the Dakota column, you said he went to Chicago. Actually, he went by way of New York. I was wondering if you recall an article in the *New York World* on May 2, 1876, in which Custer was interviewed and in which he claimed that neither you nor General Sherman agreed with President Grant that he be relieved."

"I recall the article," Sheridan says in a choking voice, his face still red.

"Was what Custer said true, sir? Did you not agree with the President that Custer should be sacked?"

"It was not true. I agreed with the President."

"Thank you, General," Gardiner says gently, and Jacobson shakes his head in admiration. Like coaxing a recalcitrant child.

"One more point only, General Sheridan. When Custer came to you, I believe you said you would not intercede to have that position changed—his being sacked."

"No! It was between Grant and Custer."

"Custer had been one of your favorites during the war and in fact afterwards on the Plains, is that correct?"

"He got the job done."

"Why, then, would you not intercede for him in a time of trouble?"

"I told you . . ." Sheridan starts, bending forward as though ready to leap out of the chair. "It was a matter between Grant and Custer."

"Isn't it true, however, that you felt his actions had indeed caused much too much embarrassment for the Army?"

"No!"

"In fact, hadn't your disillusion with him begun before the war was over, when you discovered he made false reports?"

"I don't know what you are talking about, Major." He spits out the words and his eyes are narrow as he studies Gardiner.

"Let me refresh your memory, sir. The Battle of Five Forks. Do you not recall that after he had captured a Rebel baggage train he reported to you that it had been defended by a full Confederate division? And in fact it had been defended by only half a dozen worn-out cannons?"

Sheridan seems to shake himself and lower his head for a charge. He looks at Gardiner through his thick brows and then his glance goes to Custer, beyond him to his wife.

"Well, sometimes he was a little over-enthusiastic," he says, and the harsh, short laugh comes like a bark. But now few people in the room even smile with him, the tension is so heavy.

"Over-enthusiastic? Wouldn't a better term be 'liar'?"

"No, by God, I did not say that, and I will not sit here any longer and have you put words in my mouth, do you understand that?" Sheridan's voice is an octave higher, and once more he grips the arms of the chair and leans forward.

"I do apologize, General, I certainly had not intended to put words into your mouth," Gardiner says, backing away. Then he smiles suddenly. "It was not you, but I, who mentioned that non-existent southern division that the brave Custer subdued."

Jacobson is up at last, having until then been so intent on the play between Gardiner and Sheridan that he has let it ride too long. But before he can voice it, Gardiner waves his arms in the air.

"Oh, very well, Mr. Jacobson, I withdraw that last and I am finished with this witness."

I suspect he is not finished with you, Jacobson thinks.

Lieutenant Edward Godfrey, commander of Company K, 7th Cavalry, enters the courtroom. He has an enormous nose, piercing brown eyes, and long, talon-like fingers, all of which, combined with his tendency to quick movement, gives him the appearance of a predatory bird. He explains that he was the training officer in the regiment for the year prior to the expedition against the Sioux. Once more in the center of the bull ring, a cheek full of tobacco, Jacobson holds his open jackknife in his hand, bouncing it like a baton as he speaks.

"Lieutenant Godfrey, as training officer, how did you report to your superiors the fighting trim of the unit—if you will excuse an old Navy term?"

"Not in the best of shape, through no fault of any officer or man serving with it. About as good or bad as any other frontier regiment at the time. Due to Congressional reluctance to appropriate the funds required to sustain an Army, the men, animals, and materials were not of the best quality."

"Specifically, how did this manifest itself in your regiment?"

"We were ill equipped for combat. Our pack mule situation. Most of those we had should have been condemned. Our remount problem was actually worse. We could not maintain a reserve of newly acquired animals in training. We had to use them as we got them.

As a result, we went to Montana with horses which had never been trained to gunfire. We didn't have the ammunition for it either. The training, I mean. In fact, we never had enough ammunition to train our recruits properly before they were committed."

"Can you testify to actual results of this in the fight?"

"Of course. In my own company there were a number of instances in the Little Bighorn campaign of horses' bolting under fire. It was our next-to-worst problem. Our worst was the recruits' lack of training in fire discipline because we had not had time."

"You continue to mention recruits. Could you clarify that?" As Godfrey answers, Jacobson sprays tobacco juice into a handy spittoon.

"Yes, sir. In some units the percentage of men not yet in service over three months was thirty to forty percent. And when we fought dismounted, the horse holders—one out of every four men —were always veterans because we needed men there who could handle four horses under fire. That made the percentage of recruits on our firing lines even higher. In my company, almost sixty percent. These men had simply not been with us long enough to teach them much about fire discipline. It's a difficult task anyway when ammunition issues are so short."

"With what weapons were you armed at the Little Bighorn, Lieutenant?"

"We didn't take sabers. We had the Colt revolver, of course, a reliable weapon, but for close range. Our primary weapon was the single-shot Springfield breechloader, 45-70. It's a .45 caliber weapon, the rounds loaded with 70 grains of black powder. It's excellent for a few shots. But in sustained fire, the chamber quickly becomes caked with burnt powder and the extractor won't pull the empty case from the weapon—and soldiers have to dig each casing out with the point of a knife or bayonet."

"Did that happen on the Little Bighorn?"

"It happened to every soldier I know who fired more than a few rounds."

Jacobson paces back and forth in front of the bench, his limp pronounced but not distracting. He has great confidence in this witness and feels no necessity for constant eye contact.

"To another subject, Lieutenant. On the evening before you left

LT. EDWARD GODFREY

the Yellowstone and marched up the Rosebud, did you have occasion to hear anything relative to the orders of the regiment?"

"I heard a conversation aboard the *Far West* late in the evening of that day. I was on board posting the regiment's mail. A previous mail courier had overturned his boat in the river, losing all the mail and drowning one of the regiment's sergeants. So many of the men had written letters again —most men like to write a letter just before leaving on a march——"

"Of course they do. Please continue, Lieutenant."

"Yes, sir. I overhead General Terry speaking with some other officers——"

"Objection. Hearsay," Gardiner says from his place, not looking up.

"I will take it to the extent that a certain thing was said," Schofield says. "Lieutenant Godfrey, you may answer."

"Yes, sir. I couldn't see who the others were. They were at the rail and it was dark. They were taking a smoke before bedtime. General Terry said, 'I hope Custer ties into them if he can whip them.'"

"And, Lieutenant, as a company commander with the column, what was your greatest concern the next morning as you rode out?"

"That the hostiles would escape. I was concerned that Major Reno had alerted them with his scout previously."

"Oh, you were unhappy with Major Reno's conduct on the scout?"

Godfrey hesitates only a moment, looking squarely at Jacobson, who now stands still before him.

"I must admit, sir, that I have never been completely happy with Major Reno's conduct, official or otherwise."

"Mr. President." Gardiner is up now. "I move that be stricken. We are not here to judge Major Reno's conduct, nor am I as prepared to accept as expert the testimony of Lieutenant Godfrey as I was General Sheridan's. I think it obvious that he is too closely involved."

"Sustained. The court will not take any of that about the witness's opinion of Major Reno's conduct."

But Jacobson knows the newspapers will print it.

"Do you understand what is to be stricken, Ben?" Schofield says quietly to the reporter, and he says he does. Jacobson says nothing but indicates by resuming his seat that he is finished with the witness.

Gardiner remains seated as he begins. "Lieutenant Godfrey, did I understand you to say that General Terry wanted Custer to tie into them—*if* he could whip them? Now how does one determine that of a force he has never seen?"

"There is only one way, sir. You just tie into them. You join battle."

"With that philosophy, I'm amazed that the United States Army hasn't suffered more disasters than it has. But never mind. You were training officer during all those months before the campaign. A critical time for a unit, from a training standpoint, is it not?"

"Extremely so."

"During the winter months, after it was known a campaign would be forthcoming and the companies of the regiment were being assembled at Fort Lincoln, was Custer on station?"

Godfrey glances at his old commander, but Custer seems unaware of the direction the questions have taken and sits picking invisible specks from his trousers leg.

"Well, he was absent for about two months."

"Where was he?"

"He and Mrs. Custer were visiting New York."

"During the last weeks of training, just before the regiment departed for the field, was he on station then?"

"No, sir," Godfrey says, obviously uncomfortable with it. "He had been called to Washington——"

"Thank you," Gardiner cuts in. There is a long pause and Gardiner taps a pencil on the papers scattered on the table. "In the

7th Cavalry, Custer gathered about him intimate friends and rela-
tives, did he not—his brothers, Lieutenant Calhoun, Captain Keogh?"

"Yes, sir, he socialized a great deal with that group you mention."

"Were you not one of the members of this—shall we call it the
Custer admiration clique?"

Godfrey stares at him. Jacobson is trying to keep his expression
blank, but the corners of his mouth twist up and he chews rapidly.

"My God! I admire General Custer as a soldier. I think this
trial is a sad comment on the Army's sense of justice. . . ." Godfrey's voice trails off and he looks at the Custers once more. They
both watch him now with no visible hostility. "Many of those
officers you refer to were killed on Custer Hill."

"But were you not one of those included in the Custer circle?"

"Sir, I believe General Custer to be a good officer," Godfrey
says. He is embarrassed. "But . . . personally, I do not enjoy his
company."

Someone in the press gallery laughs. Gardiner nods, his eyes still
on the papers before him. Jacobson sees a muscle twitch in the
trial judge advocate's cheek. It has not been a completely satisfactory
answer for either side, and Gardiner is unhappy that he has put the
question at all.

"I appreciate your candor, Lieutenant Godfrey," Gardiner says,
looking up. He pauses for a long moment before continuing. "May
I say that I am happy you and other commanders on the frontier
are finally receiving the supplies and equipment you need. That's all
I have."

Schofield calls a twenty-minute recess and Jacobson hurries out
to see one of his next witnesses. But the press is already there.

Colonel Nelson Miles, 5th Infantry, has had considerable success
as an Indian fighter since the Little Bighorn sent its shock across the
frontier. He has chased a great many hostiles back to reservations
and whipped a few as well. Many of his operations have involved
infantry troops, which a great many people had thought useless
against Plains Indians. He apparently has the respect, if not the love,
of his associates. In his success he has become self-serving and arro-
gant. He will be a general officer soon, a powerful and ruthless one.

Miles is a handsome man, his dark hair well trimmed and kept, as
is a moderate moustache. He has a large chin, a solid jaw, a look of

being always ready to smile. His blue eyes are direct and clear. Now and then he uses a pinch of snuff. He is a rather large man who knows how to set off his imposing frame with well-tailored clothing. He arrived in New York wearing a buffalo cape and a Russian-style fur cap, both of which the newspapers duly reported.

Newspaper correspondents are crowded around him in the anteroom as Jacobson sees him for the first time since the two met the previous summer to discuss the case. That had been in Chicago, where Miles had managed to visit between Indian skirmishes. They had discussed his testimony, and Jacobson had been convinced at the time that for an expert witness on Indian fighting he could do no better.

Yet he had a feeling of apprehension when he talked with Miles, and now the same uneasiness returns.

He still holds a note left on his table by the provost sergeant during Sheridan's testimony: "Allan, I am here. Arrived late last night from the West. Too late to see you at your hotel. Arrived there this morning after you had gone. Am ready. Nelson."

The press people around Miles are a yammering pack, but Jacobson notes with some admiration that they are being well handled. With aplomb, Miles answers questions he wants to answer, turning aside those he dislikes, all without irritation and with great good humor, which is reflected in the courteous treatment he gets from the normally raucous group. Miles has shed his buffalo robe and is splendid in a doeskin jacket with long fringe and shoulder boards showing the eagles of his rank.

It is impossible to break through the circle now, and Miles shows no inclination to break out of it. Jacobson turns back to the courtroom with considerable irritation, and Major Winthrop meets him there with the information that Elizabeth Custer has been feeling light-headed and has slipped out through the court conference room. She will return to her hotel, where, Winthrop explains, she has great confidence in the house physician whom she had met socially on previous trips to New York.

"Likely just a slight head cold," Winthrop says.

Jacobson's irritation becomes more acute. He hurries back to the front of the room and shuffles through his papers, Winthrop following directly.

"Try to get some of this stuff in order, for God's sake," Jacobson growls. As the court reconvenes, he glances back at Libby's empty seat.

Much of the press gallery is empty as well, many of the correspondents more interested in talking to Miles in the anteroom than in hearing the next defense witness, Lieutenant Charles Varnum. Normally a member of Company A, during the Little Bighorn campaign he had been assigned as commander of a group of Crow scouts. He is a tall, slender officer, with a rather pinched handsomeness. His nose is thin, his eyes dark and deep-set. His hair is slicked back with oil from a part in the middle, and his moustache is a small, short-cropped patch above thin lips. Among his fellow officers he is noted as a hot-blooded battler, but apparently nothing short of mortal combat touches his emotions. He sits in the witness stand unconcerned, unmoved, almost unblinking.

"I was at the Crow's Nest with General Custer. There was a morning haze in the valley of the Little Bighorn but I saw nothing I could characterize as either village or horse herd."

"While at the Crow's Nest, were you informed of the day's plan?"

"I was. The regiment would rest that day, attack the next."

"And what happened to change that?"

"As we rode back to the regiment, a number of Sioux were seen watching us. Officers were called together and General Custer said we would attack immediately in view of our having been discovered. Because we were not sure exactly where the village was located, he ordered the 'movement to contact' formation—battalions in line. He impressed us with the necessity to move quickly before the Indians escaped."

"How does a movement to contact work?"

"Battalions are on line. They cover a wide area as they move in this fashion, some distance between. When one strikes something, the rest react. It's a formation that sweeps a wide area, as it were. Locating the objective quickly."

"And this formation was adopted because of the need for speed and because you were not sure where the enemy lay?"

"That is correct."

"Once General Custer had given the order to move into the

valley of the Little Bighorn, did you hear a single officer indicate that there was anything strange or unusual about it?"

"No. That morning I had considerable conversation with officers of the Custer battalion—Captain Keogh, Captain Tom Custer, Captain Yates, Lieutenant Porter. None expressed the least surprise that we were going immediately to the attack."

"Thank you, Lieutenant Varnum."

Gardiner stalks around his table to the witness chair, his hands behind his back. He looks for a moment at the medal on Varnum's chest. "Lieutenant Varnum, I would like to express my personal admiration for your conduct on the day of the battle. It has been well documented and reflects great credit on the Army."

"Thank you, sir," Varnum replies, no show of emotion on his face.

You will not soft-soap that one, Jacobson thinks. He is as hard as a cavalry bit. But then, possibly that's a disservice to Gardiner's sincerity.

"Did you personally see any of those Sioux who discovered the regiment?"

"Yes, sir, I did."

"Did they appear in great haste to depart, once they had discovered you?"

"Not particularly."

Custer is out of his chair and apparently about to walk over to the front of the bench, but wheels and strides to one of the windows looking out on Manhattan. Once more everyone in the room stares at him, Schofield with his mouth partly open. Jacobson flushes and starts to rise, but Custer as quickly spins about, and, his limp still obvious, stamps back to his seat. With a loud clearing of his throat, he starts to sit down, then glares at Jacobson.

"Where is my hat?"

"In the vestibule, George."

Custer stands another instant, all eyes on him in astonishment. Then he abruptly sits down.

Schofield is obviously perplexed and perhaps a little angry. But he shakes his head and points a finger at Jacobson. "Sir, I must insist . . ." He pauses, looks at Custer, who now sits quietly, looking back into Schofield's eyes with a vacant stare. "Well . . . never mind. Let's get on with it, Major Gardiner."

It is apparent to everyone that Jacobson is upset with the scene. More and more it has come to irritate him when Custer is on his feet before this crowd, for he is aware that comparisons are being made between himself and the Golden Cavalier because of their limps. Jacobson has tried to underplay his own as the trial has progressed, but his courtroom manner—long developed to take advantage of the clubfoot—frequently slips into the proceedings without being summoned. Gardiner is sensitive to the defense counsel's distress and somehow does not wish to capitalize on it. So he turns quickly back to his witness and resumes.

"Lieutenant Varnum, as commander of scouts, were you at the time of the movement into the valley far enough in advance to warn the main body of whatever you might find? I mean, were you far enough ahead for the regiment to react to anything you might report?"

"I doubt they could have reacted in any great degree. I also doubt that I could have gotten my scouts any farther ahead of the main body than they were."

There is a mutter of approval in the room and some of the Army officers are looking at one another and nodding, whispering to their ladies.

"They might well have been apprehensive, then," Gardiner says, returning to his table. He pauses and turns back. "Oh, one more thing, Lieutenant Varnum. Each of those officers you mentioned who had no question about the regiment's attacking a day early— they were all killed, were they not?"

"Yes, sir, but——"

"That is all, thank you, Lieutenant Varnum."

As he is dismissed and salutes the president of the court, Varnum clicks his heels loudly.

19

Winthrop calls Colonel Nelson Miles, and as the doeskin warrior marches down the aisle, Jacobson glances once more at Libby Custer's empty chair, half expecting her to have reappeared. He fidgets in frustration, a little unnerved that Libby's sudden departure has created some gnawing doubt in his head.

Miles salutes the court, smiling a greeting, and the members seem well disposed toward him. Perhaps his driving ambition has not touched any of them yet, but Jacobson bets it will soon. Before Gardiner finishes administering the oath, Jacobson has moved to the stand, somehow anxious to have this testimony done with.

"Colonel Miles, I would expect that if there be an Army officer who could be classified as an expert witness in regard to Indian fighting, you would be that officer. In your experience, what is the single most obvious characteristic of Plains Indian hostiles in battle?"

"They use the tactic of strike and run, strike and run. They are an effective force in that tactic."

"Why do they use such a tactic?"

"Because in most instances, even though they outnumber us, our weapons and our fire discipline make a stand-up fight very expensive to them."

"Have there not been pitched battles before?"

"Oh, yes, before the war and since, as well. In a few instances.

But the hostiles have generally suffered heavily, too. Beecher's Island, the Wagon Box Fight, others. At the Little Bighorn their numbers were so overwhelming. And this particular group had just seen that a stand-up fight could suceeed. This was important, that they were not apprehensive of a pitched battle. Plains Indians fight as individuals and the warriors must each feel there is a chance of success. Their chiefs do not order them into a fight unless they want to go."

"When did they see that a stand-up fight could be made?"

"On the Rosebud against Crook on June 17, I believe, when Crook was unable to force a decision and could not scatter or rout the Sioux. But of course Custer and Terry were not aware of this."

"So as he ascended the Rosebud, General Custer was acting on his knowledge of Plains Indians—excluding the Crook fight."

"Absolutely. The northern column knew nothing of the Crazy Horse success. And knowing nothing of it—or perhaps even *had* he known—Custer's main concern would have to be catching the Sioux before they escaped."

"How would you have conducted the operation?"

"As Custer did. March quickly, if unable to locate the hostile camp from the divide, attack immediately. With all speed."

"You would have followed the Indian trail at once when it turned west?"

"Absolutely."

"Would you have made a detailed reconnaissance first?"

"Not under the circumstances. Such a reconnaissance would have given the hostiles more time to disperse. You must understand, this is their normal reaction to a column approaching a village. Once more—unknown to Custer—they felt unafraid and were just taking their time about reacting to the presence of troops."

"Colonel Miles, you imply they had no plan, necessarily, to stand and fight."

"Of course not. After the Crook fight they expected only extreme caution from our troops. I have spoken with a number of Cheyenne chiefs who were there and have come in since, and they tell me the camp was very casual about it all. Riders had come in reporting soldiers on the Rosebud. But on June 25, Two Moons was cutting tobacco in his tepee. One chief was out with his wives picking some early blackberries on the east bank of the river. A number of them

COL. NELSON MILES

were discussing what action they might take in response to a column of troops coming too close. They were in a brush arbor near the big eastern bend of the Little Bighorn. Then suddenly Custer was upon them and they reacted.

"From what I learned from them, they were surprised that Custer came on so fast. Custer was surprised they reacted directly against his formations. They were excited, but still they felt a new power—a medicine—they had never felt. It was the largest gathering of tribesmen ever seen on the North American continent. Nothing had prepared us for their numbers. Even so. We might have won . . ."

"How might we have won?"

"Except for the conduct of certain officers in his regiment, Custer might have——"

"I object," Gardiner says, challenging Miles directly with his eyes.

Well, after Sheridan, Miles is of small consequence to him, Jacobson thinks.

"The prosecution can accept Colonel Miles as an expert witness in certain circumstances, but to hear accusations against brave men not here charged is most assuredly not acceptable."

"Sustained. I realize there is a thin line here, Mr. Jacobson, on what a so-called expert witness can say. But we will not get into this . . . business."

"I can accept that, General," Jacobson says. "One more question, Colonel Miles. You have seen the written order General Terry gave General Custer?"

"Yes, you were kind enough to show it to me last summer when we were discussing the case."

"Of course." Jacobson smiles sourly, for he would as soon Miles had put it some other way. "Had you received that order, how would you have acted?"

"I would have followed the trail, turned with it, and on being discovered, attacked at once. The order was discretionary! I do not know why General Terry has now decided it was not. I don't know the pressures that that fine officer and gentleman is under, but——"

Gardiner is on his feet, but before he can object Schofield breaks in. "Colonel Miles, please confine yourself to the question."

"Very well, sir. I would have done as General Custer did."

"Thank you, that will be all," Jacobson says, and starts for his seat with a sigh of relief. But he is stopped short as Miles reaches inside his doeskin jacket and produces a long envelope.

"If I may, sir," he says to the court, "I have evidence here which clearly indicates that General Terry intended his order to be discretionary. I hesitate to introduce it, because I realize it may cast some doubt on what General Terry has said, but then I must assume that at the time General Terry was so occupied with other things he forgot or that——"

"What is that?" Jacobson snaps, taking a step toward the witness stand.

"Just a moment, Mr. Jacobson, if the witness has evidence he feels should be introduced . . ." Schofield says.

"I'm not saying it should be ignored, General, I want to see what it is. This is, after all, the defense portion of the case."

"Let me see it, Colonel Miles," Schofield says, reaching out a hand.

"General, I'm not sure you have the right to look at whatever——"

"Mr. Jacobson, please take the envelope from your witness and hand it to me," Schofield says hotly, and Jacobson, red-faced, does as he is told. Gardiner has risen, ready to interpose his own objection as Schofield rips open the envelope and pulls forth a legal-size sheet of paper folded twice. He quickly spreads it on the bench and reads it, frowning.

Schofield hands the paper to Jacobson and the defense counsel reads it as well. His reaction is much the same—a deep frown.

"Mr. President, may I confer with my client?"

"Of course. Do you desire a recess?"

"No—only a moment."

Jacobson kneels beside Custer and shows him the document. He waits as the cavalryman reads. Custer rubs his head and acts as though he is in pain. Jacobson looks past his shoulder to the empty chair and swears under his breath.

"I can't recall," Custer whispers, stammering slightly. "My head wound. It has made my memory so faulty on many things."

"For God's sake, George, you should be able to recall this."

"I can't recall . . ."

Jacobson snorts and grabs the paper from Custer's hand. "General Schofield, may I ask a few questions of the witness before I make a decision on this?" He waves the paper.

As Schofield nods, Jacobson says, "Colonel Miles, where did you come by this?"

"A Mr. Frederick Whittaker. I had met him some time ago in Chicago and asked for an autographed copy of his book. On my trip to the East he joined me on the train from Chicago to Columbus, Ohio, and gave me the book I had asked for. He said he had read in the newspapers that I would be coming east to testify and that he had been working in Custer's behalf. He gave me the paper."

Jacobson looks at the paper again.

"It's an affidavit. Mr. Whittaker obtained it himself."

"I am aware that it is an affidavit," Jacobson snarls. "But why did I not know of it?"

"I have only had it the past two days, and I arrived too late last night to contact you."

"Yes, but why . . ." Jacobson turns and stares at George Custer and at the empty chair behind him. With a sudden jerking movement he flings the paper on the bench before Schofield and, dragging his foot across the floor, goes to his seat. "General Schofield, I cannot introduce it."

Schofield is plainly nonplussed. His eyes move from Jacobson to Custer to Gardiner and back again to the defense counsel. The forgotten cud makes an unsightly bulge in Jacobson's cheek.

"This is a sworn statement," Schofield says, lifting the paper. "I cannot understand why you will not introduce it."

"Mr. President, I will not introduce it."

The courtroom is silent as Schofield reads the document again. Both McDowell and Pope have by now seen enough of it to know what it is, and they each whisper for a moment with Schofield.

"All right, all right," Schofield says quietly, then addresses the witness. "Colonel Miles. This gentleman to whom you refer—was he the Whittaker I recall writing a book—a biography of Colonel Custer?"

"Yes, sir. And, General Schofield, I can vouch for the notary public appearing on that document. I don't mean I have spoken with him about this—but I know he is indeed a Bismarck notary."

"That is helpful," Schofield says with a hint of sarcasm. He leans back, scratching his muttonchops. At last he takes a deep breath and straightens in his seat. "Mr. Jacobson, do you object to the court's introducing this document?"

"To what could I object?"

"Very well. Lieutenant Jones, mark it court exhibit B, pass it to the trial judge advocate, and when you have finished with it, Major Gardiner, give it back to Colonel Miles."

Jacobson squirms in his seat. He looks at Custer once, but the cavalier still rubs his forehead, his face down. While Gardiner reads the document, a buzz of conversation starts in the courtroom but subsides as Miles takes the paper once again.

"Colonel Miles, please read the document."

Miles clears his throat. The document as entered into the trial record reads as follows:

Territory of Dakota:
County of Burleigh:

Personally came before me Mary Adams, who first being duly sworn deposes and says: she resides in the city of Bismarck, Dakota Territory. That she came to Dakota Territory with Genl. George A. Custer in the spring of 1873. That she was in the employ of Genl. Custer from 1873 until the time of his wounding and removal from Fort A. Lincoln, D.T. That while in his employ she accompanied him on military expeditions in the capacity of cook. That she left Fort A. Lincoln in the spring of 1876 with Genl. Terry's expedition in the employ of said Genl. Custer and was present in Genl. Custer's tent on the Rosebud River in

Montana Territory when Genl. Terry came into said tent and spoke to Genl. Custer: "Custer, I don't know what to say for the last." Genl. Custer replied: "Say whatever you want to say." Genl. Terry then said: "Use your own judgment and do what you think best if you strike the trail. And whatever you do, Custer, hold onto your wounded." Further respondent saith not.

X

MARY   ADAMS

(Her Mark)

Subscribed & Sworn to Before me
This 16th day of January 1877
[*Notary Seal*]

George P. Flannery
Notary Public
Burleigh County, D.T.

The room is quiet, everyone watching as Gardiner rises. He shows only moderate concern, which unnerves Jacobson even more.

"If it please the court," Gardiner says, "this sudden and unexpected revelation—not only to me but to others as well"—and he turns momentarily and looks at Jacobson, who stares back sullenly—"requires some research on my part, and I would respectfully ask the court for an opportunity to do that."

"We cannot stay here all winter, Major Gardiner," Schofield says. "What is the nature of your research? Would you be required to leave the city?"

"All that is needed, Mr. President, is a search of my own files. If we could recess for the remainder of the day."

"I see no objection to that. Unless defense counsel does." Schofield looks at Jacobson, who shrugs.

"Of course not," Jacobson says. "I would like to ensure that the record shows all of this to be on the court's initiative and not mine."

Schofield frowns. "Mr. Jacobson, I don't completely understand your attitude. Do you know something about this affidavit that you have not revealed to the court?"

"No, sir, I do not. That is my concern. That I have just now been made aware of it."

Schofield turns back to Miles. "The date on this document is January—"

"Yes, sir, January 16."

"Why was it held back so long?"

"General, I cannot say what Mr. Whittaker's motives might have been. All I know is that I had it in hand only two days ago."

Schofield fingers the cue ball, rolling it back and forth. Gardiner still stands, and across the room Jacobson empties his mouth into a spittoon and wipes his lips with a large white handkerchief.

"Colonel Miles. What do you know of this Mary Adams?"

"I know that she is a black woman who has been with the Custers for many years. I am told she departed Dakota Territory as servant to a family named Thompson, or Thomas, or some such thing. They were en route to British Columbia."

Schofield turns back to Gardiner. "Major, does it appear to you that General Terry will have to be recalled from his station in St. Paul?"

"If I cannot impeach that document, I see no alternative."

"Yes, well, make up your mind quickly on that so that we waste as little time as possible getting him here."

"General, may I ask a court ruling on the property of hearsay that is obvious in the affidavit?"

"Yes, it is hearsay, but admissible as testimony to the effect that those words were in fact spoken, and a sworn statement has essentially the same weight as sworn testimony from the witness chair." Schofield leans back in his chair, his palms flat on the table before him. He looks at the members of the court, the witness, trial judge advocate, and Jacobson. "Very well. The court is in recess until the usual time tomorrow."

20

The snow has stopped but nearly six inches have collected in the streets. As night comes on the wind dies and it is moderately warm in the city. Horses and wheeled vehicles have churned and chopped the snow into brown mush, and pedestrians walking too near the edge of the sidewalks must take care or they will be splattered with slush as the evening traffic moves through the streets. Because passing crowds beat down the snow as it was falling, store and theater owners have had no chance to sweep their walks clean, and the footing in places is treacherous.

Jacobson walks along the Bowery, in the old theater district. By 1877 much of the show business world of New York has moved farther uptown, but there are still vestiges of it here. The lights on the buildings along the street are reflected and magnified on the patches of snow still remaining and there are gas lamp posts at ten-yard intervals, all of it illuminating the broadsides plastered on every square inch of wall not taken up by windows. As he walks along, his shoulders hunched against a chill more imagined than real, the defense counsel glances up at them.

DOCTOR LICHTIE'S SALVE
Made From Buffalo Tallow & Healing Herbs
A perfect cure for skin disorders. Pimples! Erysipelas! Blotches!
Scald Head! Barber's Scratch! Corns! Itching Piles!
At All Drug Stores   15¢ A Bottle

The walls are covered with them. Vivid reds, blues, and greens. The copy is in boldface type, often ten inches high. Some have illustrations. A rearing horse, a mother and child. Some are risqué. There is a young and buxom lady in her underclothes:

DOCTOR WILSON'S MAGIC BELT FOR LADIES
Better than Quack Nostrums or Harsh Drugs!
Will positively cure Back, Stomach, and Intestinal Troubles!
Heart Disease! Dyspepsia! Indigestion! Malaria! Constipation!
Female Weakness! Menstrual Irregularities and Other Complaints
Peculiar To Women!!!!!!
Price $3.00

But they can amuse him for only a while. He is depressed and the feeling has not gone away with evening, although he has just finished a supper of baked ham and orange marmalade, with more than the usual two glasses of Jamaican rum before.

He had pumped Nelson Miles for more information about the damned affidavit, but nothing had been forthcoming. Of all the insane, self-centered, overblown-with-his-own-importance jackasses . . .

Coming across from the island, he had gone at once to the Grand Central Hotel. But it was exactly as he had expected. Elizabeth confined to her room and some goat-faced lackey barring his entry, saying she was asleep. Custer, of course, still suffering a loss of memory. Jacobson suspected that as soon as he was out of sight, the Golden Cavalier would bound off gaily for the Jockey Club or the theater.

There are more intrigues in this case, he thinks, than in the Arabian Navy. And I'm on the dry tit. What's even worse, it's expected that I perform like a monkey on a string as a favor to the firm and family of Bacon, with not a penny for my efforts.

He stands absently reading a garish poster. P. T. Barnum's Museum, with the freaks and midgets, live animals, and Oriental eunuchs. A vendor with his steaming cart passes along the sidewalk selling hot chestnuts and Jacobson buys a bag. Following the cart are two small boys, their long coats mostly rags, their shoes sizes too large and probably retrieved from the trash heap, their soft-billed caps pulled down over their eyes.

"Why'n cha share wid me and my sick brudder?" the larger boy challenges in a hard voice. Jacobson looks at them and buys two more bags. He hands them to the boys, but the older one snatches both the striped sacks.

"Watch ya han's, ya snot, ya'll get ya share."

They hurry off with no sort of "thank you" through a crowd of people just disgorged from a trolley. Jacobson watches them go as he munches the hot nuts, feeling the salty grit between his fingers.

Mary Adams. The Mary Adams affidavit, they're calling it—already in the *Evening Post* and certain to be in all the morning newspapers. What is Miles doing wrapped up in this thing? Something wrong, badly wrong. He wants to help Custer so much that his reason is out of whack. He could have given me the damned thing and I could have introduced it once I was sure it was on the square. But he had to do it himself. Take the limelight. The Army is full of these brilliant officers who can't seem to constrain the urge for strutting and scene-stealing . . . for appearing suddenly in the nick of time . . . each trying to outdo the next.

Elizabeth? She certainly would have known if that black woman had left Fort Lincoln with George. Of course she could have no knowledge of the conversation between Terry and Custer. But that cold? Had it come on so conveniently in order that she not be available to testify? A wife cannot be made to testify against her husband. But if she could verify the affidavit, her testimony would not be against George, but *for* him. So were she asked to take the stand and refused, most certainly the court would be other than human if it did not assume she was avoiding perjury.

And Custer himself? Perhaps he had forgotten one conversation—although that's doubtful—but certainly he would have recalled if that cook was with him on the expedition. So why hasn't he just told me, "Yes, she was there"?

And Terry! Right in the middle of this somehow. Could he have forgotten saying such a thing? Could he sincerely think, now, that Custer had disobeyed? Or had he simply ignored it in his effort to shift the blame for the disaster?

Mary Adams! Simple, intensely loyal to George Custer. Under the influence of a man dedicated to the cavalryman . . . How did she know what she was swearing to? She can't read!

His head is bursting with it. He stops before a brightly lighted theater, thinking, let Gardiner try to unravel it. He looks at the bright lights, the box office, the colorful playbills. On the sidewalk under the tattered marquee that identifies the place as the Bowery Theater, a man walks back and forth, the stump of an unlighted stogie in one corner of his mouth. He is swathed in a bright red blanket, his face is stained unevenly with walnut juice. Around his head is a beaded band holding a bedraggled turkey feather. He wears a sandwich sign:

BUFFALO BILL'S LAST SHOT
or
Doe Eye, The Lodge Queen
Thrilling, Sensational!   Hero of the Plains Battles Hordes
of Savage Indians!
25¢   25¢   25¢
Epic Tale of the Prairie by Major Wm. Burt

21

November 15. Miles on the stand, much more subdued. He wears the less flamboyant regulation blue now, with a double row of brass buttons down the front. Gardiner rises to indicate that he does not wish to cross-examine. He has been unsuccessful in locating what he needs to rebut the Mary Adams affidavit. Schofield is plainly irritated that Miles must be cautioned to remain available. Jacobson can hardly suppress a smile, feeling that perhaps his frustration and sense of foreboding have been without cause.

As Miles is excused, Major Winthrop calls the next witness. It creates a stir in the courtroom, and a number of newspaper reporters who have started out behind Miles quickly turn back to take their places. Schofield waits until the room is still.

"Colonel Custer," he says to the defendant, now standing rigidly before him. "I am required to explain your rights."

"I understand my rights, sir," Custer says, and his voice makes a high crack in the room. There are a few snickers in the rear.

"Nonetheless, I must explain them," Schofield says. He reads from a manual open on the table before him. "As the accused, you may remain silent. If you remain silent no inference may be drawn from it. You may make an unsworn statement upon which you may not be cross-examined. Or you may take the stand and be sworn and be cross-examined like any other witness. However, you may only be cross-examined on that evidence which you yourself testify to in direct examination."

Schofield closes the book and looks at Custer. "Do you understand these rights as the accused?"

"Yes, sir."

"And what is your decision?"

"I will testify under oath."

As the trial judge advocate administers the oath, Custer and Gardiner look directly into each other's eyes for one of the few times during the course of the trial. Jacobson moves in quickly, interposing himself with a quick shuffle between his client and the prosecutor.

"George, tell the court what happened on June 25, 1876."

"Our regiment had marched up the Rosebud River for some time, following a wide Indian trail. The trail turned west toward the Little Bighorn late on June 24 and was so fresh that I was concerned that the Sioux might discover us and escape if we proceeded farther south along the Rosebud as planned. Therefore, as the trail turned west, I directed the regiment to follow." He pauses and once more looks directly at Gardiner. "The written order of General Terry had given me wide latitude. It indicated clearly that if I saw reason to deviate from the plan, I should do so. As the commander on the scene, I felt strongly that I should follow the trail.

"What was perhaps more important, I saw that if I marched farther south before turning to the Little Bighorn, I would arrive late—if I could get there at all by the 26th, when Gibbon was due up, the regiment would be jaded. Therefore, I felt strongly—I ordered the regiment to follow the trail.

"From a high observation post on the morning of June 25, I was unable definitely to locate any village in the Little Bighorn valley. I had determined to rest the regiment that day, then strike toward the Little Bighorn on the 26th, in concert with Gibbon. But while we were at this high point observing, it came to my attention that we had been seen by the Sioux. I determined that we should immediately attack and engage the hostiles before they could escape to the southwest. I ordered the regiment forward.

"Benteen I sent to the left to prevent the Indians' escaping around that flank. Unfortunately, he wandered around in the Badlands, apparently lost for most of the day. He was entirely too far from the main body. Benteen never carried out my orders with dispatch. He always seemed to question my decisions. . . . May I have a glass of water, please?"

Jacobson has watched the trial judge advocate throughout the testimony and is satisfied with what he sees. Gardiner sits slumped in his chair, taking no notes, frowning as he seems to study the floor. It is no matter that Jacobson still smarts over the Mary Adams affidavit, he still has the best interests of his client at heart and he stands close to Custer always to lend moral support.

"Reno I kept in the center because if he is not watched closely, there is no telling how he will react to an order, no matter how clear-cut it is. I sent him straight forward across the river, instructing him to wheel right and attack—I expected the village to be exactly where it was, in fact. I expected him to charge the village with vigor, holding their warriors while I could strike in support. With my battalion on the right, I swung north, parallel to the river. Soon we heard the fight in the valley. I rode to the bluffs with my staff and saw the location of the village. Immediately I perceived that it should be struck in flank and that the possibility of such a move was obvious because there was a level ford some distance down river from where Reno was making his attack.

"I led the regiment across Medicine Tail Coulee. We had begun to take fire from the direction of the river. We saw a number of mounted warriors in that direction. We crossed two or three low ridges, and the fire against us was becoming intense. We rode down into another draw, much wider and not so deep as Medicine Tail. I swung the regiment toward the village. But within a short distance we could see masses of Sioux horsemen to our front. The fire was becoming hotter. Being in column, I could bring very little weight against my front so I turned to the north again, riding out of the draw to ground where the regiment could be deployed. But quite suddenly we were under heavy pressure."

Custer pauses, taking a linen handkerchief from his pocket and wiping his forehead, his mouth, and his moustache. He has begun to stutter ever so slightly.

"Riding out of the draw, I saw high ground to the north and slightly west. A little more than a mile away, I would guess. I made for that ground, for it was apparent that Reno had failed to push his attack and that we must defend ourselves until Gibbon arrived. The hostiles were in strength around us. Many were riding parallel to us and out of range, setting up their unholy howl. Nearer, mostly unseen, were dismounted warriors, shooting at us as we rode.

"The head of the column had started the long climb up the hill I had chosen to defend, when a great burst of firing broke out back along the line of march. I had already dropped off messengers to bring up my company commanders for orders. I had no way of knowing at the time—later I learned that the Sioux had struck the column hard, cutting it in two. The ambush had been so deadly that the trailing two companies—Keogh and Calhoun—had veered off to the right. That same pressure continued to eat away at the rear of Company E, and I am told that their dead were scattered for almost a mile up the approaches to the hill.

"As I came to the crest, officers and their runners were joining me. I discovered that we had a number of Company F troopers in the command group as well. Looking back along the route of march, I could see that most of that unit had been struck in flank, torn in half by Sioux and Cheyenne on horseback and on foot. What was left was still under violent attack. The dust was so thick we could see little, but it was obvious the entire column had been hit while on the march—from both sides. They were trying to fight their way to the crest. . . . They were fighting for their lives.

"Captain Yates was beside me and he was looking back down the slope. 'My God, General, they're slaughtering my company,' he said to me, and it was true. The slope between us and the river was swarming with mounted Indians, and having just passed that way ourselves, we knew there were at least that many more on foot in the brush and rocks."

Custer pauses once more, wipes his face, takes a deep breath. He is controlling himself well, although his pinched nostrils and the darkening blotches under his eyes indicate that he has still not recovered his normally robust health.

"Within a few seconds of crying out in anguish, Captain Yates was hit and fell mortally wounded. At about that time I saw Company I—Keogh's company—coming up along the south ridge that ran out from our position. We had some sniping, but mostly we were not under great pressure. . . . At first I had no idea who the riders were on the ridge. Then Lieutenant Cooke called that it was Keogh. It was then I realized the last two companies had been cut off and had taken a different route. . . . Keogh was in good order. He had not been hit hard on the march. He began to deploy his company.

"We saw his men dismount and horse holders start to the rear— he had his line facing east—when suddenly from that direction there was a great volley of fire and . . . I don't think the horse holders ever got back out of the firing line before they were hit. They were hitting Keogh hard from the east. My heart sank then. We never did see Company L. I've since learned they were badly butchered in column, scattering their dead over a wide area. . . .

"It had become very dusty, and we couldn't see how Captain Keogh's fight ended. We had our own trouble by then, anyway. Captain Custer had arrived earlier and had formed our group into a hollow square, after a fashion, horses in the center. Pressure increased sharply as the Indians crawled closer and delivered an intensive fire. The ground cover was good for them as they dashed closer. Then they made a number of forays on horseback. Many of our recruits were hit and crying for help. Doctor Lord was already down himself, but the other surgeons did what they could—until a few moments later when they took up weapons and joined the fight.

"Horses, even well trained, go mad in many instances when they are wounded. Lieutenant Cooke went about having all our horses shot, but he was down himself before the job was finished. Many of our horses bolted out of the circle and were immediately caught by Sioux rising up out of the brush and catching their reins. The crest of the hill was absolute bedlam. Within a few moments, all were using their pistols, hot cases jammed in the breeches of the carbines. My own revolvers were so hot I could hardly reload them. As our number decreased, a few of the bolder warriors tried to ride in and use lances. They were closing in tight around us and they must have hit one another with their fire on many occasions. . . ."

He stops and breathes deeply, his forehead beaded with moisture. His pale eyes seem to protrude and they have turned glassy.

"I was struck in the thigh. A hard blow. I felt no pain, however. It was a sudden shock—I was seated on the ground against a dead horse, firing a pistol. I became dizzy and had difficulty holding the gun up. Then I was hit in the head, and I recall being knocked back by the force of the ball. That was all I could—that is all I can remember of the fight."

The courtroom is deathly silent, everyone leaning forward except Gardiner, who continues to stare at the floor. Jacobson waits, allowing Custer to catch his breath and to wipe his face once more. He

LT. COL. GEORGE ARMSTRONG CUSTER

speaks gently. "George, do you remember how long the fight lasted?"

"It went on for some time. From the first shots fired against us in the coulee through the fight at the crest. I suppose our fight was the last to be finished. Keogh couldn't have lasted long. From the time we saw him until I was hit in the head, I'd say it was twenty minutes, but I don't know how long the fight went on after. . . ."

He has controlled his stammer well through most of it, but now the words seem to struggle to get out. He is aware of the affliction and it upsets him. Jacobson allows him plenty of time to control himself.

"One more thing, George. What do you recall after the fight?"

"I was vaguely aware of someone pulling off my pants and underwear," Custer says. "The sun was down. It was near dark. But light enough to see. My eyes were full of caked blood. I felt nothing. I suppose it was a woman undressing me, scavenging the battlefield. I recall nothing after that until I was wakened by the cold. My wounds hurt me terribly by then. There were animals around—

wolves I suppose—among the dead. I had good sensibility in my hands. There was a canteen beside me, I assume placed there by one of the lads before he was . . . I drank a little."

He bends his head and brushes his hand across his moustache a number of times. He is obviously strongly moved by the memory.

"I regained my senses the next day. Midday, I suppose. The battle-field was empty. I was dizzy. I recall thinking the crows would eat me alive. I have no idea why they and the buzzards . . . it was a miracle! A true miracle!

"Late in the day I woke again. My skin was on fire with sunburn. I may have taken more water. I don't know. I recall nothing more until I woke on the *Far West* with two of General Terry's fine sur-geons bending over me."

"Thank you, George. Your witness," Jacobson says. He returns to the front of his table and remains standing there, bent slightly forward.

As though on a single string, heads in the courtroom turn toward the trial judge advocate as he rises slowly. He does not move out into the bull ring, but remains behind his table, hands resting lightly on it.

"Colonel Custer, did General Terry ever indicate to you that you could follow the trail when it turned west if you saw fit?"

"I object," Jacobson cuts in quickly before his witness can an-swer. "He has not testified to oral instructions."

"Sustained."

"Colonel Custer, according to the written order from General Terry, was it not clear that he desired you to go farther south along the Rosebud in order that you come up south of any Indian village on the Little Bighorn?"

"His order stated that he desired I do that, but he also said he trusted my judgment and that if I saw sufficient reason I could de-viate from it," Custer says. As he replies, he looks at the members of the court, avoiding Gardiner's eyes.

"Colonel Custer, why did you not make a reconnaissance of the Little Bighorn valley to determine size and location of the enemy force before you committed your regiment?"

"It was my command decision! I made it on the ground, in ac-cordance with my best judgment. I was concerned with speed of movement. No matter what was there, I felt I had to attack in order to prevent them escaping. Quickly."

"Why did you not instruct Benteen and Reno more thoroughly in your plan?"

"They are soldiers of experience. I do not expect to have to provide volumes of instructions for experienced officers."

"Did you see Reno's fight when you were on the bluffs?"

"Objection. Not addressed in direct examination."

"Sustained."

"Did you see the Indian village from the bluffs?"

"Yes. I have testified that I did."

"Do you honestly think a force of less than 150 troopers could successfully charge a village of that magnitude?"

"Of course." His voice is becoming squeaky and his stammer is pronounced. "If Reno had put the pressure on them, holding them, I could have cut through them from the flank."

"You have said you expected to find the Indians in that valley—in fact you found them where you expected to find them. Why, then, did you split your command into four units—in which, I would point out, the train had more soldiers with it than did Reno's battalion?"

"It was a command decision. In Indian country, Major, you must protect your trains. As to the formation, not knowing an enemy's exact location, you will often use a formation of battalions on line. That formation sweeps a wide area. From it, a regiment can deploy in any number of ways to meet the situation as it develops."

"Apparently you did not discover the right way."

"I object," Jacobson shouts, bounding out into the bull ring.

"Sustained," Schofield says. "Major Gardiner, save your summations for closing argument."

"You had said you would support Reno's battalion. You gave him to understand that you would support him, did you not?"

"I object," Jacobson says, still in the center of the room.

"No, I will take that, Mr. Jacobson. I think the witness did imply as much," Schofield says.

"Yes, I told Reno I would support him. When he was ordered to attack."

"But you did not support him."

"I made every effort, and if he followed out his orders . . ."

"But you failed to support him, isn't that true?" Gardiner is around the table now, advancing on Custer.

"How could I support him——"

"You left him and those men of his to die in that valley, and they all would have died there for your efforts, would they not have, Colonel Custer? Isn't it true, Colonel Custer? Had Reno not taken an initiative, would his men not be dead, all of them, along with those troopers who accompanied you?"

"*I object.*" Jacobson stumbles over and stands before his witness. "This is unthinkable. This man is trying to make General Custer admit errors that rightfully fall on his subordinates."

"Sustained. Major Gardiner, I think your attitude and manner here are completely uncalled for," Schofield says.

Gardiner heaves a sigh and throws out his arms. "All right, I am finished with him," he says. Obviously glad it is over, Jacobson extends his hand to Custer as the cavalryman comes off the stand. It was better than I thought it would be, he thinks. Much better. All that fine bravery and almost nothing bearing on the charges against him. George may be many things, but he is not a stupid man. Jacobson turns and smiles at Gardiner.

"The defense rests."

22

With Custer's story finished, many of the newspaper reporters dash out of the courtroom. They are the evening paper correspondents who want to ensure that the account of what happened on Custer Hill gets into this day's news even though it means they may miss something to follow. The reporters for the morning papers sit and curse the timing.

In the hubbub, only a few people notice that one of Gardiner's assistants comes into the building and hurries to the trial counsel table. Jacobson's smile turns sour as he sees the three officers talking quietly, their heads together.

"Very well, Major, are we going to get on with the trial?" Schofield asks testily. Gardiner rises, and now for the first time Jacobson sees he holds a paper in his hand.

"Sir, I have a document to be placed in rebuttal," he says.

As the document is marked prosecution exhibit H, Jacobson shakes his head. He cannot help but admire Gardiner's tactic. He had that damned thing all along, he thinks, whatever it is. As a rebutting statement it will stand out like Custer's nose!

"Major Gardiner, will you read your deposition into the record?" Schofield asks. He hands a copy to Jacobson, who now sees that Lieutenant Beakin is passing out a copy to each member of the press.

"Mr. President, what is happening here?" he asks, pointing toward Beakin.

"Mr. President, it is an open court." Gardiner smiles. "Why make the gentlemen of the press copy all of this?"

"I see nothing objectionable, Mr. Jacobson."

Jacobson sits down as Gardiner begins to speak.

"If it please the court. During the preliminary investigation on this case, both I and my assistants took depositions from a great many persons involved with the 7th Cavalry in the campaign of 1876. Much has not been used because it is repetitious or irrelevant. When Colonel Miles introduced what is now being called the Mary Adams affidavit, the name recalled a deposition taken by Lieutenant Beakin at Fort Lincoln last year. We have found that document and present it now in rebuttal to the said affidavit."

Schofield waits without a word, and Gardiner reads.

"Deposition of William S. McCaskey, Captain, 20th Infantry, Fort Abraham Lincoln, Dakota Territory.

"Being duly sworn, respondent testifies as follows:

"I was in command of Fort Lincoln during the absence of the Terry expedition in the spring of 1876. At about 1 A.M. on July 6, the riverboat *Far West* pulled into the Fort Lincoln dock, having already stopped at Bismarck about six miles to the north. When the boat had tied up. Lieutenant C. L. Gurley, the officer of the day, brought to me Captain Edwin Smith, General Terry's staff adjutant. He informed me of the disaster on the Little Bighorn and said that as soon as it was light, he would require assistance in moving the wounded to the station hospital. He informed me of General Custer's condition and said he would be among the first moved.

"I called the officers of the post together and gave them the information I had. I asked the post surgeon, Doctor J. V. Middleton, and the officer of the day to accompany me to the quarters of General Custer for the purpose of informing the women. By that time it was about 5 A.M. and getting light.

"We arrived at the rear of the Custer home and there woke the housemaid, Mary Adams, telling her to wake her mistress and to go collect the other 7th Cavalry officers' wives. Soon most of the women had gathered in the Custer drawing room and I gave them the news of the disaster. Mrs. Custer at first consoled her sister-in-

law, Mrs. Calhoun. She then asked that we gather the sergeants'
wives and inform them of the sad news as well. Taking a light
shawl, she then went to the station hospital, escorted by Lieutenant Gurley.

"Further respondent saith not.

"Signed William S. McCaskey.

"Taken before me this 19th day of October, 1876, Fort A.
Lincoln, Dakota Territory, Lieutenant George Beakin, Adjutant
Generals' Corps, Summary Court Officer."

For a long time the room is silent as General Schofield studies
his copy of the document.

"There can be no doubt it is the same woman?"

"No, sir."

"I see. Do you desire now to cross-examine Colonel Miles?"

Gardiner indicates that he does, and once again Miles marches
in to take the stand.

"By this time, sir, I realize that you probably feel like a rather
large shuttlecock, going back and forth . . ." The laughter interrupts Gardiner's comment and Miles flushes. ". . . meaning no
offense, sir. I have given you a copy of this document, have I not?
And you have read it, have you not?"

"I still object to this passing out of documents to everyone,"
Jacobson starts, but he knows before he is finished it is of no use.

"My dear Mr. Jacobson," Gardiner protests, "it was you, I believe, who gave this witness a copy of General Terry's order before
he appeared in direct examination. The prosecution did not want
him to feel slighted."

Laughter once more interrupts him and Schofield tries not to smile.

"Colonel Miles, sir," Gardiner says, turning to the witness. "In
the light of this document, how do you now view the so-called
Mary Adams affidavit?"

"I am still inclined to accept it."

"You do not believe the sworn deposition of an officer in the
United States Army?"

"I am not saying that at all. I believe the Mary Adams affidavit.
She could have left the *Far West* as soon as it docked at Fort Lincoln and been in the Custer home when this"—he waves the document—"officer arrived there."

"Of course, but while we are supposing, is it likely, Colonel Miles, that this housemaid, after being away from Mrs. Custer for a long period, would return in the wee hours and tuck herself into bed without a single word to her mistress about the terrible disaster that had occurred?"

For a long time Miles sits mute, staring at Gardiner. He has made himself another enemy I would not like to have, Jacobson thinks.

"I believe the affidavit."

"No more questions," Gardiner says. Jacobson shakes his head. Get him out, out, out as fast as possible.

Schofield waits until Miles has passed from the room before he addresses the trial counsel. "Major, do you feel we should recall General Terry?"

"I see no reason for it at all," Gardiner says.

"It is your decision. It is your rebuttal."

"It is unnecessary."

Schofield scratches his whiskers, frowning.

"Very well. I don't know about other members of the court. But I need time to digest some of this. I must say, it is unusual for the advocates in a case to balk at certain points as these two have done."

"Mr. President, I suggest your comments are prejudicial and I move the charges be dismissed," Jacobson says.

Schofield stares incredulously at the crippled Michigan lawyer. "Mr. Jacobson, don't try my patience. Now. As I was about to say, does the prosecution have any other rebuttal witnesses?"

"The government does not," Gardiner says.

"Very well, gentlemen. We will hear arguments tomorrow. I will set no time limit on you, but try to be reasonable. The court is recessed until 9 A.M."

Jacobson leans back in his chair, toying with his open jackknife. It feels fairly good! I may not have gotten all of them, but I suspect most will remember the powder smoke on that hill and ignore Gardiner's deposition.

Holding the document by one corner, he slices neatly through it with the sharp edge of the blade.

23

The sun is out and the blanket of snow begins to disappear. By afternoon none will be left except along sheltered walls facing north. On Governor's Island the air is crisp, smelling of salt and fish. With the court opening one hour later than usual, the sun is up and only light mufflers are needed by the time the courtroom fills for the final act in the drama that began over a year ago on the Greasy Grass.

Although Schofield has managed to maintain an even pace throughout the trial, the tension has built up, and among the regular spectators there is a feeling of personal involvement. They are subdued—even the press people—as they file past the provost guards. Many have changed a little during the trial. Some came hating Custer and now are not sure why. Others came adoring him, but have been shocked as the veneer was peeled back here and there to reveal a different man from the one they thought they knew. But regardless of whether they are for or against him, all have been caught up in the almost mystic attraction of the man. There is no denying that simply by sitting there, running his fingers back through his hair from time to time, in some strange way Custer draws the eye, the mind—creates affection or hatred.

Today Custer shows his old flair for upstaging. He enters late, wearing a beautifully handworked buckskin jacket, somewhat like those worn by officers on frontier service, but much more elaborately fringed. He wishes as he strides down the aisle. Across each shoulder of his tailored jacket he wears his insignia boards—and today they show the silver leaf of a lieutenant colonel against a background of cavalry yellow. About his neck Custer wears a yellow silk bandana. The sunburn and peeling skin on his nose, so obvious on the first day of the trial, have disappeared completely, but as he passes down the aisle a number of people suspect he has rouged his cheeks to create the wind-beaten color that was there when he led his troops on the Plains.

Elizabeth's place is still unoccupied. As always, Custer has arrived in court with a retinue of New York friends, but today the party is larger than usual. One of the women is a famous actress whose name Gardiner cannot recall. Jacobson, bending over his notes and wearing a pair of small wire-rimmed spectacles, pays no attention as his client arrives.

Schofield raps for order and the courtroom becomes still.

"All parties to the trial who were present when the court was recessed are now present," Gardiner intones.

Opening argument is reserved for the government, followed by defense summation, followed by prosecution rebuttal. In practice, opening argument is usually waived, and it comes as no surprise to anyone—least of all Jacobson—when Gardiner expresses no desire to open. Immediately the big man from Michigan, his lame foot dragging awkwardly, moves into the bull ring, positioning himself squarely before the president of the court. He has slipped his glasses back into a vest pocket, and his cheek does not bulge with tobacco. He bows and smiles, looking directly at each member of the court in turn.

"Gentlemen. Almost eighteen months ago, on a dusty, barren plain, this man led his command into battle under the flag of his country, as he had so often done before." Without turning he extends an arm back toward Custer, palm up.

"It was a fateful Sunday as he rode down into that broad valley. A Sunday that will be recorded forever among the tragic milestones of our history. Because the battle was lost that day."

He walks over and stares for a moment at the map of the battlefield behind the witness stand, then turns once more to face the court.

"A tragic day because the battle was lost. But doubly tragic because it was lost through neglect. *Our* neglect, gentlemen. For we sent this brave man and his troops into mortal combat with untrained men, untrained horses, with faulty weapons and spavined pack mules. But we did worse! We sent them to that fight without giving them the vital information they needed for their task."

Jacobson pauses, looking slowly around the room, as though everyone in the building is a juror. His eyes finally come to rest on Custer, who stares back at him unblinking, his head held high.

"A sad result, gentlemen, destined by our own miserly short-sightedness—and the complete and utter confidence we had always placed in this man and his ability to do anything on a field of combat."

He walks the width of the room, turning finally at the windows opening toward Manhattan. There he pauses once more, looking about, challenging everyone with his eyes.

"But then the awful butcher's bill arrived, and we suddenly were sickened and afraid, and we discovered a dreadful need within ourselves to salve our consciences. We had to find someone to blame! We had to have a scapegoat! And, gentlemen—there he sits." His finger stabs toward Custer and continues to point as he speaks. "A man who, because of his fame, has made powerful enemies, political and military! Can you doubt it after the parade of witnesses who have come here to vilify him? Can you deny it after the sly attacks in the newspapers? Can you deny it after reflecting for a moment on the high and mighty? Sherman—who first cast doubt! Sheridan—who consented to let his old comrade go to the block! Terry—who on second thought accused him!

"And so he was charged. The man who for years has been your darling. The man who for years has been the public hero." He walks over and places a hand on Custer's shoulder. "And charged with what, gentlemen? With disobeying! For having a newspaper reporter in his command."

He glances back at the press gallery.

"Yet the government could not prove Mark Kellogg went along at the bidding of this man. All it could prove was that Kellogg died and that, in fact, Terry had issued the invitation. Kellogg or anyone else could have slipped into the column as it left the Yellowstone on June 21, unbeknownst to a busy commander.

"Charged with what, gentlemen? With disobeying Terry's order, an order you have seen is discretionary. Discretionary! I need not explain to you, gentlemen, what that means. It means the commander in the field makes the final decision."

Jacobson leaves his place near Custer and walks again to the bench, where he stands close to the members of the court, looking at their faces, bending toward them. But even though he is close, he speaks loudly, clearly, so that no one in the room has any difficulty hearing what he says.

"Charged with what, gentlemen? With neglect. He made no proper reconnaissance, the government contends! He posted no security, the government contends! He did not make his orders to subordinates specific enough, the government contends! Gentlemen, if Reno had pressed his charge—if Benteen had not gone too far to the left—if the Sioux had been routed—would we be here accusing this man of those charges? You are soldiers. You have been on many battlefields. You have made decisions there. Could anyone make them for you? Of course not! The commander must make them—based on *his* judgment! Based on *his* duty! If we take away the commander's prerogative today, does it mean that henceforward, officers beware? Are we going to set the precedent of loading our commanders down with responsibility and at the same time strip them of authority?"

He takes a deep breath and wipes his eyes with his fingertips. He is beginning to sweat.

"Charged with what, gentlemen? Political ambition creating prejudice to good order. What does that mean? In your wisdom, what does it mean? I have come here, a civilian far out of touch with your Army, but I had hoped during the course of the trial that someone would explain what that charge means. I still do not know! And where is the proof of any political ambition? More importantly, where is the proof that any such ambition—if it did exist—affected this man's decisions at the Little Bighorn?"

Jacobson throws out his arms and lets them flop back at his sides. He backs away from the bench slowly.

"Examine these charges, gentlemen. Those which are militarily criminal have not been proven. The rest are nothing more than the slander of an officer's judgment on the field of battle. They are combat decisions, made by the man responsible for making them and after the fact branded criminal because the battle was lost. We, who have never set foot on that field, are here to judge those decisions! We, who sit comfortably on Governor's Island eighteen months after that dreadful afternoon! Is that how we judge military decisions in battle? From two thousand miles away in space and eighteen months in time? We may criticize, oh, yes, gentlemen—but judge?"

He stamps over to his table and leans against it for a moment, not looking at notes, but seeming to rest his eyes as he holds his fingertips against his forehead. As he faces about, he does not look at the court, but at Gardiner.

"If we are to begin trying our generals for failures—for losing battles and men's lives—why have we started only now? Why have we suddenly started to make criminals of commanders who have done their duty but have failed somehow? Why do we start with this man, who won so many of our battles, but finally, through the neglect and ineffectiveness of others, finally lost a fight?"

He walks to the bench once more, a hand out in supplication.

"We did not court-martial Burnside after Fredericksburg. How many soldiers did we lose? About ten thousand? We did not court-martial McClellan when he failed to take Richmond and with terrible loss."

There is not a person in the room who is not aware that two of the members of the court had dismal defeats at First and Second Manassas—McDowell and Pope. They sit now, stony-faced.

"And what of the great slaughters? Grant at the Wilderness, Spotsylvania, Cold Harbor? Or McClellan again, at Antietam? We lost ten thousand men in a single day. Is the rule 'Win and there is no matter the blood cost—lose and we hang the commander'? Is that what we are doing here, is that what is happening, is that the terrible precedent we are establishing? Why do we bring this man to account, when we did not all the others from the beginning of our history?"

He waves his fist above his head.

"Do we say to our battle leaders, 'Win! Or you will be branded a criminal!' Do we tell them, 'If you lose horses and men, no matter how hostile to life a battlefield may be, we will imprison you!'"

Jacobson turns again to Custer, moves behind him, and places both hands on the cavalryman's shoulders.

"How can we accuse this man of fault on the battlefield? Was it not we who time after time thrust the responsibility into his hands, and was it not he who time after time brought home the victory to us?"

He slowly drags his crippled foot into the center of the bull ring, shaking his head sadly as he moves. He twists and stares at Custer, a small smile on his lips. He nods.

"Yes. Take it, we said." He thrusts both hands toward Custer. "*Take it!* Take the responsibility."

He straightens and looks at the court.

"What is to become of military discipline indeed, when we bring our former heroes after their first defeat before a bar of justice and accuse them with charges dredged up from petty hatred and jealousy, charges happily agreed to by those who would profit if they could point the blame elsewhere and sworn to by every malcontent and sluggard this brave man has ever offended—offended by trying to see that his duty was done. No, gentlemen, the prejudice to good order will be done today, in this courtroom, if by a finding of guilty you show to our citizens, to our leaders, to our newspapers, to our military officers, and to all the world, that in the United States when a god falls, we let loose the tigers to devour him!"

Jacobson stands for a moment before the court, his arms outstretched, his face gleaming with moisture. Then he drops his hands, lowers his head, and turns to his table. The sound of his dragging foot is loud in the silent room.

24

___

Unlike Jacobson, Gardiner stands behind his table throughout the summation, speaking clearly and distinctly—rather slowly—his fingertips resting lightly on the surface before him, and not once looking at Custer.

"If it please the court. At the outset, I am compelled to state an unpleasant fact of which I am sure you have all become aware during the course of this trial—if you were not aware of it before. Lieutenant Colonel George Armstrong Custer has enjoyed too long in the Army and among the public a reputation as our most able cavalry leader. Unfortunately that reputation has been established largely by an over-exuberant press, generally misinformed as to the true nature of this man and, I suspect, willing to overlook gross inadequacies in order to perpetrate a myth of their own making.

"It is most dangerous! For Custer himself has begun to believe it. But he is not our most able cavalry leader." Gardiner looks squarely at MacKenzie. "As a leader, Custer is monstrously inadequate! Through sheer good luck he has time after time blundered through what would seem impossible situations—situations brought on by his own impetuous, brash, and unthinking spasms of action. His victories have almost always been the result of high-velocity, blind movement against enemies whose chief characteristic has been that they were even less aware of the situation than was Custer. The time has now come when we must resolve that the lives of our soldiers and the good name of the Army can no longer be trusted to the antic convulsions of what has to be a demented mind."

The effect on the courtroom is instant. There is a gasp and then loud muttering. Schofield bangs his cue ball against the bench. Gardiner can feel the hostile glares of the press gallery against his back. Custer, too, is looking at him, head up, neck extended. He has the startled look of a turkey gobbler peering over a log.

"It has been said here in defense of Custer that, due to the fault of others, his unit was ill prepared at the Little Bighorn. How terribly concerned he must have been! He absented himself from the regiment during the most critical times of its training!

"In the history of war, I doubt if there has ever been a commander who went into battle completely satisfied with the condition of his troops, his arms, his equipment, his animals. Yet go into battle a commander must. And use intelligently what he has. No matter what other name you may place upon it, what we are concerned with here is whether George Armstrong Custer did indeed use his resources intelligently. Or did he squander them through his own brashness? Did he waste them by his headlong dash to be alone at the kill? Did he allow them to be plundered because he was so eaten with the greed for recognition that he had to plunge in—no matter what the odds? No matter what the cost? From the evidence presented here, you know he *was* impetuous. He *was* brash. He was greedy for the kill—extremely so, in fact. For if he felt his command inadequate to the task, would that not have been all the more reason for any prudent man to survey the battlefield before plunging onto it?

"Did Custer survey the battlefield? Did he look at it carefully? He gave it hardly a second glance before he flung five hundred men against a force of thousands—thousands of well-armed warriors. And . . . more than half of those soldiers were destroyed—killed. Butchered!

"They have told you he was misinformed. If he was—and we have presented evidence which suggests strongly that the Army knew, and that Custer knew, there were a great many more hostiles out there than the Indian Bureau would admit—but if indeed he was misinformed, and uncertain of what he faced, is that not all the more reason a commander should proceed cautiously? Does it not compel a commander to see for himself what is there? And did he attempt to see for himself? Did he make the slightest effort to assess the enemy or the terrain? He did not! He did not know where high ground was! He did not know where fords on the river were! He did not know the size of the village or its location! He did not know the village was making no move to escape! In short, he knew nothing! He simply lowered his head and rode in. If that is not neglect of a commander's recognized duty, then there is no such thing!

"We have heard it said that in the formation Custer adopted in this headlong thrust, there was the best possibility of reacting to any eventuality—a statement which events disproved most dramatically. How could any commander in control of his senses suppose that he could concentrate a regiment after it had been split in four parts, dispatched beyond signaling distance of each other? After Benteen left the main body, there was but one way to reach him—by mounted courier. After the pack train had left the main body, there was but one way to communicate with it—by mounted courier. After Reno and Custer parted, there was but one way to signal between them—mounted courier. Is this how a regiment of cavalry is quickly massed for attack against a superior foe? So badly split that it could only be concentrated again after hard-riding messengers on jaded horses had stumbled over miles of unfamiliar terrain? What did Custer expect the Sioux to be doing while he assembled his troops? Smoking?"

There is not a murmur of laughter—nor any other sound. Gardiner pours himself a glass of water and drinks it slowly. Then, equally deliberately, he takes a handkerchief from his pocket, wipes his lips, and replaces it. Every member of the court watches him closely, but Custer now looks straight ahead, pulling his head down into his collar. He stares at Schofield's boots and scowls, the muscles along his jaw working visibly.

"It has been hinted here that the newspaper reporter killed with Custer's battalion slipped into the column unknown to Custer. If that be the case, it is another example of neglect—for a commander is supposed to know what is happening in his unit. Here is a civilian, well known to Custer, attaching himself to the regiment, and we are told Custer was unaware of his presence? What was Kellogg doing, hiding in one of the bread boxes?

"I have no intention of dwelling on the disobedience to General Terry's order because it is obvious. Regardless of all else, Terry told Custer to go south of where the Indian trail might leave the valley of the Rosebud. But he did not. He followed it immediately. Before he had any evidence of being discovered! Immediately! And thus destroyed the very foundation of Terry's plan. Custer disobeyed, and no amount of rhetoric concerning discretionary wording can change that fact. Custer disobeyed before the time Terry had allowed his discretion.

"Custer disobeyed intentionally and with forethought. Do not forget what he told Colonel Ludlow on the streets of St. Paul—that he would swing free of Terry just as he had done from Stanley years before."

Gardiner pauses, but he remains where he is, leaning forward slightly, his head still as his eyes move back and forth along the line of court members.

"And now, ambition. Of which a great general has said Custer has only the required amount. I cannot help but wonder, if General Sheridan agreed with this court-martial, why did he appear in Custer's behalf? But that is a mystery only you can resolve. The ambition of Custer is no mystery. An Army officer who elected himself the public prosecutor of a Secretary of War. A man who for years has strained to keep himself in the public eye—even to writing of his own exploits for publication. Instantly leaping to any controversy in the press. Using a great newspaper to criticize a court-martial finding. Using another to try to pressure a President of the United States to change his decision and reinstate him to his command. What but blind ambition drives a soldier to so violate the chain of command, to so ignore the courtesies of the service?

"There was an election coming, in the fall of that very year when he rode up the Rosebud. What better way to attract attention than to defeat the mighty Sioux—singlehandedly? And, as General Sheridan tried to convince us, if his ambition was solely for military position, what better way to impress superiors than with a victory over the mighty Sioux—singlehandedly?"

For the first time Gardiner raises one hand, clenched into a fist.

"As surely as one man becomes intoxicated on whiskey, so the next may become drunk on his own overpowering aspirations, on his sense of infallibility—even his attorney called him a god! We do not condone forfeiture of the lives of soldiers on the altar of a commander's worship of the grape—should we allow our men to be slaughtered as they follow the dictates of a commander's ambition?"

Gardiner lowers his clenched fist, and with his palms on the table leans far forward, toward the court.

"Each of these charges should be a clear signal to this court. The signal that Custer is dangerous! That the Army must rid itself of a commander who will squander troops! The bones of every soldier buried on those lonely hills above the Little Bighorn rise up from their shallow graves and cry out against him, and they shout, '*No more!*'"

He slams the tabletop with the flat of his hand.

"No more war emperor's palaces on the Missouri, kept by enlisted men! No more conceit! No more brutality! No more horse killer! No more of this—bragging, strutting, primping, preening peacock! No more Custer."

He strikes the table again and the water glass bounces off onto the floor, somehow does not break, and rolls noisily into the center of the bull ring. Gardiner straightens and takes a deep breath.

"Custer is guilty. He is guilty in fact and in spirit! I do not ask you to be vindictive. We are not accusing him of losing a battle. We are accusing him of being inept in the use of men's lives. There are 14 officers and 233 men lying in their graves now in Montana, and the Sioux and Cheyenne did not kill them. Custer did. I ask you, find him guilty. Thank you."

For an instant there is total silence in the room except for the puffing of the stoves. Then a collective sigh.

Schofield raps gently, appearing to come out of a deep reverie. "Thank you, gentlemen—Mr. Jacobson, Major Gardiner. The court will be closed."

There is an explosion of activity and a babble of voices as the people rise and start toward the door. The court quickly disappears into the rear of the building. Custer's party collects about him and they slowly move up the aisle behind the crowd. Major Winthrop is with them, but Jacobson remains at his table, whittling off a chew now and looking out the windows toward New York. Gardiner and his two young associates remain, too, until the room is clear, and then they hurry out as well. Jacobson sits alone in the great room, leaning back, slowly chewing.

25

The court must vote on each charge and specification after whatever argument they may have amongst themselves. Everyone is sure that the process will consume the rest of the day and that perhaps a verdict will not be forthcoming until Saturday. Many go back to Manhattan for lunch, expecting to return later.

Solomon Buckley of the *Herald* walks calmly down to the slip and boards the ferry, aware that most of the other reporters will do as he plans. He will report to his office, write in longhand his account of the arguments, have a short lunch of Welsh rabbit, a few ounces of brandy to ensure against the unpredictable whims of New York weather in November, and return to Governor's Island by mid-afternoon. In his newsroom his schedule is somewhat disrupted by other members of the staff on duty, who crowd around and ask questions. Soon there are bets being laid, the odds running eight to five for conviction. An editorial writer sits down to pen tomorrow's front-page blast to the effect that Custer has been shanghaied by high brass, Grant-lovers, and other malevolent Republicans.

On Governor's Island, Gardiner strolls about, unwilling to socialize with anyone, including his two assistants. He stands for a long time on the south ramparts of Fort Columbus, looking out toward the Narrows, and becomes chilled from the cold wind that is picking up as the day wears on. He has been informed by the provost sergeant that Custer and some of his friends have begun a card game in the guard room.

What outrageous confidence. Playing poker while a group of officers, some decidedly unfriendly, deliberate on one's future. For Gardiner knows that if this court finds for conviction, the Army will never be the same again for George Armstrong Custer. They might cashier him—but that is doubtful. Something less than that, but even so it would be ruinous. This time Sheridan would not be rushing off to Washington to have his favorite reinstated so that the Golden Cavalier might lead the charge into some snow-swept Cheyenne village, as had happened in 1868. This time Sherman waits like a fox at the hen coop, no longer sympathetic to the hero of a hundred battles—so the newspapers claim, but Gardiner knows Custer's real fights can be counted on the fingers of a man's two hands. Already command of his beloved 7th Cavalry has been given over to Wesley Merritt, who is truly one of the Army's best.

What a blow that must have been! Gardiner has never commanded a combat unit and he finds it difficult to imagine the emotions connected with such a relationship between a man and a military unit. He has seen it frequently—the moist eye, the stiffening lower lip when an old regiment is mentioned. The very passage of the colors of an outfit of long-ago association could cause speechlessness in hardened veterans. Now it was Custer's time to face the fact that he was no longer leader of the "Garry Owen" regiment.

The 7th Cavalry had been formed immediately after the Civil War to police the Indian frontier. Actually, it had been used extensively on occupation duty in the South. But the frontier and the Indians and the 7th and Custer—they had all gone together in people's minds. It is hard even for me, Gardiner thinks, to imagine the regiment without him. Even after these weeks of stripping away the facade . . . How devastating it must be for him.

Gardiner truly does not know—cannot guess—how the court will find. He knows what it should find, if there is any justice. Or if the Army is to benefit. Custer has to be judged guilty and removed from any position that would ever allow him to command troops. God help us if that doesn't happen, Gardiner thinks.

He thinks of Sherman, sitting in that great chair in the office of the Commanding General of the Army, frowning, his eyes cold, jaws bristling with the wheat-stubble beard that is turning white. If this court does not do it, Gardiner thinks, then Sherman is the Army's last chance. He must destroy Custer if the court-martial does not.

Somehow the thought that Sherman is waiting makes Gardiner feel better. Yet it disturbs him that, even though convinced of Custer's guilt, he can think in terms of "destroying" another officer. Well, he muses, there are brutal solutions to brutal problems.

Once again, his thinking about the trial ends with Elizabeth. It is a disquieting thought—that Elizabeth Custer had intentionally avoided the courtroom in order to be unavailable as a witness to establish the truth of the Mary Adams affidavit. It would have assured her husband's acquittal on at least one charge. So, he thinks, if she was indeed avoiding the opportunity to testify, it could only mean she *knew* the document was a fake.

But of course she had nothing to do with creating the fake deposition. He shakes his head, frowning. Of course not!

Well, he thinks, she needn't have worried. I took care of it for her. Of all things that happened in the trial, that I feel best about. I discredited that damned Mary Adams affidavit and I hope Nelson Miles chokes on it. But still, it makes Elizabeth look bad, and I'm somehow disappointed. Yet what else is a wife expected to do? What is the least she can do but refuse to show herself in an embarrassing situation?

Gardiner descends the parapet and walks back toward the courtroom. He walks across the parade ground and through the west sally port and on toward the old mess hall that has been the scene for this trial. He looks at the building, thinking of the members of the court deliberating there. He can imagine the junior member—Colonel Sykes—tearing paper into small ballots, passing them around. And after arguments and discussions, each officer marking his ballot "guilty" or "not guilty." Passing the slips, now folded, back to Sykes, who counts them off, aloud, everyone keeping tab.

Gardiner is suddenly very cold and he hurries on into the vestibule. A provost guard opens the door for him and he enters the courtroom. As he walks forward, he sees Jacobson still at his place, apparently asleep.

But Jacobson is not napping. He is too hungry to sleep, and besides, he is playing a guessing game about the members of the court. He is guessing who will vote for conviction, who for acquittal. Now and again his jaw moves quickly on the cud bulging in his cheek.

Behind his closed eyelids he visualizes each member. Sykes, an infantryman, tough, high-principled. A veteran combat leader. He'll go for conviction. So will MacKenzie, with his cold stare and the hands constantly clasping and unclasping on the bench.

Chris Augur, his whiskers like a white cloud around his jaws, he might go either way. But he's smart—slow but smart, and he can recognize the consequences of such a trial's going against the officer who has lost a battle.

The preacher and psalm-singer, O. O. Howard, one-armed, mean. But with years of hard experience and an Army man first and always. He would vote not guilty. He's stringy as baked buzzard, but the Army will come first and he'll think the Army can survive Custer, or any other mortal man.

My favorites, Jacobson thinks: Pope and McDowell! How could either of them vote guilty after I put them right on the block with Custer? And for once, even McDowell got the point. I thought they'd squirm out of their seats when I started yelling about outrageous casualties that gained nothing. I think they actually felt indebted to me for not mentioning their names outright. Not guilty, without a doubt.

And Schofield? Jacobson smiles to himself. Nobody could guess how he'd go, it was a good bet. And I don't know how much he'll influence the others, he thinks. But there has to be a two-thirds guilty vote for conviction, and that means five of them will have to say thumbs down to George, and I don't think there are that many who will. Also a good bet, he thinks.

Jacobson rouses as the rear door opens and Sykes sticks his head out and signals the provost guard at the rear of the room. The soldier disappears and soon the sounds of gathering people disrupt the silence, and the rear doors are held open. Custer limps back in, his leg obviously giving him some pain. He quickly slumps into his chair, tugging the cape tight around his ears. His eyes are glassy with fever and his cheeks have an unnatural flush. He stares fixedly at the floor, and as the doors open and the court marches in, he does not look up.

Schofield is frowning. He remains standing for a while after the others are seated, glaring back at the press gallery where the reporters are now crowding into their places. He turns his back once to wipe his nose with a large bandana handkerchief. He turns back in time to see Major Winthrop hurrying down the aisle and his frown deepens. Slowly the noise in the room subsides and Schofield remains on his feet, looking down the aisle as though expecting someone else to enter. Then he nods and the provost guards close the doors. Schofield finally speaks. "The court is open." He sits down, then, with a loud grunt.

"All parties to the trial present when the court was closed," Gardiner says, "are now present."

"The accused will rise and face the court," Schofield says.

Custer and his civilian attorney rise, then Winthrop stands up as well, but he remains at the defense table as Jacobson and Custer move into the center of the bull ring, facing the court. Custer stands stiffly at attention, his eyes focused on the flag above Schofield's head. Schofield shuffles a number of papers before him and looks down at the open *Manual for Courts-Martial*.

"This court, in closed session, with two-thirds of the members concurring in all votes of guilty, finds you, Lieutenant Colonel George Armstrong Custer, of all charges and specifications, not guilty!"

There is an instant of electric silence, and then the press gallery bursts out into the bull ring. Custer, his face drawn, turns to the congratulations of his friends, who have also rushed forward.

Schofield leaps up and shouts, "Sit down, sit down there, this court is not . . . trial judge advocate, have you any further business for this court?"

Gardiner is on his feet and shouting as well. "I do not, Mr. President."

"This court is adjourned to meet at the President's call." He slams down his cue ball and wheels to leave the room. Before he follows, MacKenzie looks at Gardiner and shakes his head. The trial judge advocate shrugs. He has already guessed the truth—that MacKenzie voted for conviction.

As the members of the court disappear into the rear, the courtroom becomes bedlam. Friends and former enemies now crowd around to shake hands with the Golden Cavalier. Ladies are laughing shrilly. Members of the press crowd in, shouting questions. Gardiner catches a glimpse of Major Winthrop standing next to Custer, his hand on the cavalryman's shoulder. Custer looks somehow pained, as though the strain of the trial has finally caught up to him.

Hurrying, Gardiner and his friends elude the crowd and escape to the front walk and down it to the causeway. They say nothing. Gardiner's face is bleak. Sommers shakes his head, and Beakin spits repeatedly over the rail of the ferry after they board it.

Back in the courtroom the

DRUM MAJOR

crowd is milling noisily, but the members of the court have long since disappeard into Fort Columbus. At the defense table Jacobson sits, quietly pulling papers together and shoving them into a small valise. He empties his mouth of tobacco for the last time in this room, making the spittoon rattle. Wiping his lips with his fingers, he purses them and whistles a small tune. He avoids the crowd still lingering around Custer and moves out of the building.

The garrison of Fort Columbus, in dress blues and capes, is forming for the weekly Friday afternoon parade. The soldiers watch the figures coming through the west sally port from the old warehouse area, officers and their ladies, the ladies' colorful skirts billowing in the freshening wind. There are whispers along the lines as some claim to recognize Custer.

The band—which comes over from Fort Hamilton once a week—blares "Adjutant's Call." The adjutant struts out to take his post at the end of the line of troops. Breaking into a martial air, the band marches out and troops the line, each company standing to attention with bayoneted rifles at the order.

As the band resumes its place at the end of the line, the adjutant marches out to the center of the field, facing the post commander and his staff. A sharp command and a single bugle plays "Retreat." As the last note dies, a cannon shot rattles every window in the old fort. The adjutant commands, "Present arms," and as the troops snap their rifles up, the bugle plays "To the Colors." The sound whips across the parade field, distorted and warped by the wind, and as all stand motionless, the flag is lowered at the far end of the quadrangle. A detail of the guard catches it and folds it quickly, the adjutant bellows, "Pass in review." As the troops march off, their weapons at right shoulder, the band plays another lively air.

On the long veranda of the officers' mess, some of Custer's party have paused to salute the colors. Custer stands at the head of the group and for a long time after the last sounds of the bugle are gone, he holds his hand to his hat brim. As the companies march away, he drops his hand slowly to his side.

The bandmaster, not unaware of who is watching, raises his hands as the air is finished, looks toward the officers' mess, and jerks down his baton. The band bursts into "Garry Owen." They wheel and follow the troops through the far sally port, and Custer watches as they disappear, the sound of the music growing fainter and finally dying. The members of his party are subdued now, for they can see that his cheeks are wet with tears.

26

General Hancock's table has always been a delight. His charming wife knows how to supervise a kitchen as well as anyone in the Army, and the majestic spread of her husband's belly proves it. The baked flounder and parsley potatoes were delicious, the wine chilled to perfection. But Schofield was in no mood to display his not inconsiderable reputation as a gracious dinner guest. Now he hurries through the cold wind and the gathering darkness toward his quarters after a minimum of polite converse.

Sergeant Hill greets him at the door of his quarters and helps him off with his overcoat. It gratifies the general to see that his instructions have been carried out—the bags are packed and tied and waiting near the door. It will be late, but he wants to be back at West Point tonight.

"Did you leave out a shirt?"

"Yes, sir, on the bed," Hill says. "You had a caller, sir."

"Oh, who was that?" Schofield watches as Hill produces a long package from behind the door. He hands it to the general along with an engraved calling card: "Solomon Buckley, the *New York Herald*."

"What the Sam Hill?" Schofield has it unwrapped in a moment and pulls from the paper a walnut walking stick with a head shaped as an owl. He inspects it closely.

"I'll be damned." The head is sterling silver. Across the tail feathers of the owl, Schofield sees an inscription cut into the metal. He peers at it.

"To Major General John M. Schofield, with great respect and admiration. James Gordon Bennett, Jr. and staff, the *New York Herald*."

He shakes the stick and laughs. "Well, I'll be damned!"

As Hill gathers up the brown wrapping paper, Schofield goes to a small writing desk, still admiring the cane. Standing it against the desk, he takes a wallet from his inside pocket and produces a calling card of his own.

"Hill, I need to write two short letters. Get whatever done that still needs doing," he says.

"We're ready, sir."

Schofield takes a quill pen and frowns. He sets down an address on one envelope. "General William T. Sherman, The Commanding General, War Department, Washington City."

The pen makes loud scratching noises as he quickly writes. His penmanship is jerky, somewhat cramped, but also highly legible.

The Commanding General
United States Army
My Dear General Sherman:

You will soon be in receipt of the official transcript of the court-martial of Lieutenant Colonel George A. Custer. It would be the height of impropriety for me to disclose the vote of the court on acquittal. However, I must tell you that there were certain members of the court with whom I was greatly displeased.

Realizing the outcome will be a disappointment to you, I would recommend that no fault be found with Major Asa Gardiner, the trial judge advocate. Under the circumstances, he did as well as could be expected.

My staff and I are looking forward to your Christmas visit to West Point.

I am, sir, your most humble servant.

Respectfully,
John Schofield
Friday, November 16, 1877

The second envelope he addresses to James Gordon Bennett, Jr., the *New York Herald*. He looks at the cane leaning against the desk and smiles. On the back of the calling card he scribbles his message.

"All right, Sergeant, get these sealed and over to the post mailroom," he says, rising and rushing toward the bedroom. "I'll just change my shirt and we'll be off. Don't waste time."

"Yes, sir." Hill goes to the desk and lights a candle, finding the sealing wax and holding it over the flame. Before he sets the hot wax to the paper, he glances at the back of the calling card where his general has written, "My Dear Mr. Bennett: Thank you for the walking stick. But I feel you should know, I voted for conviction."

27

Jacobson leaves a note at the Grand Central Hotel for Elizabeth. He hopes she is feeling better and that the verdict has made her happy. For himself, he is leaving in the morning for Monroe and will visit with her and George there after they return from New York.

He stands for a long time in front of the hotel, watching the evening traffic. There will be parties this night, he thinks. In fact on Governor's Island there was a lively one going on within an hour after the verdict was announced. But Custer would soon leave that, coming in to the city he so adores and the people he so admires. There will likely be a banquet at the Fifth Avenue Hotel, followed by the theater—*Macbeth* is playing at Booth's—then a midnight supper at the Hoffman House, dancing in the grand ballroom of the Manhattan, and a breakfast of kippers and cream at Delmonico's.

It is the way of trials and of court-martials. The life of an Army prosecutor must be filled with despair. He does not decide who will be tried for what—he is simply handed the bill of fare, as it were. There was little question that Custer had done everything the government accused him of having done. But the court refused to classify any of it as criminal. And who could expect anything else? After all, if such a precedent was set, the Army might drag

Pope and McDowell to justice for those dismal battles they had engineered. Jacobson chuckles, thinking of McDowell in the dock, trying to stay awake. What is the statute of limitations on stupidity?

He turns toward midtown and walks briskly. It is a time for celebration! And he will celebrate by buying his wife a gift. And perhaps for his grandson one of those clever little monkeys on two sticks that jump and tremble as though alive. He turns up Broadway and sees that it is, indeed, broad. In places there are grassy islands down the middle of the thoroughfare.

I must go some day and visit that battlefield, he thinks. Perhaps George would be kind enough to give me the grand tour. He snorts. Give me a tour, indeed. After the verdict today, not a word of thanks or a kiss-my-ass. And dear Libby, of course, still indisposed. Like hell! I would bet my last four-bit piece that for tonight her illness will go away as suddenly and as strangely as it came.

He had known from the beginning—at least he had suspected— that the sickness was the best way for Libby to avoid having to talk about the Mary Adams business. Old Schofield would have jerked her fanny up on the stand in a minute if Gardiner had made any further fuss about the affidavit's validity. But he seemed to think he had destroyed the thing with his own rebuttal. Perhaps he had. But then, perhaps not. Some of those people on the court just might have believed Mary Adams instead of Gardiner's deposition.

In a way, it is too bad Elizabeth was not called to the stand to establish the whereabouts of Mary Adams at the critical time. Better than a Greek drama, to watch her under those circumstances. Would she lie to support the Mary Adams statement? Because Jacobson knew the statement was not true, and to protect George, Libby would have been forced to lie.

He pauses and watches a brightly painted hansom draw to the curb across the street. Four ladies dressed in high fashion but with a little too much bare arm showing under flowing capes tumble out and go into a dimly lit vestibule. Jacobson laughs and people on the sidewalk turn to look at him.

How about a woman, he thinks, for a celebration? Well, hardly that, not after all these years. Twenty years ago, perhaps. He shakes his head. No, not even then. There have been opportunities. Monroe has its women of the street. Old Lottie Samples, and she was not always old. But I was only her lawyer, never her client. And she was a good looker. What does a whore do for a living when she grows old? Or do they ever get that old? New York would be the place to find out, a city so big. There must be a hundred of them. Perhaps even a thousand.

The thought leaves him muddled, and he turns off Broadway into a small side street, thinking suddenly of a large, warm glass of Jamaica rum.

28

————

Even the strong rye in Ned Stokes's Gentlemen's Bar does not seem to warm them, and after only two they walk out into the dark street, going toward Gardiner's flat three abreast, not speaking, their heads down.

Newsboys on each corner call the news. "General Custer not guilty! Read it in the *Evening Post!*"

"Little buggers," Sommers grunts.

On 33rd Street in front of Gardiner's apartment, they stop and stand on the sidewalk. Gardiner takes cigars from his coat and they light them, holding flaring matches in cupped hands against the wind.

"Our ferry leaves soon," says Beakin. The younger men are going back to Washington, where they will await new assignments.

"I could walk to the slip with you," Gardiner says.

"No need for that," Sommers says. "We've learned your city well in the past few weeks."

They shuffle their feet, puffing their stogies. The smoke is immediately whipped away.

"Well . . . I suppose it's goodbye, then," Beakin says.

Gardiner nods. "I expect to be back in Washington the first of next week," he says. "For my own court-martial."

They all laugh hollowly. There is another long pause and they puff on their cigars again.

"It was well done," Sommers blurts.

"Nobody could have done better, sir," Beakin adds.

"Well, the Little Bighorn left a lot of casualties, and you're looking at the latest one." Realizing they will stand there all night unless he makes a move, Gardiner reaches out his hand. Each clasps it, nodding, saying nothing. He turns into the doorway and as he closes himself into the vestibule he hears one of them say, "Good-bye, sir."

Passing the landlady's quarters he can smell clam chowder and he hopes she will not bring him any. His flat is cold and he leaves his overcoat on as he lights a fire in the small stove.

Closing the stove and opening the damper, he turns to his view of the river. The weather is clear and the lights on the Jersey shore are brittle and sharp. He moves close to the pane and it begins to cloud with the room's growing heat and his breath.

There has always been some evil star over the enterprise, he thinks. Since the bad weather forced a postponement of the expedition out of Dakota last year and Custer managed to get back in time to make the trip. Nobody has won.

He shrugs, then walks across the room. He must pack. No need putting it off and waiting for some message from the War Department. Yet he feels more relief that the trial is finished than he does apprehension about losing it. He is still convinced that Custer is guilty of criminal neglect. Yet he has come to understand, too, that it is the way of all armies—sometime, somehow, no matter how carefully they are selected, the wrong man emerges on some battlefield and the result is horrifying.

He goes to his bed, sliding out the huge leather suitcase and placing it on the table. He opens the suitcase and leaps back as a mouse scrambles out, bouncing once on the table and then onto the floor and away under the bed. In one corner of the bag is a crumpled paper nest—he had carried a wine bottle wrapped in excelsior and butcher's paper. It is now a nest and it squirms. He spreads it open with his fingertips and finds six newborn mice, eyes closed, hairless, pink. He scoops them up, nest and all. He can recall that when he was a boy, his mother would conduct periodic mouse hunts in the house, always coming up with the little pink, squirming things from the sofa or the overstuffed chairs. She always threw them into the fire. Gardiner yanks open the stove.

Tomorrow is Saturday, he thinks. I can be in General Dunn's office Monday morning if I take the train. That damned Winthrop will likely already be there, looking down his nose. Then, I suspect, to General Sherman's.

There is a soft pecking at the door and Gardiner opens it to his landlady, a tiny Irish woman who has apple cheeks, a large toothless smile, and a tureen in her hands.

"I thought you might like some chowder, General."

29

Libby opens the window a crack and the wind brushes through, cold and sharp. Custer sits facing the draft as he slides off one boot. Libby moves about the room, dropping the scarf from her neck to the bed, unbuttoning her blouse. She speaks lightly of the evening ahead at Delmonico's. She carefully avoids any mention of the trial. Custer sits listening, watching the sheer marquisette curtains brushing against the heavy taffeta draperies. The boot is still in his hand, undropped. The curtain makes a soft rustle. Like a guidon fluttering on the staff . . .

Red and white in the Montana sun, whipping back, snapping, dear brother Tom riding under it, coming up fast in a cloud of white dust, three troopers with him. Behind Tom a muffled rattle of fire from the long ridge leading down toward the river.

Libby, now in nothing but chemise, black stockings, and high-button shoes, is selecting her dress for the evening, still chatting idly. Custer sits nodding at first, but as the curtain gently moves, he hears more clearly the guidon's intimate whisper over the heavy, muffled stamp of a thousand hoof beats, a regiment moving in deep dust of the High Plains country, in an empty world.

There are the lines of troops, still in column, coming along the low ground. White feathers with painted tips. An arrow arches high above the plunging horses. Captain Yates reports, his guidon-bearer holding a wound in his thigh, the blood running bright into his boot top. A horse is screaming somewhere, heard sharply above the sounds of heavy firing. The smell of sulfur and dust rolling up the ridge from Company F, and behind them Company C and then E. All being drowned in screeching savages. . . .

Get them up on the ridge, for God's sake, they're being butchered there. Sioux and Cheyenne, through all the high grass of the hill. They have repeating rifles. The dust boils up. . . .

And here are Stuart's men, swirling around Yellow Tavern, all dressed in gray. They flash a hollow, haunting yell as they come, but we kill Jeb even while we run back from them, there by the wall, and he goes off his horse with a bullet through his liver, good old Yankee lead in his vitals, and he will not see another day.

Look at those damned cones, cones of buffalo hide, there must be five thousand of them, each with blackened top and the lodge poles strutting up in disarray. A sunbeam on the river is blinding and the ponies ride close in with tails caught up in knots and bright feathers streaming from them. Manes interwoven with rattlesnake skin. Sergeant Whitney sitting on the ground, holding his neck in one hand where he bleeds, methodically firing his .45, rolling back the hammer of the single action as though he is on the pistol range. . . .

Get your damned company up, Yates. Stop bleeding from the mouth, you fool, and get your company up here on the high ground. Dear brother Tom. Lying there under that foolish dead horse, turning the yellow sand of the Montana prairie crimson. Foolish, fooling everything, foolish. The pistol in his hand, gripped in that delicate hand that has been inside so many perfumed blouses. Oh, dear brother Tom, you will be the death of me yet. Poor Libby, Tom. Poor Libby. Your dear, dear brother and sister love you very much you goddamned, lady-humping rounder. You sweet dog of a man grinning at me and blowing those red bubbles and still teasing me that you have that nasty little bauble to wear on your chest, the Medal of Honor.

There's Wade Hampton, with three brigades of cavalry. How the hell do they get such speed from those bags of bones they ride? We'll be sacked if Sheridan doesn't get some artillery into action from those trees . . . those black-topped tepees, the cones of the Cheyenne. And the Washita is cold and blue. There lies the baby in the snow, its bloody mother over it, glaring defiantly as we ride over her and she shoots trooper Gilpatrick in the back after he runs past and it takes him three days to die. Gallant Elliott, left for dead to rot in glory in the Indian Territory, the bastard.

Play the "Garry Owen," play it while we march up the Smoky Hill. If you catch a deserter, tie him to a wagon wheel in the sun and if you can't catch him, shoot him from far off, playing the "Garry Owen." The dust so thick you can hardly hear the alto horn, and magnificent Billy Cooke on the end of a Cheyenne lance like a pin cushion. The flat, desolate plain stretching away forever. But take care—it is not as empty as it seems. They can hide less than a pistol-shot away, two hundred of them, suddenly out and onto you with whoops and screams, faces black and yellow, mouths open.

Then look at those others come. Tattered gray uniforms flapping about naked legs like the billowing pantaloons of circus clowns, coming out, marching to surrender, to lay down their arms. There had been thousands of them. The reporters said so. Then why, when they came, their blood-red banners whipping over their heads, had there been so few? The 2nd Corps there at Appomattox had been no larger than a single Union division. The hollow eyes, still glaring in defiance. Most of them had been barefooted.

Close up the column, goddamn your eyes, keep the horses in tight and a clear eye to the flanks. Out-riders! Out-riders, muffle your bit chains or else tonight your hair will hang in an Oglala lodge. Ah, Montana summer, Kansas snow. The shallow streams in the Indian Territory running cold and clear out of the Antelope Hills. The horses hock-deep in it, drinking. The snow around Black Kettle's village hock-deep, too, but we catch him and his old woman in the stream trying to get away. No more, old man. No more will you have to worry about controlling your young men.

"Garry Owen." There was that big elk in the Black Hills and the stag hounds had caught him. They tore him apart and Boston was sick and threw up, but he said it was the trout we'd had for lunch, and not the sight of the dogs ripping away at the still-living buck. Dear Boston. Dear Tom. Dear Calhoun. Dear Libby. Oh, we all teased Boston about the puke. There he lies with his eyes wide open, staring up at the brassy sky, unblinking as the dust falls on his face in a fine powder.

Harrington! Sturgis! Porter! In the dust, naked Sioux boiling around them. Some of the hatchets are half a century old, traded to the tribe by Frenchmen coming up the river looking for hides. See how nobly the old French hatchets help us die, Libby?

The women and children come out before the dust is settled, hacking at fingers for trophies and stripping away scalps. Yammering and yapping like dogs. God, their dogs are here, too, but the hunting has been good lately and the dogs only sniff at the bloody wounds and eat only a few of us. The old women jerk off our clothes and loot the golden treasure of ammunition still unused in the fouled Springfields.

There is Myles Keogh on the battle ridge, that's it, dear Myles, face the east, face them as they come up from the draw and volley them. The east? Dear God, they are all around us . . . the Gatling guns. No, the Gatling guns are with Terry, shooting fish in the Yellowstone. . . .

The gold rattles under the horses' hooves. The Black Hills are full of gold. It says so in the *Chicago Inter-Ocean*. A belt of it thirty miles wide. Call the press. No, write it yourself. Of course. A nice story for the *New York Herald*. Perhaps for Mr. Greeley's *Tribune*, the damned old fussbudget. See my fine words, Libby? See my grand style? See my sweet grammar, Libby, see my dancing prose, Mother, watch me win the prize, Mother. Mother, may I hold you close, dear, dear Libby.

"Autie? Autie?" she says speaking loudly, her hand on his shoulder. She bends and sees his eyes. They stare straight ahead, unblinking, seeing nothing in the room. The boot slips from his fingers and strikes the floor. He sits motionless. "Autie," she says softly. The wind rustles the curtain, a gentle whisper in the red and white guidon. And he sits, hearing the soft death of his regiment around him.

PART SIX

Libby

30

Under an early evening sky the Potomac shines like quicksilver as it slides past the foot of Constitution Avenue. Sherman, on the high District of Columbia bank, can still see the structure of the bridge just to the north of where he stands. It points into the dark rise of ground on the far shore that is Virginia. The water here makes a soft rushing sound and it gives off the faint aroma of dead fish. The area along the bank is overgrown with brush and trees, but there is a bridle path that follows the river—probably an old towpath—and the Commanding General stands on the narrow, beaten thoroughfare, looking across the sluggish river. Washington City is behind him, and at this time—December 1877—it has not yet sprawled out to the Potomac.

On the high ground across the wide stream, he can still make out the shape of Arlington Hall, the old homeplace of General Robert E. Lee—and before that of the Custis family, descended directly from Martha Washington. During the war the place had been confiscated by the Federal government. The massive white building, its eight Doric columns of marble across the front, is like a Greek temple, frowning down on Washington. Sherman is not unaware—nor unmoved—by what that old hall has seen. The laughter, the marriage banquets, the Fourth of July celebrations, the stately dinners. There had been other things, too—Mrs. Lee's constant sickness, the terrible decision of Lee himself, deciding for the older allegiance and resigning from the United States Army. The grounds around the mansion are used now as a burial ground by the Army—have been so used since that spring day in 1865 when the first wagon loads of dead came back from Manassas and were planted in Lee's ground. Some said for spite. That was before the area had been designated a National Cemetery by Congress in 1864.

Why do I think of the war so consistently of late? Sherman asks himself. It is long since over, and the sooner forgotten the better. But, he thinks, I suppose that each man generally has one high-water mark in his life, and ghastly as it all was, the war was mine.

It is not unpleasant here along the river in the growing night. After a blustery November, Washington has turned almost to spring, and it appears that there must pass many long weeks yet before any possibility of sleigh rides along the Anacostia River. The Congress is ready to adjourn for the holidays, and most government business is grinding to its annual halt.

Sherman scratches his stubbly beard. It is short, and he keeps it that way intentionally, even though he looks like a man who wears no beard at all but has simply forgotten to shave for two days. As his nails make loud scraping noises through the stubble, he ponders the strange invitation that has brought him here. He has arrived early—which he has always tried to do on a battle ground.

Since the trial George Custer has been in Monroe, letting his wounds heal, it is said. He has a new assignment from the War Department whenever he desires to go back to active duty. Sherman cannot suppress a smile when he thinks of it—military observer to Costa Rica. But since such orders cannot be kept secret, they have become known and wept over in the pages of many newspapers. Custer or somebody near him has begun making the old noises again in the printed columns of the land. All of it to the effect that although the gallant general has been found innocent of any wrong in the mismanaged campaign of 1876, he is being pilloried by a vindictive Army out of pure meanness, political backbiting, professional jealousy, or some other motive. Knowing the quickness of the Custer family to draw the pen, Sherman is suspicious of the authorship of much that has been printed, especially in the *New York Herald*, which appears to be leading the charge for its own Boy General.

Since the trial no one has seen Custer—no one in public life. His officer friends have not been able to talk with anyone but Elizabeth when they have gone to Monroe to pay their respects. Sherman knows that a number have been there, but have been turned away after only short talks with Elizabeth—their old commander was not feeling well. How is it that such a flamboyant man will not at least speak with his former subordinates? It is strange, damned strange!

But perhaps it will now be cleared up. The note had come today in the delicate hand of Elizabeth Custer, asking that the Commanding General give her a private audience here on the bridle path south of the bridge. Like two conspirators, intent on the destruction of good order and discipline. It is distasteful to him. He waits impatiently and at one point turns and looks back into the trees. He can see nothing, although he knows that there, somewhere, are the horses and his aide, Colonel Nelson Wright. He has to reassure himself that Wright cannot be seen, for Mrs. Custer has specifically asked that their meeting have no audience.

This may be a damned bad mistake, he thinks. She's as sly and tricky as Albert Sidney Johnson was, before he bled to death at Shiloh.

There is the sound of a small vehicle on the road, stopping short of the bridge. Sherman waits, watching in that direction, and soon two figures appear moving down the path toward him. One is short and he knows it is Elizabeth Custer. She moves up close to him, the second figure close behind.

"General Sherman?"

"Yes, madam, it is I."

"General Sherman, this is Mr. Whittaker."

"Yes, I have heard of the biographer of your husband." His voice is cold, as is hers. He makes no move to extend his hand to the gentleman. "I had assumed that if I were to be alone, then you would be as well."

"Of course, General. Mr. Whittaker has only escorted me here," she says. Turning toward the shadowy figure behind her, she speaks softly. "Thank you, Frederick. Please wait at the cab."

"May I inquire into the state of your husband's health, madam?"

"Thank you, he is stronger each day," Elizabeth says. "He has stayed in Monroe, but he is aware of my being here and the reason for it. But, General. I would appreciate your discretion. I have no desire that anyone else should know I have come."

"I understand," he says, but of course he does not.

They turn and walk down the bridle path, two dark shapes. They lean toward one another as they speak. There is a cool courtesy at first, but a great deal of suspicion on the part of both. Soon, regardless of their differences, they are in animated conversation, a state of affairs Sherman always enjoys—except with politicians or newspaper reporters. He listens attentively as she makes her point. She walks with her face turned up to him, her pale cheeks framed in a black lace bonnet that seems to cup her entire head and shadow her brow. They are two people who create powerful magnetic fields —both are sometimes charming, always powerful, frequently ruthless. And now, although each has good reason to distrust the other, there is some kind of strange bond. It is a sensation, Sherman thinks, not unlike what he felt before Atlanta toward John Bell Hood, the magnificent Texan—who really came from Kentucky.

Watching them, his hands gripping the reins of the two horses, Colonel Nellie Wright has the feeling of watching a staff meeting from too far away to hear what is being said. His feet are cold, too. His feet are cold from November to March, even though he wears woolen socks year-round. The cold creeps up like a Potomac fog, from the tips of his toes to the instep and the ankle. He wiggles his feet, stamps them, and the horses snort and try to pull back.

"Easy, easy," he whispers.

The two dark figures on the bridle path have gone out of sight into the trees downstream. He watches through the tree trunks, which are silhouetted against the brighter background of the water.

It has not been a pleasant time for him since the court-martial ended in acquittal for Custer. Sherman has been irascible and cross, and nothing has seemed to please him. Only once in all that time— over a month—has the Commanding General asked Nellie to join him in morning coffee and cigars. That one time lasted only long enough for the Chief's diatribe against the press, where those damned Custer stories had begun to pop up again. Custer! The thorn in the Army's foot has not been plucked out, Sherman had roared, but remains to fester and rot the good flesh around it.

Somewhere in the darkness along the river, Wright sees the flare of a match and is somewhat surprised that Sherman would smoke while speaking with a lady. Could it be some odd familiarity bred of mutual hostility? Who knows what the Chief now thinks of this woman? Of his thinking on Custer, he leaves no doubt. And one hardly thinks of Mrs. Custer without thinking also of the Golden Boy General. Yet Wright knows a number of officers who despise the man but enjoy the company of the wife. There is nothing so strange about that, he thinks.

A carriage crosses the bridge with a clatter of steel tires and trace chains. Two riders are close behind. They come off the wooden bridge and onto the road where hoofbeats are muffled as they move on toward the city. Wright digs a cigar from his pocket—he always carries a few in case his Chief runs out. The horses snort in the sudden flare of light, and he holds them in close. Their eyes shine dully in the orange light. Then the match is out and the tip of the glowing cigar is like a bead of red on the velvet blackness of the night under the trees. He sighs unhappily as he inhales the thick smoke. His feet are cold up to his knees—up to the bottom of his flannel drawers, in fact. He wishes he had worn the long ones.

There is the murmur of voices and he sees the two figures appear again, pausing and speaking together for a long time. The taller bends down to listen intently. Wright believes he can see them touch hands. Then Elizabeth walks alone back toward the bridge and her cab. Sherman stands for a long time watching after her and soon there is the sound of a horse moving up the road toward Washington City. Wright moves out of the trees, pulling the horses, and Sherman turns as he comes up. Wright sees that there is no cigar in Sherman's hand.

"I saw your match, sir, and thought you were smoking," he says, dropping his own cigar to the bridle path and grinding it under his heel. He never smokes near Sherman unless Sherman is smoking, too.

The Commanding General hands his aide a folded paper. "No, Nellie, I was inspecting this document to be sure it was real," Sherman says. "Be careful with it. I want it in the safe tonight."

"Yes, sir," Wright says. He slips the paper into an inside coat pocket. It startles him when Sherman laughs.

"Do you know what she gave me?" Sherman asks. "An undated

resignation from the Army. Signed, Nellie, by George Armstrong Custer."

"My God," Wright blurts. "Custer is resigning——"

"Oh, she didn't give it to us free of charge," Sherman says. "She made a bargain with us. Damned if she didn't."

Sherman takes the reins of his horse and is quickly in the saddle. Wright mounts, too, and follows his chief along the path toward the road. Before they enter the thoroughfare, Sherman pulls up and Wright comes alongside. Sherman is looking at him in the dark.

"Nellie, she wants the Medal of Honor for Custer."

Wright gasps. Since the war, when there had been a great many of these medals passed around, the award for valor has become highly prized, coveted by Army men. On the Plains it became scarce, given usually only to those who had risked their lives to save others.

"That's absurd."

"No, it isn't," Sherman cuts him off. "I told you. She struck a bargain. She is a horse trader, that one. I don't know if living around a cavalry regiment all these years has done it, but she is a horse trader, Mrs. Custer. And a rough one at that."

"But, sir, a Medal of Honor . . ."

"It won't be easy, Nellie, we've got our work ahead. Sheridan will recommend of course. He is well thought of in the Congress. And I am not without means and methods, either. Once we have the thing in motion on the Hill, I am authorized to date and publish the resignation."

"You mean she trusted you, sir?"

"Nellie, I'm surprised at you." Sherman laughs again. Harsh and short. "Of course she did. Why shouldn't she? Let's get back to town, I want to see my brother and some of his friends. Perhaps at the Union League Club."

They spur out into the road, then Sherman pulls in to a walk, not wanting to catch Mrs. Custer's hansom cab. He shakes his head from time to time and grunts, and Wright knows he is thinking rapidly, setting all the names straight in his head, those people he needs to see before the Christmas recess of Congress.

"Nellie, do you know? We may have compromised our honor a wee bit here and there along the way. But I think, finally, we are going to be rid of the bastard!"

31

In the hansom, Frederick Whittaker, biographer of the Golden Cavalier, can sense Elizabeth's need for introspection. He sits silent in his corner as the driver whips the cab horse into a slow trot that will take them to the Willard.

Elizabeth feels no triumph, no sense of victory, although she knows that she has won a considerable one. Her general will never realize the significance of the beribboned bauble his government will present him—provided Sherman can make the bargain work on Capitol Hill. Custer's mind grasps little now. It reaches back along dusty routes of march in a treeless land, where he and his troopers search for a savage enemy almost never found. As in some tortured dream, he rides constantly under the regimental colors, chasing across an endless plain.

General Sherman is a well-informed man. Elizabeth cannot help but suspect that he knows—at least a little—of Autie's malaise, knows he can never wear again the badge of responsibility in the Army. Yet why would he agree to something so disagreeable to him if he had known—if he knew—his beloved Army was already shed of her Bo?

The horse's hoofbeats and the rimmed wheels of the hansom on the street newly paved with brick make a soft chattering in her consciousness, recalling the sounds of a cab very much like this one in which she and Autie had ridden to the train station in Monroe that February evening in 1864, only hours after they were married. They had been a little light-headed with the gaiety of it all, like children on their first merry-go-round. He had been twenty-four then and already a general. He had hardly any real beard at all—only a light fuzz the color of his long golden curls.

She could recall when the *Harper's Weeky* magazine arrived and he would insist they read it together in the study of their quarters in Austin, Texas. And she would stop her reading and stare at his yellow hair, then touch the ringlets, and he would look up and smile and admonish her for allowing her mind to wander from the printed page.

Texas! She could still hear the mockingbirds singing in the evening, from the pecan grove near their camp at Hempstead, where she had lived for weeks out of an Army ambulance that her general had especially designed for her comfort while traveling. There had been much traveling back and forth, from post to post. And often the quarters were completely inadequate and she had been forced to live like a gypsy out of a wagon. But everything her Bo could do to make it comfortable, either in movement or in serving as a home, he had done.

The mockingbirds! Before they left Texas Autie had hired two Texas boys—who surely thought he was mad—to trap one of the mockingbirds. They had taken it to Kansas with them after the 7th Cavalry was formed at Fort Riley. But, caged, it refused to sing, and once released it immediately flew away toward the South, braving the hawks of the Indian Territory to be back in its pecan grove, Autie had said. A true Rebel bird.

She had crossed Kansas so often she felt she knew each bump and rock, each treeless knoll, each dry stream bed. Fort Riley to Fort Harker to Fort Hays and back again. Packing, loading the ambulance, clouds of dust, never sure a Cheyenne war party would not appear and fall on the small detachment of mounted men detailed as escort from her husband's command. On one such trip they had seen Indians, and the regimental adjutant, Lieutenant Cooke, had said he would shoot her if there was any chance she might fall into their hands. She had asked him if he would have given her so little chance of life. He had replied it was the general's wish. Lieutenant Cooke, dead on the Little Bighorn.

There were wonderful times. Dreadful times as well. The thrills and excitement of a match buffalo hunt, when the officers of the regiment were divided into teams and went out to shoot buffalo with Colt pistols. After a specified time the chase was ended and the tongues counted to determine which team had won. Only the tongues were taken from the slaughtered beasts, the rest left to rot. But then there had been an endless number of them. What a horrid day when Custis Lee, her own dear saddle horse, had been killed by an accidental shot during one of those hunts.

When Bo was on scout he wrote her constantly, the Army couriers riding across dangerous Indian country to bring the letters back to Fort Riley or Fort Harker. He had always addressed the envelopes: "To Mrs. General Custer." He confided to her in all things. Even his love of gambling. What a struggle he had had stopping the evil habit. And poor Captain Keogh, spending months paying back to him losings from a single night at cards. Keogh, dead on the Little Bighorn; and of all of his company, only his horse, Comanche, found alive, bleeding from many wounds.

They are passing gaslit streets and buildings now. She can see the dark Christmas wreaths in the doorways. It seems an unreal season, with the singing about sleighbells in air as warm as springtime. And to the south, she has heard, they set off firecrackers on the Yuletide. What a dreadful custom! Yet her legs are chilled and she draws the lap robe tighter around her knees.

"Mrs. Custer?"

"Not now, Frederick. Please don't talk now."

It was a brutal life. Short and brutal. She could still remember her terror when two of the general's dogs—Turk the bulldog and Rover the big hound—had broken from their leashes during a storm and had gone at each other. Officers had run up and tried to separate them. It was only after a long struggle that the dogs were pulled apart, bloody and torn by then from ear to flank.

And the constant fear of pox and cholera. Or a soldier's mutiny. They had once threatened to shoot Autie, but he faced them down. The dust. The scorpions. A brutal life. Those seven men swept away in a flash flood at Fort Hays. Their cries were still fresh in her mind as though it had been yesterday.

The time she caught cold and dear Doctor Lord had ministered to her as though she were his only child. Dear Doctor Lord, nothing left of his worldly self but bone and buckle in the dust of Custer Hill. Captain Yates, finest dancer in the regiment. Bo had loved to watch as she and dear George did the polka, the regimental band huffing and puffing. The gallant leader of Company F, lying on the high ground now above the Greasy Grass. How delicate his step had been.

The time when old Mr. Custer had finally given his blessings for the marriage of Margaret—Autie's sister—and Lieutenant Calhoun! What a celebration! A new brother in the regiment along with dear Tom and dear Boston, now Jimmy as well. All . . . all dead at Little Bighorn.

She had not cried. Not when she first heard of the disaster, when she first saw her George, torn and sunburned on the stretcher as they carried him up from the *Far West*. Nor the first time he regained his senses, gripped her wrist, and glaring at her gasped, "Where have you put the artillery?" Nor comforting her sister-in-law, nor when the Army decided to court-martial her Bo, nor over all those dreadful things they said and printed about him. Nor yet even when she first saw the vacant glassiness of his stare. And she would not cry now. She had had a few golden years, and for the rest of her life she could relive those. Golden years, in the midst of a brutal life. But their contact had been a shining thing, like a gemstone among the beans of an Army breakfast. She smiled at that thought. I must write that down. I must write down all the good thoughts. The others do not matter.

Dear, gallant Bo! Sweet, charming Autie! Unable to hold back his innocent, boyish pleasure in the company of women, seeing something in each of them to praise, to desire, to appreciate. But always turning back to me, like a small child looking over his shoulder anxiously to see that mama is close behind. Perhaps it would have been different if children of our own had been possible. But with Autie, it was not. . . . He had never had the chance to stop being a child so he could become a parent.

But how the ladies loved him. How they flocked to him. The

pride was like a sweet taste in my mouth, because everyone knew he was mine. He was a brittle flame, and they all flew only as close to it as they dared, not realizing there was no danger. For his light was brilliant and bright, but it was a flame without heat.

They are on K Street, and the early evening traffic makes a clatter around them. As she steps from the cab in front of the Willard, she pauses to gaze up and down the street. The tears almost come then. She had stood like this in the month of her marriage, Autie beside her. She had been charged with excitement. Now she is only tired.

I must be getting old before my time, she thinks. Too much, recently, I dwell on things gone by. The bittersweet recall of happenings in another day, a day of muster rolls and bugles distantly heard, of martial airs and flags snapping, of all the places once called home, of names and friendships, tender longings, secret desires, unfulfilled promises, of faces withered now and gone. Like a lonely spinster in her rocking chair, opening books on faded and crumbling flowers pressed between the pages long since, in a youthful time of laughter and stolen kisses.